Paul Tillich's Dialectical Humanism

Paul Tillich's

Dialectical Humanism

Unmasking the God above God

Leonard F. Wheat

THE JOHNS HOPKINS PRESS   Baltimore and London

To David

Contents

List of Abbreviations

The following abbreviations are used in the footnotes to cite works by Tillich (including lectures and collections edited by others):

Absolutes: *My Search for Absolutes* (New York: Simon and Schuster, 1967).

Biblical: *Biblical Religion and the Search for Ultimate Reality* (Chicago: University of Chicago Press, 1955).

Boundary: *On the Boundary* (New York: Scribner's, 1966).

Courage: *The Courage to Be* (New Haven: Yale University Press, 1952).

Culture: *Theology of Culture*, ed. Robert C. Kimball (New York: Oxford University Press, 1959).

Dialogue: *Ultimate Concern: Tillich in Dialogue*, ed. D. MacKenzie Brown (New York: Harper & Row, 1965).

Dynamics: *Dynamics of Faith* (New York: Harper & Row, 1957).

Eternal Now: *The Eternal Now* (New York: Scribner's, 1963).

Foundations: *The Shaking of the Foundations* (New York: Scribner's, 1948).

History: *A History of Christian Thought*, ed. Carl E. Braaten (New York: Harper & Row, 1968).

Love:	*Love, Power, and Justice* (New York: Oxford University Press, 1954).
Morality:	*Morality and Beyond* (New York, Harper & Row, 1963).
New Being:	*The New Being* (New York: Scribner's, 1955).
Perspectives:	*Perspectives on Nineteenth and Twentieth Century Protestant Theology*, ed. Carl E. Braaten (New York: Harper & Row, 1967).
Protestant:	*The Protestant Era*, trans. James Luther Adams (Chicago: University of Chicago Press, 1948).
Religion:	*What Is Religion?*, trans. with introduction, James Luther Adams (New York: Harper & Row, 1969).
ST-1:	*Systematic Theology*, Vol. I (Chicago: University of Chicago Press, 1951).
ST-2:	*Systematic Theology*, Vol. II (Chicago: University of Chicago Press, 1957).
ST-3:	*Systematic Theology*, Vol. III (Chicago: University of Chicago Press, 1963).
World:	*Christianity and the Encounter of the World Religions* (New York: Columbia University Press, 1963).

Preface

This study is an indirect outgrowth of my graduate years at Harvard University (1955–58). Paul Tillich, already acclaimed as the number one Protestant theologian in this country, was teaching there at the time. He held the rank of University Professor, an honor reserved for six of the most ultra-distinguished faculty members. This in itself made him a personality of some interest. More important, two of my dormitory friends were among his students. Although I never met Tillich or attended any of his lectures—my degree was in Political Economy and Government—he became a frequent topic of conversation. Apparently he had the entire class in a state of confusion as to what he was saying. "Ultimate concern" and other Tillichian expressions became the subject of considerable jocularity on our floor.

In subsequent years, while pursuing an avocational interest in religious subjects, I often encountered references to Tillich. To judge from some of these, scholars were having the same trouble as Tillich's students. It seemed that Tillich was indeed a puzzling thinker, also a very deceptive one, and liberal well beyond the standards of liberal religion. My curiosity piqued, I decided to develop a firsthand acquaintance. A random but fortunate selection from among several of Tillich's paperbacks had me reading *The Courage to Be*, possibly the most enlightening of the more popular works Tillich wrote. This book, subtle in meaning but hardly too subtle for comprehension, confirmed Tillich's deep antipathy toward basic Christian beliefs. In addition, it led me to wonder whether Tillich had something particular in mind, something beyond variegated human concerns, when he spoke of "the God above God."

Intrigued, but too lazy to plow through the three volumes of

Systematic Theology, I read a book about Tillich. Surprisingly, the writer, who thought he was explaining Tillich, was completely disoriented as to Tillich's position. Yet abundant quotations and delicately worded paraphrases were adequate to provide tentative identification of Tillich's God above God. I became even more curious and, at the same time, suspicious that the whole theological world might be in the dark about Tillich's message. More books, both by and about Tillich, followed. Here my background in political science and economics gave me an unanticipated advantage over earlier interpreters, virtually all of whom were trained in theology. For in Hegel and Marx, a couple of political and economic theorists with whom members of the theological camp have evidently escaped close contact, I found the key to Tillich. His thought is rife with concepts borrowed from Hegel and Marx, mostly Hegel. It would be an overstatement to describe Tillich as simply a reworking of Hegel, and not just because Marx and some other philosophy are involved: fifty percent of Tillich derives from classical theology. Still, Tillich's thought is as much as anything a matter of giving new substance to formulations and concepts taken from Hegel; the basic outline of Hegel's thought is retained intact. Master some analogies to Hegel and you have come a long way toward mastering Tillich.

As I read, my suspicions jelled. Certain aspects of Tillich's thought, but not the fundamentals—not his unqualified ("unconditional") No and not his Yes to the higher God—were understood by his theological colleagues. Equally important, existing interpretations of three methodological building blocks of the Tillichian system consistently proved to be wrong or else so superficial as to be meaningless. The building blocks are symbolism, correlation, and dialectics. Of these, dialectics is the most crucial. It is also what gets you from Hegel to Tillich. To understand Tillich you must understand dialectics, and this means Hegelian dialectics. Other writers have acknowledged that Tillich's thought is dialectical, but it has been done in passing, without special emphasis, interpretation, or illustration, and often in a way suggesting that the writer was thinking of Barthian dialectics, which is something else. There has been no recognition of the many novel and cleverly disguised dialectical formulations that permeate Tillich's thought, no pointing out of crucial parallels between Hegel (and Marx) and Tillich, and no suggestion that dialectics is the necessary basis for understanding Tillich. These observations convinced me that another interpretation was needed.

In attempting to meet this need, I have sought to provide for casual readers—laymen and others who know Tillich chiefly through his published sermons and other popular works—as well as serious students of philosophy and theology. Occasional digressions designed to clarify certain elementary theological terms, terms which the professional theologian takes for granted, will therefore be found. Perhaps the commentary on such topics as the Holy Spirit will not only facilitate comprehension of Tillich but help some readers to gain a generally better understanding of theology.

There is no one to implicate in this enterprise but myself. I would nevertheless like to acknowledge two authors who proved especially stimulating and helpful. First, Walter Kaufmann, in *The Faith of a Heretic*, more than anyone else kindled my interest in Tillich and provided a useful preliminary orientation to his thought. Kaufmann's insights certainly helped me to look in the right direction for answers. His influence can also be seen, among other places, in my use of the concept of two audiences. Since Kaufmann is on record as opposing the view that Hegel's thought is dialectical in the usually accepted sense, it is only fair to add that he is not responsible for what is said about Hegel. Second, Robert Tucker (who as far as I know has no interest in Tillich) has published valuable background material on the concept of alienation, as developed by Hegel, Marx, and several other philosophers whose bearing on Tillich has not received proper appreciation. Alienation is as fundamental to Tillich's system as dialectics, to which it is intrinsically related; and no one has explained alienation better than Tucker. His *Philosophy and Myth in Karl Marx*, despite its unlikely sounding title, should be required reading for anyone seeking to understand Tillich's ideas about estrangement and self-realization, ideas which *must* be understood to understand Tillich. In addition to these two gentlemen, Donna Webster deserves recognition for her extremely competent performance in typing the manuscript. Finally, I owe my wife copious thanks for being so patient with the family theologian.

Paul Tillich's Dialectical Humanism

CHAPTER 1

Shaking the Foundations

Paul Tillich was a philosopher-theologian concerned about the meaning of life. His readers and critics, however, have generally been more concerned about the meaning of Tillich. And that is what this book is all about.

German born, Tillich came to the United States in 1933. Within two decades he was firmly established as (with the possible exception of Reinhold Niebuhr) America's leading Protestant theologian. Tillich's theological eminence has been widely acknowledged—for example, in his selection as the first subject of the *Library of Living Theology* series. Professors Kegley and Bretall, editors of the series, write, "The adjective 'great,' in our opinion, can be applied to very few thinkers of our time, but Tillich, we are far from alone in believing, stands unquestionably amongst these few."[1] Tillich, they continue, belongs in a class with Dewey, Whitehead, Russell, and Santayana, yet stands solidly on Christian soil.

The theology which won Tillich this acclaim revolves around the notion that God is not a being but "being-itself." Alternatively, God can be referred to as "the ground of being," "the power of being," or one's "ultimate concern." This Tillichian God is not the traditional Heavenly Father but "the God above the God of theism." A companion doctrine holds that man is estranged from God but, through the saving experience of New Being, can partially

1. Charles W. Kegley and Robert W. Bretall, eds., *The Theology of Paul Tillich* (New York: Macmillan, 1952), pp. ix-x.

overcome his "existential predicament." The formula for New Being is "dialectical."

IN SEARCH OF THE KEY

These ideas and others subordinate to them have produced end-less confusion regarding what Tillich is trying to say. Students, ministers, theologians, philosophers, and laymen find Tillich not only difficult to understand but frequently incomprehensible. Once, after Tillich had read a paper to some professional colleagues, a distinguished member of the group was moved to comment: "Now really, Mr. Tillich, I don't think I have been able to understand a single sentence of your paper. Won't you please try to state one sentence, or even one word, that I can understand?"[2]

Ambiguity Compounded

The vague and often misleading quality of Tillich's thought stems from two related attributes: (1) his redefinition of the terms and concepts of traditional theology and (2) his failure to adequately define numerous other words and phrases he employs, often symbolically. Tillich, though he means what he says, usually doesn't mean what he *seems* to be saying. Without making it clear what he is doing, he has drastically altered the meaning of virtually every term, "God" included, in the traditional theological vocabulary. Familiar words and doctrines no longer mean what they have always meant. "He" in reference to God, for example, really means a very impersonal "it"; "revelation" refers to a value judgment; and "salvation" becomes a philosophical concept, the content of which is shrouded in mystery. Tillich's ambiguous use of theological concepts is reinforced by his equally ambiguous use of other terminology. He blithely plays with words like "infinite," "unconditional," and "nonbeing" and, in effect, challenges the reader to guess their intended meaning in a given context. His claim to be correlating "questions and answers" has been taken literally by practically all of his expositors, whereas Tillich privately means that theological and philosophical concepts (e.g., Eden and essence) are being analogically correlated to produce synthetic symbolic

2. John Herman Randall, Jr., "The Ontology of Paul Tillich," in *ibid.*, p. 133.

meanings. Ambiguity is piled upon ambiguity until the reader is at a complete loss to interpret. Tillich euphemistically describes this verbal legerdemain as consciously relating each connotation of a word to all others and centering them about a controlling meaning.[3] Whatever it is, the effect can be overpowering.

This pervasive ambiguity and the overall fuzziness of Tillich's thought have naturally caused much disagreement and misunderstanding among commentators and critics as to what Tillich is saying. He has been variously regarded as a theist, deist, pantheist, panentheist, metaphysician, and mystic. He has also been implicitly and explicitly treated as too obscure to interpret. And he has been labeled an atheist. In order to appreciate the full extent of the confusion about the meaning of Tillich, we can profitably survey the salient views on his doctrine of God, a doctrine on which all of his other concepts hinge. Our survey must perforce exclude most of the minor commentaries. We can, however, cover the major works on Tillich and a few lesser ones which help to illustrate the variety of opinion which has emerged.

Before proceeding, we must reject the example of Tillich by pausing to define a few terms. Several interpretations will be classified as theistic; hence an understanding is necessary as to what is meant by theism. Some writers seem to regard theism as connoting anthropomorphism or, even more narrowly, wrath and vindictiveness on the part of God. This is supposedly all that Tillich denies when he speaks of the God above the God of theism. A more accurate definition of theism describes it as the belief in a rational, self-conscious supernatural being who created the universe, takes an interest in human affairs, and providentially watches over us. A theistic god is not necessarily the physical image of man; most often he is viewed as a spirit. Neither must a theistic god have a temper or occupy finite space. But "God" has always implied personality. Specifically, the God of theism has always had the rational faculty of a person, although of course his reason has been considered infinitely superior to that of mortals. God has had the power to observe, comprehend, remember, organize facts, think, plan, and make decisions. He has also been aware of himself as an entity

3. *ST-1*, p. 55.

standing in relation to man and the rest of the universe. And—this is optional—God has usually manifested manlike emotions, including love. A god constructed along these lines is a being, a theistic god, whether or not anything else can be said about him.

Deism, a close relative of theism, is seldom attributed to Tillich and can be treated very briefly. It postulates a creator god who takes no interest in and does not intervene in human affairs. The usual analogy likens a deistic god to a watchmaker who builds a watch (the universe), winds it up, and then sits back and lets it run forever under its own power.

A larger number of interpretations can be described broadly as metaphysical. Metaphysics is sometimes employed loosely in place of "supernaturalism." Properly applied, however, the term avoids traffic in popular superstition (elves, ghosts, broken mirrors, magic, and the like) and focuses on abstruse matters concerning supernatural material found at the cosmic level. Usually metaphysics is taken to mean inquiry into a presumed supernatural reality that lies hidden from experience. Usages often embrace cosmology, or theories regarding mysterious forces thought to shape the universe and guide its destiny. Sometimes metaphysics is used more narrowly to mean ontology, or thought about a presumed "essential" (and by implication supernatural) nature of "being," that is, about a concealed reality which underlies observable reality. Theology is occasionally treated as a branch of metaphysics, but for our purposes a metaphysical god can be defined as a supernatural god which, because it is not a self-conscious being, lies beyond the usual range of theology.

Pantheistic and panentheistic gods are more or less members of the metaphysical household. Pantheism is popularly held to mean that God is nature. Actually the term suggests a sort of organic unity between the parts and the whole, a hidden nature or essence which underlies observable nature, and sometimes even consciousness belonging to reality as a whole. This makes it supernatural. Panentheism is roughly a cross between pantheism and deism. It holds that God includes the universe (immanence) yet also stands beyond it (transcendence); the universe is part of a supernatural whole.

A metaphysical god can also be mystical. Mysticism involves

4

belief in an ineffable supernatural reality—a power, force, or god—which can commune with the human mind through mystical experiences. In one form, especially common in the orient, these experiences are called "visions" or "religious ecstasy" and may be accompanied by visual or auditory stimulation. The experience is quite real, sometimes resembling the "trips" produced by hallucinatory drugs, and apparently results from biochemical disturbances in the brain. When not actually induced by drugs, the mystical experience is precipitated by intense emotional preoccupation with or concentration on religious subjects. The mystic assumes he is in the grip of a universal power. In a looser sense, and more pertinent to opinions about Tillich, mysticism describes religious ideas resulting from intuitive insights thought to emanate from the supernatural. Here intellectual elements tend to replace emotion. But whatever the nature of the experience, the "reality" appearing to the subject is characteristically so nebulous and indescribable as to be mysterious.

Theistic Interpretations

The logical place to begin our survey is with the view that Tillich is a theist of sorts, if not exactly an orthodox one. An early theistic interpretation comes from David Soper. He devotes a chapter to Tillich in *Major Voices in American Theology: Six Contemporary Leaders*. According to Soper, Tillich can bridge the gulf between irreligion and religion because he understands that there "is only one way to know another personality—to become united with that personality through love."[4] Love unites, and union brings knowledge. "God knows me because he loves me" is Soper's paraphrase of Tillich. God is thus another personality and is capable of loving. Soper also ascribes to Tillich the belief that "in so far as the human Jesus has become an idol, rather than an incarnation, he must be dispensed with."[5] Obviously, Soper believes that Tillich accepts the doctrine that God became a man, which again implies that God is a supernatural being.

In *The Systematic Theology of Paul Tillich: A Review and*

4. David Wesley Soper, *Major Voices in American Theology: Six Contemporary Leaders* (Philadelphia: Westminster, 1952), p. 112.
5. *Ibid.*, p. 121.

5

Analysis, Alexander McKelway offers a comparable but less enthusiastic interpretation of Tillich. His view is that Tillich's God is a being—rational, self-conscious, and concerned about man—whom Tillich doesn't want to call *a* being because "He" is far more than an ordinary being. "Tillich has emphasized correctly that the knowledge of revelation is not the reception of information, but is the participation in an encounter between man and God, and as such is synonymous with salvation."[6] Here Tillich speaks "correctly" and, since McKelway personally thinks revelation involves a supernatural being, we can safely infer that Tillich's "correct" view is similar to McKelway's. Continuing: "We wholeheartedly accept Tillich's description of God as the ground and power of being-as-being-itself."[7] Coming from one who believes in "the self-manifestation of God in Jesus" and speaks of "God the Father,"[8] this plainly suggests that Tillich's ground of being bears a strong resemblance to the traditional God. Elsewhere McKelway laments that Tillich "unfortunately led many critics to believe" that his thought was deistic.[9] This notion he refutes, and not simply because he thinks that Tillich's God is even less personal. McKelway, it is true, stresses that the Tillichian God is "not *a* being or *a* person, for he transcends all particular beings."[10] But all McKelway means is that God is not on the same plane as man, "cannot be placed in a category with other beings,"[11] and "is the basis of, and includes, all personality."[12] "Tillich argues for a view of God as 'suprapersonal,' "[13] summarizes McKelway. "For Tillich, God transcends the personal, but he nonetheless includes it. He is person."[14] The phrase "not *a* being," in short, becomes semantic quibbling.

A third theistic interpretation, that of George Tavard, gives a Catholic slant on Tillich. Father Tavard's *Paul Tillich and the Christian Message* also takes the position that Tillich's God is a being who shouldn't be called a being. Early in his study Tavard makes the point that Tillich is a supernaturalist whose repudiation of the supernatural merely indicates that the supernatural realm is

6. Alexander J. McKelway, *The Systematic Theology of Paul Tillich: A Review and Analysis* (Richmond: John Knox Press, 1964), p. 95.

7. *Ibid.,* p. 138. 8. *Ibid.,* p. 98.
9. *Ibid.,* p. 155n. 10. *Ibid.,* p. 137.
11. *Ibid.,* p. 123. 12. *Ibid.,* p. 137.
13. *Ibid.,* p. 126n. 14. *Ibid.*

not something beside the natural but *is* natural.[15] Having semantically prepared the way for a supernatural God, Tavard implies that Tillich's denial that God is a being is purely linguistic. God is not to be called "a being" because "he is beyond the realm where 'a' is meaningful, beyond singular and plural";[16] but God is still a "he," not an "it," and can still be described as "the living God."[17] God is not only within but beyond man, and love drives both toward union. Unlike certain other writers, Tavard nowhere suggests that Tillich is a metaphysician or pantheist. Indeed, he has no serious quarrel with Tillich's views on God. After reading volume 1 of *Systematic Theology*, in which Tillich develops his concept of God, Tavard felt that Tillich's position could be reconciled with a theistic view, specifically that of the Roman Catholic Church. Only after inspecting volume 2, containing Tillich's Christology, did Tavard find Tillich's view un-Christian. But what upset Tavard is the fact that Tillich's Christ is not God; Tavard launches no attack on Tillich's doctrine of God.

Carl Armbruster provides a second Catholic interpretation. The first half of Father Armbruster's *The Vision of Paul Tillich* flits from one to another of Tillich's superficially contradictory statements about God, leaving the reader in the dark about what the author thinks. God is "whatever" concerns a person ultimately. An artistic work seems to fit the description, and Armbruster eventually brands the concept of ultimate concern "all but impenetrable." God is not a being, yet revelation, whatever else it implies, includes "intellectual communication" with God. God can only be described by analogy, which is why Tillich uses personal terms to describe "him"; God is really personal only in the sense that the divine "participates in all beings as their ground."[18] But, most emphatically, Armbruster denies the validity of deistic and pantheistic interpretations. One begins to doubt that he has any substantive opinion. Finally, though, he sensibly asks if Tillich's God lacks intelligence, direction, and directing power and therefore resembles electricity. His reply is negative. Tillich could say that God is a

15. George H. Tavard, *Paul Tillich and the Christian Message* (New York: Scribner's, 1962), p. 20.

16. *Ibid.*, p. 55. 17. *Ibid.*, p. 26.

18. Carl J. Armbruster, *The Vision of Paul Tillich* (New York: Sheed and Ward, 1967), p. 140.

person "without sacrificing any principles" but hesitates to do so because it would make God sound too much like other beings.[19]

Shifting now from the religious right to the left, we have Duncan Howlett's Unitarian views on Tillich. What Howlett writes in *The Fourth American Faith* is particularly interesting, for his competence as a scholar equals his prominence among free thinkers; certainly he is not a person to be described as credulous. In the chapter "The Return to Orthodoxy," Howlett characterizes Tillich as "supremely the apostle of the faith of stability" and "the leading theologian of Protestant orthodoxy today." Tillich is essentially not a philosopher but "a theologian whose system of thought, while heavy with metaphysics and ontology, is theological in its final analysis." He can even acknowledge "that Jesus Christ is the incarnation of the universal Logos of God." Tillich therefore is not too far removed from Augustine, Aquinas, Calvin, and Barth.[20]

For a philosophy specialist's reading of Tillich we have Ernst Breisach's succinct 14-page analysis, found in his *Introduction to Modern Existentialism*. Much of what Breisach says about Tillich's God is highly ambiguous: God is a "power" and the "absolute reality" which concerns man. Do these terms refer to a self-conscious power resembling the traditional God, a metaphysical one like the Logos, or a figurative one like money? Breisach definitely has the first in mind, for he finds it "clear" that Tillich "stands in the Christian tradition." To be sure, Tillich's God is not the biological sort of being visualized by some and therefore shouldn't be called a being, but "he" still "speaks to man as a person." The God-man relationship is therefore "between person and person." Tillich may reject most of the Christian tradition, but he manages to maintain a "careful balance" between questioning and faith. Consequently, he belongs relatively close to Kierkegaard on the believing end of the existential spectrum, at the opposite end from such atheists as Nietzsche and Sartre.[21]

19. *Ibid.*, p. 153.
20. Duncan Howlett, *The Fourth American Faith* (New York: Harper & Row, 1964), pp. 119–24.
21. Ernst Breisach, *Introduction to Modern Existentialism* (New York: Grove Press, 1962), pp. 136–50, 218.

Metaphysical Interpretations

Just as often, Tillich's interpreters treat him as a metaphysician of one kind or another. The most cautious exponent of this position, George F. Thomas, actually adopts a compromise interpretation combining theism and metaphysics. In *Religious Philosophies of the West*, Thomas expresses doubt that Tillich's references to "the God above God" constitute an out and out rejection of Christian theism. This is a "hasty assumption" in view of Tillich's disavowals of pantheism and mysticism.[22] At the same time, Thomas joins company with the multitude of others who can find no precise meaning in the terms "being-itself," "the power of being," and "the ground of being." Acknowledging that Tillich wishes to transcend mystical religion, Thomas nevertheless regards "the God above God" as "closer to the 'Godhead' of the monistic mystics than to the personal God of Theism."[23] Thus: "When Tillich speaks of 'being-itself' as 'beyond' the polarities which characterize the structure of being, e.g., the 'split' between subject and object, he reflects this monistic mysticism."[24] This Tillichian mysticism, Thomas contends, is a form of pantheism. Tillich, he believes, "seeks to synthesize the pantheistic element of immanence with the theistic element of transcendence in a way that seems to point to *Panentheism* rather than Pantheism."[25]

J. Heywood Thomas (not to be confused with George F.) is less circumspect. His book, *Paul Tillich: An Appraisal*, affirms that Tillich's doctrine of God "is not at all clear and seems even to suggest that Tillich is holding some doctrine of God as being the Absolute of the metaphysicians."[26] Conceding that Tillich has rebutted the charge that he is engaged in old-fashioned metaphysics, Thomas charges that what Tillich calls "ontology" is really metaphysics in disguise. "What can he hope to achieve by abandoning the name if the business he carries out is the same?"[27] Continuing:

22. George F. Thomas, *Religious Philosophies of the West* (New York: Scribner's, 1965), p. 416.

23. *Ibid.*   24. *Ibid.*, pp. 421–22.

25. *Ibid.*, p. 411.

26. J. Heywood Thomas, *Paul Tillich: An Appraisal* (Philadelphia: Westminster, 1963), p. 57.

27. *Ibid.*, p. 35.

"McTaggart defined metaphysics as 'the systematic study of the nature of ultimate reality'. This has been the intention of all the classical metaphysicians from Plato to Bradley, and Tillich seems to be undertaking exactly the same task."[28] Thomas also finds Tillich's discussion of man's predicament to be on "the borderline of religion and metaphysics."[29] All told, it "becomes clear that Tillich is concerned with metaphysical questions and more particularly with the commendation of a faith which is one element of the metaphysical answer."[30]

Kenneth Hamilton, whose *The System and the Gospel: A Critique of Paul Tillich* is strongly antagonistic toward Tillich, elaborates on the J. H. Thomas theme. Hamilton calls Tillich's thought "metaphysical," "pantheistic," and "mystical" all at once. The term "metaphysical" he employs in what has become its pejorative sense of speculative inquiry into matters alleged to lie beyond experience. Hamilton declares that Tillich's "defence of the metaphysical system"[31] places him "squarely among the traditional metaphysicians."[32] Tillich's brand of metaphysics "is not pantheistic in that it does not identify the Universe and God." Yet, "because God is identified with the reality *of* the Universe," Tillich's system "must be classified as a monistic system standing in very close relation to pantheism, differing from the latter in the detail of its ontological analysis but sharing with it a common vision."[33] Hamilton continues, "The God of the system . . . . conforms more closely to the pattern of pantheism than to any other."[34] At the same time, God is viewed in "mystical terms."[35] "Actually, what Tillich rejects is not mysticism as such, but the type of mysticism characteristic of the East."[36] This mystical element in Tillich's God is as "unmistakable" as the pantheistic element and is its twin.[37]

Easily the most imaginative interpretation of Tillich is that of Guyton Hammond, whose two books[38] on Tillich develop the thesis

28. *Ibid.*   29. *Ibid.*, p. 126.
30. *Ibid.*, pp. 157–58.
31. Kenneth Hamilton, *The System and the Gospel: A Critique of Paul Tillich* (New York: Macmillan, 1963), p. 37.
32. *Ibid.*, p. 14.   33. *Ibid.*, p. 85.
34. *Ibid.*, p. 87.   35. *Ibid.*, p. 88.
36. *Ibid.*, p. 221.   37. *Ibid.*, p. 222.
38. Guyton B. Hammond, *Man in Estrangement: A Comparison of the Thought of Paul Tillich and Erich Fromm* (cited below as *Estrangement*)

that Tillich's God is life. This is not life as you and I know it but Life, visualized as a metaphysical power in which the universe is rooted. Hammond, in effect, characterizes this power as desperately insecure (but apparently more instinctively than emotionally so); Life is constantly driven by an insatiable impulse to affirm and reaffirm its own being through the creation of mortal beings. "Life can only maintain itself against the threat of death or nonbeing by continually creating itself beyond its own present limits."[39] It therefore "moves out from itself into relative nonbeing in order to achieve its full realization."[40] Fulfillment occurs in man, who is supposedly the only being that can experience self-consciousness (self-realization). Whenever man recognizes himself as a separate being apart from his environment, Life is affirmed. Unfortunately, the process of becoming self-aware sets Life apart from itself: his own self-awareness blinds man to his essential oneness with the ultimate. This "metaphysical . . . separation"[41] is necessary but carries a tragic implication: the separation of man from God. Through this analysis Hammond is led to the conclusion that Tillich views the world as "an aspect of the divine life" and that, therefore, "pantheism has not been avoided."[42] Because Tillich believes that estranged man can achieve only fragmentary reunion with God, however, Hammond's pantheistic interpretation is qualified. "It might be said that Tillich's thought sustains a tension between pantheistic elements and the more orthodox position that finitude is good even in separation from the divine life."[43]

Further echoes of the preceding appraisals appear in David Hopper's *Tillich: A Theological Portrait*. Hopper's principal interest is in tracing the development of Tillich's thought over the years; he is concerned more with surface aspects and thought forms than with the inner substance of Tillich. Accordingly, he avoids being very specific about meanings. (This approach not only allows him to skirt many pitfalls but actually leads to more insights than are found in any other book about Tillich.) Hopper can nevertheless

---

(Nashville: Vanderbilt University Press, 1965), and *The Power of Self-Transcendence: An Introduction to the Philosophical Theology of Paul Tillich* (cited below as *Power*) (St. Louis: Bethany Press, 1966).

39. *Power*, p. 37.　　　　　　40. *Power*, p. 36.
41. *Power*, p. 42.　　　　　　42. *Estrangement*, p. 167.
43. *Estrangement*, p. 170.

refer to a "basic metaphysical interest" in Tillich's thought.[44] He is also willing to identify "pantheism" as one of many "problems" one encounters in Tillich.[45] More broadly, Hopper finds that "Tillich makes room in the life of faith, not only for the whole tradition of mysticism, Christian and non-Christian, but also for the important 'pantheistic element' that he insisted should be part of a Christian doctrine of God."[46]

Not surprisingly, philosophy has witnessed the same division of opinion as religion on the question of whether Tillich is to be interpreted theistically or metaphysically. A metaphysical interpretation not specifying "pantheism" or "mysticism" comes from William L. Rowe, in *Religious Symbols and God: A Philosophical Study of Tillich's Theology*. Rowe begins by linking together two terms Tillich uses to designate God. These are "ultimate concern" and "being-itself." Tillich's pluralistic descriptions of ultimate concern, observes Rowe, make it sound as if an ultimate concern can be practically anything. Yet Tillich also adheres to "the view that we are ultimately concerned about the metaphysical ultimate, being-itself."[47] The seeming contradiction is overcome by making ultimate concerns the medium through which being-itself is experienced: "Since man can encounter being-itself only through the concrete, his infinite quest for being is focused on something concrete through which the power of being is experienced."[48] The result is metaphysics: "Given this metaphysical background, the phenomenon of ultimate concern focused on sacred objects can be explained as the way in which man's striving for being-itself expresses itself in actual life."[49] The upshot is that Tillich's explanation of religion "is given in terms of a particular metaphysics," but one which can be criticized on grounds that the "truth of the metaphysics is not answered by any description, however accurate, of religious experience."[50]

Sidney Hook, representing atheistic philosophy, is another phi-

44. David Hopper, *Tillich: A Theological Portrait* (Philadelphia: Lippincott, 1968), p. 103.
45. *Ibid.*, p. 179.   46. *Ibid.*, pp. 181–82.
47. William L. Rowe, *Religious Symbols and God: A Philosophical Study of Tillich's Theology* (Chicago: University of Chicago Press, 1968), p. 17.
48. *Ibid.*, p. 19.   49. *Ibid.*, p. 22.
50. *Ibid.*, p. 24.

losopher holding the opinion that Tillich is a metaphysician. In his essay on "The Atheism of Paul Tillich," a somewhat misleading title, he finds in Tillich's thought "the recognition of atheism as a religion among others, with truth claims that seem better warranted, on Tillich's own showing, than its rivals'." Hook is using "atheism" here in the restricted sense of unbelief in a *theistic* (intelligent, self-conscious) god; he ultimately perceives in Tillich the "watery metaphysical mists" of another form of supernaturalism. "The God whom many millions of men have worshiped is dead, according to Tillich, because He has been conceived as *a* Being instead of being-itself or being-as-such." In place of the old God, Tillich offers an ontological concept of man "according to which our individual selves are part of the Universal Self or Ego which is the Teutonic correlative of being-as-such." There is a "Cosmic Egoism from which our egos are painfully separated—and in which we find peace and security when our egos are dissolved and reintegrated." Therefore, "Tillich's God is the all-in-all of pantheistic spiritualism." As such, it is not an entity among other entities; rather, it resembles the gods of Spinoza and Hegel.[51]

Hesitant Interpretations

Several other writers have found Tillich so obscure that they hesitate to ascribe any definite theological meaning to his concept of God. James Luther Adams, author of *Paul Tillich's Philosophy of Culture, Science, and Religion*, is among these. His analysis is of interest both for its specific rejection of allegations that Tillich is an atheist and for its forthright acknowledgment of the difficulty of interpreting him. After examining a certain quotation from Tillich, Adams says, "These words come very near to expressing the sentiments of the existential philosopher Heidegger, though Tillich does not agree with Heidegger's atheistic position."[52] A little later, Adams notes that some German theologians once accused Tillich of atheism. These accusations, he indicates, are attributable to Tillich's socialist activities; Adams does not take

51. *Religious Experience and Truth: A Symposium*, ed. Sidney Hook (New York: New York University Press, 1961), pp. 59–62.
52. James Luther Adams, *Paul Tillich's Philosophy of Culture, Science, and Religion* (New York: Harper and Row, 1965), p. 12.

13

them seriously.[53] In classifying Tillich as a believer (without regard to the specific content of his doctrine of God), Adams is more or less in agreement with the previous writers, but he is not as willing to classify the Tillichian God. In a chapter on Tillich's philosophy of religion, Adams complains that he can find nothing in Tillich's writing about "the character of God and his relation to the world."[54] Adams' last chapter is a protracted struggle to make sense of Tillich. Its general tenor reflects the view that Tillich is often empty, nonsensical, or contradictory. For example: "What particular character in God it is that impels him to fulfill a purpose in history is not made evident by the assertion that nothing can 'prevent us from community with the infinite and unexhaustible ground of meaning and being.'"[55] Again: "Even if we grant that God is not an object and that the term 'personal' is a symbol, still we are left in doubt as to whether God has a character somehow suggested by the symbol or is merely said to have it in order that our loneliness, anxiety, and despair may be overcome."[56] He concludes that "it is because Tillich has been so prone to show that God is not an Object or a Supreme Being that he has inadequately dealt with the question of the character of God—at least, when considered under the rubric of the Unconditioned."[57]

The Fabric of Paul Tillich's Theology, by David Kelsey, is a book predicated on the belief that one should take seriously Tillich's claim to be a Christian theologian and not a mere metaphysician with religious interests. Yet Kelsey sometimes wonders whether Tillich's God is more than philosophical. As he sees it, Tillich presents two conflicting conceptions of God: form and power. Both relate to the biblical picture of God. When Tillich explains this picture in terms of form, God becomes an imaginative impression formed by the revelatory experience. Here there is a formal analogy between the picture and God, but one which leaves us with no clear description of God. When the picture is explained in terms of power, the analogy is functional. In this case power, or the courage of self-affirmation, flows from the symbolic picture and is the meaning of "God." This, thinks Kelsey, "turns Tillich's ontology

---

53. *Ibid.*, p. 16.
55. *Ibid.*, p. 268
57. *Ibid.*, p. 270.

54. *Ibid.*, p. 226.
56. *Ibid.*, p. 269.

into a philosophical anthropology";[58] courage enables man to "affirm" himself despite nonbeing. From these deductions Kelsey reaches the conclusion that Tillich offers what amounts to two Gods, one supernatural (by implication) and the other philosophical. Neither approach to explicating the biblical picture tells us anything, he says, because a picture is merely esthetic and cannot make claims.[59]

Robert Scharlemann may well object to having his book, *Reflection and Doubt in the Thought of Paul Tillich*, grouped among "hesitant" interpretations, for he elucidates in confident tones suggesting anything but hesitancy. But the reader, striving to discern whether Scharlemann's rendition of being-itself harmonizes with a God who is rational and self-conscious, has a rough time of it. The book's introduction hints at a theistic slant: Armbruster, who we recall decided that being-itself *was* intelligent and personal, is cited as a work that "succeeds in catching Tillich's vision" to a laudable degree. Later, dealing with Tillich's Christology, Scharlemann mentions "the two extremes anticipated in Jesus—a decision for the will of God, and a decision against the will of God."[60] That sounds like the God of theism, a God with a will; and if "will" is being used in some figurative or fictional or pantheistic sense, the context fails to bring this out. The word "anticipated," referring to something subsequently repeated, seems to rule out the possibility that this "will" exists only in the biblical story. Nevertheless, another passage suggests an allowable pantheistic interpretation: "In the self's [man's] thinking God, God is thinking himself." Does this mean that an external intelligence projects itself into man's intelligence, or do we face a pantheistic concept holding that God participates nondirectively in man and man's mind, in which (among other things) the universal essence flows? Most of Scharlemann's book suggests the latter interpretation. There are several references to the "metaphysical spectator," which seems to indicate that Tillichian reality can be viewed as a metaphysical system. God "is not a third kind of being but the ground of the two irreducible

58. David H. Kelsey, *The Fabric of Paul Tillich's Theology* (New Haven: Yale University Press, 1967), p. 61.

59. *Ibid.*, pp. 174–75, 196–97.

60. Robert P. Scharlemann, *Reflection and Doubt in the Thought of Paul Tillich* (New Haven: Yale University Press, 1969), p. 106.

kinds of being [man and the rest of the universe]."[61] To which one can only comment, if "ground" had any obvious meaning, we would not be writing books about Tillich. "God is not a supernatural being [in how narrow a sense?], but he is not the unity of self and world in a larger whole either [pantheism]."[62] It begins to sounds as though God includes—metaphysically participates in—the universe yet also stands beyond it. Are we back to George Thomas' pan*en*theism? Or might not the traditional Creator (ground) be said, as McKelway would have it, to be something other than a being yet not the universe either? Unlike Armbruster, Scharlemann simply hasn't faced and tried to answer for us that crucial question: does being-itself have mental attributes resembling those of a person?

The next observer, a rabbi, supplements Howlett in representing religious viewpoints outside the Christian church. Interestingly, he comes nearer to the truth than any of the preceding writers. Bernard Martin, in *The Existentialist Theology of Paul Tillich*, is concerned primarily with Tillich's doctrine of man. He therefore confines himself to a brief review of Tillich's doctrine of God, which he considers to be separable from that of man. This review leads Martin to the very tentative position that Tillich's God may not be supernatural at all. What, he asks, can Tillich mean by God but "an inward drive in all individual beings?"[63] But when Martin discusses Tillich's concept of revelation, one can't be sure whether he construes it supernaturally or not. On the whole, his writing suggests uncertainty, though perhaps his caution is more a matter of inter-faith courtesy. His final thoughts, at any rate, lean in the direction of a philosophical interpretation: "Tillich's doctrine of God, in short, appears to us to be not an explication of the God of the Judaeo-Christian tradition, but rather a philosophical [metaphysical?] doctrine that uses most of the traditional terms but reinterprets them through the use of a radical symbolic method."[64]

A final critic with no definite idea as to what Tillich means by God is David Freeman. "Tillich certainly uses the term God, but

61. *Ibid.*, pp. 40, 29.   62. *Ibid.*

63. Bernard Martin, *The Existentialist Theology of Paul Tillich* (New Haven: College and University Press, 1963), p. 174.

64. *Ibid.*, p. 175.

what does he understand it to signify?" Freeman's monograph, *Tillich*, is very clear on the point that Tillich's God is not the God of theism. "Tillich is an atheist, if, by 'atheist' one means anyone who denies the existence of the God of theism." Freeman is not speaking in terms of some ultra-narrow concept of the traditional God either. "The word 'God' has been understood, within the main stream of Christian tradition, to refer to a Supreme Person, the Creator, and Sustainer of the world. Christian theism never reduced God to a being on the same coordinate level of other beings." The traditional God is rejected by Tillich, who thereby "places himself outside the main stream of historic Christianity." But what, of a positive nature, can be said about Tillich's God? "At the foundation of the system is an understanding of the idea of God that is neither naturalistic nor supernaturalistic. Tillich tells us he has such an understanding. But has he told us what it is that he understands?" What Tillich does say is "unintelligible," because "divine ground" and similar phrases convey no meaning. "Maybe he's got a secret, a secret thesis, but what is it? He won't tell us." (If this sounds like sarcasm, consider the possibility that it is the best hypothesis reviewed thus far.)[65]

The Tillichian Perplex

The considerable disagreement as to the nature of Tillich's God leads to the obvious question: who is correct? This query is discomfiting, for what must now be said tends to place the present endeavor in a league with an essay from Frederick Crews's delightful satire on scholarly criticism, *The Pooh Perplex*. Therein the imaginary scholar, Harvey C. Window, proceeds with an analysis of A. A. Milne's classic in this fashion: "Neither Ogle, nor Smythe, nor Bunker, nor Wart asked himself the absolutely basic questions about *Winnie-the-Pooh*, and thus each of them necessarily failed to grasp the key to the book's entire meaning. I find myself in the embarrassing position of being the only possessor of this key, and I am writing this essay only to alter such an unbalanced situation as quickly as possible."[66]

65. David H. Freeman, *Tillich* (Philadelphia: Presbyterian and Reformed Publishing Co., 1962), pp. 9–42.
66. Frederick C. Crews, *The Pooh Perplex* (New York: E. P. Dutton, 1963), p. 4.

None of the foregoing interpreters of Tillich is correct or even close to an understanding of Tillich. There is a key to Tillich, one which opens wide all doors to interpretation, but no analysis published to date has grasped it. Happily, though, the situation with Tillich is not nearly as unbalanced as that with Pooh. For Tillich likes to speak of a "No" and a "Yes" which are dialectically united in his thought. This means there are really two keys to Tillich, one which opens an outer door to the No and one which unlocks the inner door leading to the Yes. Other critics have accurately discerned what the No means and have even made progress toward explaining the Yes. In particular, Alasdair MacIntyre and Walter Kaufmann find not a modicum of literal meaning in any of Tillich's statements that seemingly imply a supernatural God of one sort or another. Without hesitation they have bluntly identified Tillich as an atheist, and not merely with respect to the God of theism. They have understood that Tillich's No relates to *any* supernatural God and to supernaturalism generally.

MacIntyre, in a commentary on John Robinson's *Honest to God*, declares accurately that Tillich stands with Bishop Robinson as a theological atheist. When Tillich speaks of God creating and revealing himself or otherwise exhibiting the characteristics of a being, he is relying on his private concept of God. God is just a name for ultimate concern on the part of an individual. Belief in God consists of nothing more than moral seriousness; the traditional content is entirely gone. "Even if we were to concede Tillich a verbal triumph over the atheist, the substance of atheism has been conceded."[67]

According to Kaufmann, Tillich is using ancient formulations of belief to describe his own lack of belief.[68] The old creeds are reinterpreted so thoroughly that they not only stop meaning what they have always meant to the faithful but actually express the views of nonbelievers. In an antitheological passage clearly alluding to Tillich, Kaufmann notes that a theology of ultimate concern imputes gods to everyone. "God" is one's ultimate concern, and the only question is whether one's particular concern is truly ultimate

67. Alasdair MacIntyre, "God and the Theologians," *Encounter*, 21, no. 3 (September, 1963), p. 6.
68. Walter Kaufmann, *The Faith of a Heretic*, (Garden City: Doubleday, 1961), p. 44.

or merely idolatrous.[69] Only the person who lacks any ultimate concern can be called an atheist, which is why Tillich can disavow atheism; and "it turns out that millions of theists may really be atheists, while such avowed atheists as Freud and Nietzsche aren't atheists at all."[70] By redefining terms in this manner, Tillich cultivates a "double-speak" designed to convey opposing messages to different groups.[71] Thus does he say No in a way that sounds like Yes.[72]

Both MacIntyre and Kaufmann have not only identified Tillich's No but, in a very general way, have pointed toward Tillich's nonsupernatural (and nonmetaphysical, if one cares to make a distinction) doctrine of God. In two short paragraphs of an article on another subject, MacIntyre displays more insight into Tillich's God than all the previously surveyed critics pack into several books and odd chapters devoted exclusively to Tillich. Kaufmann, whose remarks are likewise of an incidental nature, devotes a little more space to Tillich and supplies what is certainly the most penetrating analysis of his thought written to date. Both writers recognize that when Tillich calls God our ultimate concern he is not talking about a supernatural being or metaphysical "what's-it"; they correctly read Tillich as referring abstractly to the concerns of particular individuals. However, a deeper, unifying ultimate concern, one which is the matrix for all "true" (nonidolatrous) concerns of the particular variety, has been overlooked. It is this deeper, or ultimately ultimate, concern that gives "ultimate concern" its essential meaning and is the key to the inner door of Tillich's thought.

UNLOCKING THE DOOR

Few who have read Tillich will dispute that he is playing a cat-and-mouse game with his readers. He is deliberately elusive where he could easily be clearer. He refuses to define terms to which he obviously attaches definite meanings. This isn't carelessness: he writes with meticulous care. Neither is it ineptitude: Tillich can write with great precision when he wants to. Rather, Tillich's elusiveness reflects a calculated effort to remain esoteric. He would

69. *Ibid.*, p. 95.
71. *Ibid.*, p. 130.

70. *Ibid.*, p. 132.
72. *Ibid.*, p. 111.

keep his deepest meaning hidden from all but a few who are prepared to receive it.

And this gives us a clue to the meaning of Tillich. It suggests that he has something to hide. Why should he hide his lamp under a bushel? Because to wield influence within the Christian church and to influence individual Christians he must be accepted as a Christian theologian, however unorthodox. Yet his doctrine of God, once exposed, is plainly un-Christian. Now there are many concepts of God not exactly compatible with Christianity. Many of these exude enough supernaturalism to protect their advocates against major censure. But one in particular must be concealed because it not only eschews supernaturalism but actually underlies the dominant moral viewpoint of those who have rejected organized religion. That viewpoint is humanism. Humanism asserts that the tests of human conduct must be found in human experience, not in superhuman ordinances; concern for man replaces concern about pleasing God. Loosely speaking, the humanist elevates man to the rank of God.

This is precisely what Tillich has done. His lamp illuminates a message, the secret message that God is man. Generic man. Mankind. Humanity. The lamp must therefore be hidden.

Before plunging into the detailed analysis supporting this interpretation, we can profitably pause for orientation by examining several basic propositions summarizing Tillich's thought. The references to Hegelian dialectics—the movement from thesis to antithesis to synthesis—will be explained to the uninitiated in the next chapter.

1. Tillich is an atheist, in the broadest sense of the word. He does not believe in a theistic God, a metaphysical God, or any other supernatural entity. Everything he says must be interpreted in a manner consistent with this fact.

2. What Tillich calls "God" has two sides, one abstract ("ultimate") and the other concrete. It is an analogical synthesis of theology's divine-human Christ and Hegel's metaphysical Spirit, with its universal and particular sides. God's abstract side, "being-itself," is humanity—man's ultimate concern. Humanity compares to the "fully God" side of the Christ and the universal side of Hegel's Spirit. God's concrete side, analo-

gous to the Christ's "fully man" side and Spirit's particularistic side, is the manifold "incarnations" of ultimate concern for humanity, i.e., diverse preliminary concerns "transparent to" the divine.

3. New Being occurs when a person embraces a preliminary concern, ambiguously called "ultimate concern," shaped from a basic concern for humanity. It represents the climax of a Hegelian dialectic moving from (a) revelation, the *thesis* which says Yes to God, to (b) reason, the *antithesis* which says No to God and the supernatural, to (c) humanism, the *synthesis* which combines a Yes to God with a No to supernaturalism, producing the Yes to the nonsupernatural "God above God." Alternatively, the movement is from God to man to God = man.

4. "Jesus as the Christ," the main symbol for New Being, represents the above three stages: (a) God's *incarnation* in the Christ represents the initial Yes, or a union of God and man, (b) man's *crucifixion* of God describes the No, rejection of the supernatural, and (c) the *resurrection* symbolizes the new life —New Being—man wins when he submits to the higher God, the synthesis of Yes and No.

5. Divine Spirit, Tillich's substitute term for Holy Spirit, is an alternate symbol for New Being. As such it is the theological analogue of the correlated philosophical concept, dialectical synthesis. (How to remember: DS = Divine Spirit = Dialectical Synthesis. A coincidence?) The analogy is union: the Holy Spirit *unites* God and man (spirit possession), dialectical synthesis *unites* thesis and antithesis, and New Being *unites* Yes and No.

6. Demonism is the moral opposite of New Being. It is having an ultimate concern, in the preliminary concern sense of the term, which is "transparent to" something less than or other than *all* humanity, e.g., a special group (nation or sect) or deity (Jehovah). Stated otherwise, it entails elevating a preliminary concern to the rank of ultimacy when it is "opaque to" man's truly ultimate concern, humanity.

7. Estrangement is humanity's state of being divided against itself (selfishness, hatred, war, and so on). Man is estranged from man, hence from God. The concept is the analogical equivalent of (a) sin, theology's version of man separated from God, and

21

(*b*) Hegelian estrangement, where the Spirit is divided against itself through failure to recognize itself as Spirit. Going by the latter model, estrangement is also the antithesis of a dialectic moving from *potential* human unity (thesis) to the *actual*—existential—separation of man from man toward the humanistic synthesis, *actualized potentiality*, or the self-realization of humanity as God.

8. The Kingdom of God is this goal: a purely conceptual situation of universal humanism—universal New Being. It is where estrangement is fully overcome and *all* men accept *all* humanity ("all in all") as God. In addition to being analogous to theology's Kingdom of God, Tillich's Kingdom relates by analogy to such philosophical utopias as Hegel's Germanic monarchy and Marx's world communism, both of which are dialectical syntheses evolving from movements of separation and return.

9. History, referring to moral history, is a vaguely dialectical process imitating on a higher plane the New Being dialectic, with "theonomy" substituted for New Being and the Kingdom of God as the ultimate goal. Moral progress oscillates between (*a*) heteronomy, or the subjugation of man to religious and political authority, (*b*) autonomy, or periods of relative freedom for reason to be exercised, and (*c*) theonomy, periods born of "kairoi" and marked by unusually strong tendencies to combine "God" and reason under the banner of humanism.

10. The Trinity symbolizes the "divine life," another ambiguous term. It refers first to the New Being dialectic, which correlates the Christ's movement of separation from and return to God with the dialectical movement from Yes to No back to Yes (belief–unbelief–new belief). It also designates mankind's "ontological" movement from essence (potential human unity) to existence (actual estrangement) back toward essence (actual unity, or essence = existence). Just as Son comes from Father, antithesis comes from thesis; and the Holy Spirit unites Father and Son, just as synthesis unites thesis and antithesis. Thus the divine life describes the God above God's life in both its general (divine) aspect and its particular (human) aspect as a movement toward moral maturity.

Unfolding within the framework of these basic propositions, Tillich's thought restates classical Christian theology in, for the most part, classical language. But the language assumes new meaning and introduces radically new conclusions. Classical theology deals with the "plight of man"—with man's fall from innocence into a state of sin, with his sinful existence in estrangement from God, and with his rescue by a divine redeemer who brings God's gift of salvation. Innocence, sin, and salvation are the three acts of a supernatural drama; man and God are the leading protagonists. The play, naturally, has a moral: life has meaning, which is that the mortal life lived in the service of God is preparation for the eternal life lived in union with God.

Tillich drastically transforms the classical drama into a dialectical one. However, the acts, the characters (with one subtle change), and the lines remain as before. The difference is in the meaning. In the new Act I, man is innocent—innocent of the knowledge that there is no God, no realm of the supernatural. But doubt insinuates itself into the scene and, partaking of the knowledge of reality, man falls. In Act II man exists in a state of sin, plagued by estrangement not only from the false God but from the true and by anxiety over his (man's) very being. In Act III a savior appears and grasps man. The savior is named God, and he looks and talks and behaves very much like the old God. But beneath the flesh he is a wholly different individual named ultimate concern. He is man's neighbor, and he whispers a message of atheistic humanism. Here the modern drama, like its classical prototype, delivers its moral: life has meaning, which is that man exists to serve man, and the mortal life lived in quest of an ultimate concern and without benefit of supernatural guidance yields fulfillment in a present "eternity"—the Eternal Now.

THE FOUNDATIONS CRUMBLE

Make no mistake, Paul Tillich is out to shake the foundations of religious belief (his No), yet to do so in a constructive manner (his Yes). "The shaking of the foundations"—a phrase based on Isaiah—is Tillich's way of describing the religious disillusionment which he and "the majority of human beings in our period" have undergone.[73] The foundations of Tillich's early belief were shaken until they crumbled. He knows that others have shared his experience. For him, the crumbling of the old foundations was ultimately rewarding, for it led to the "revelation" that God is man. But it was not an experience without distress. The widespread shaking of the foundations in our time, as Tillich views the scene, has brought similar emotional turmoil to numerous others. He speaks to these individuals: he would finish the destruction of the old and help those who are ready for help to build anew. If we are to appreciate fully the content of Tillich's thought, this aspect of it must be understood. Such understanding calls for a review of, first, the circumstances attending Tillich's own drift into doubt and, second, his view of the problems posed by society's drift into doubt.

Tillich's Drift into Doubt

The depth of Tillich's early belief, and consequently the impact of the doubt which eventually fell upon him, can be attributed in large measure to his upbringing. He was raised in a small town, which itself is usually a conservative influence. Located in eastern Brandenburg, the town had a medieval character that augmented the parochialism of the environment by giving the impression of an insular, self-contained world. Tillich's father was not only the community's leading minister but superintendent of the church district. In keeping with Lutheran paternalism, the elder Tillich was undisputed head of the family, his authority encompassing his wife, children, and servants. The general spirit of discipline that pervaded the household was reinforced in the public schools, which operated under clerical supervision.

Tillich's father was conscientious and dignified, but utterly convinced of the rectitude of the conservative Lutheran viewpoint and inclined to grow angry when confronted by doubt. Though more liberal, his mother stood fast by the strict tenets of Western Reformed Protestant morality. At the same time, a warm and loving atmosphere in the home deepened Tillich's respect for both parents. With the early death of Tillich's mother, the already dominant paternal influence was strengthened. Of it Tillich later wrote, "My

73. *Foundations*, p. 3.

24

father's authority, which was both personal and intellectual and which, because of his position in the church, I identified with the religious authority of revelation, made every attempt at autonomous thinking an act of religious daring and connected criticism of authority with a sense of guilt."[74]

At the age of twelve, Tillich was sent to board in a larger town as a pupil in a humanistic *gymnasium*, roughly the equivalent of high school and the first two years of college. Two years later, in 1900, his father moved to Berlin to accept an important position. There Tillich entered another *gymnasium*, where he passed his final examinations in 1904. Evidently the awakening of liberalism occurred in Tillich during this period. Away from home and beginning to mature intellectually, he found himself in what he has described as an atmosphere of tension between the religious and humanistic traditions. His "inward struggles with the truth of traditional religion"[75] began. In a semi-autobiographical passage, Tillich describes the situation this way: "The truth the child first receives is imposed upon him by adults, predominantly by his parents. This cannot be otherwise; and he cannot help accepting it." However, he continues, "sooner or later the child revolts against the truth given to him."[76]

In Tillich's case, full-scale revolt came later rather than sooner. His father's influence still dominated Tillich's incipient spirit of independence; theological, ethical, and political ideas contrary to what he had learned at home could be accepted only after protracted struggle. "When I would belatedly arrive at a conclusion that had long since become commonplace to the average intelligence, it still seemed to me to be shocking and full of revolutionary implications."[77] This attitude allowed the next steps in Tillich's education to be taken despite rising doubt. He enrolled in several German universities, following a theological curriculum. After passing two theological examinations, he acquired, in 1911, his Doctor of Philosophy degree. A year later he received the degree of Licentiate of Theology and was ordained into the Evangelical Lutheran Church.

Apparently it was while completing his higher education that

74. *Boundary*, pp. 36–37. 75. *Boundary*, p. 30.
76. *New Being*, p. 65. 77. *Boundary*, p. 37.

Tillich lost his faith. Shedding his remaining interest in traditional theology, he turned to historical criticism. As "documentary proof" of this reorientation Tillich cites a group of "propositions" he presented to some theological friends in 1911.[78] They involved substituting the biblical picture of the Christ for the historical Jesus to safeguard against the possibility that the latter's existence might become historically improbable. We are not told precisely what these propositions were—presumably they were vague—but their general description and his continuing interest in the problem make it virtually certain that his use of the Christ as a symbol for humanism was being tested. Confirmation that Tillich abandoned traditional religion at about this time comes from David Hopper's analysis of Tillich's 1912 treatise, *Mysticism and Guilt-Consciousness in Schelling's Philosophical Development*. It is unfortunate that Hopper was unable to match his knowledge of the German language with knowledge of just what to look for in the treatise. Nevertheless, he does show that Tillich was already preoccupied with the synthesis of opposites. Unknown to Hopper, these opposites symbolize God and man; as Hopper does recognize, the principle of "coincidence of opposites" has characterized Tillich's writing ever since. Hopper's judgment that Tillich's later thought dates back to his early treatise therefore appears well grounded. Additional evidence of the approximate date of Tillich's "conversion" is found in a 1915 pamphlet also summarized by Hopper. In it Tillich rejects the conventional belief that God is a being and speaks already of "the God above God."[79]

His loss of faith is described by Tillich in one of his sermons. The excerpt ostensibly refers to others but clearly embraces Tillich's own experience:

And there is the most fundamental kind of having and not having—our having and losing God. Perhaps in our childhood, and even beyond it, our experience of God was rich. We may remember the moments in which we felt His presence intensely. We may remember our praying with an overflowing heart, our encounter with the holy in words and music and holy places. We communicated with God; but this communication was taken from us, because we had it and did not have it. We

78. *Boundary*, p. 50.
79. See Hopper, *Tillich: A Theological Portrait*, pp. 28, 101–26, 167–69.

26

failed to let it grow, and therefore, it slowly disappeared, leaving only an empty space.[80]

In Tillich, the empty space seems to have produced an inordinate amount of spiritual discomfort. The implication of some of his later writings that he might have passed through a stage of severe anxiety, with an attendant sense of the meaninglessness of life, is open to severe skepticism. Yet Tillich's deeply religious upbringing, as manifested in his decision to prepare for the ministry, together with a sense of loyalty to his father, could indeed have made loss of faith an unusually trying experience. His own difficulties, supported by other motives to be discussed later, in turn directed Tillich's attention to the more general problem (as he chose to interpret the situation) of a society beset by doubt.

Society's Drift into Doubt

Atheism proved no barrier to a decision by Tillich to continue in his chosen field. He became an assistant pastor in the Old Prussian United Church and then, in 1914, volunteered to serve as a military chaplain. In this latter capacity he was active for four years. Preconceived opinions quite possibly colored his reaction to the wartime experience but, as Tillich describes it, his encounter with the men in the trenches convinced him of a widening gap between religion and society. At the outset, most German soldiers "shared the popular belief in a nice God who would make everything work out for the best."[81] Instead, the worst materialized, and by the fifth year of the war belief in a personal God had disappeared among the troops. During this interim, living in daily contact with men from the industrial masses, Tillich also became intensely aware of disunity among the nation's classes. The common man viewed the Church as the undubitable ally of the ruling elite. Tillich was increasingly inclined to agree.

Returning from the war, Tillich began to write about the split between the Church and the people. His literary bent was facilitated by a shift to an academic career. From 1919 to 1924 he lectured in theology at the University of Berlin. A theological professorship at Marburg and philosophical professorships at Dresden,

---

80. *Eternal Now*, p. 40.   81. *New Being*, p. 52.

Leipzig, and Frankfurt followed. (The last post was held by Tillich between 1929 and 1933, when he was dismissed by Hitler and came to the United States.) During these years Tillich produced a continuous stream of books and articles in which he explored the implications of popular discontent with religion. These and subsequent writings mirror his conviction that his own drift into doubt has been repeated over and over again within society. Many persons, Tillich understands, no longer believe in angels, miracles, hell's fire, and the divine savior. Neither do they believe that a book which attests to the veracity of such "nonsense" can be "the Word of God." Some no longer believe in God. As children they were taught to believe and they believed, but the stage of "dreaming innocence" has ended. The Church can no longer reach these people, for its message is, literally, incredible.

The problem and demands of this widening gap between religious doctrine and what modern man can believe is a favorite subject of Tillich. He feels that "the Protestant message in its orthodox form is wholly unsuited to reach the proletariat."[82] It is unintelligible to the masses, even when reduced to its simplest form (which would be the simple belief in a personal God). "Even the middle classes have become inwardly estranged from the teaching of the church—in some cases radically so, in others in a compromising way."[83] Consequently, Protestantism is faced with the question of survival.

To survive, Tillich contends, Protestantism must change fundamentally. It "arose with that era which today is either coming to an end or else undergoing fundamental structural changes."[84] The old thought patterns no longer prevail. Man no longer comprehends the old supernaturalism. "This obviously forbids that the message should be set forth in the terminology of the Reformation or in the ways prevailing in the Protestant church today."[85] It means that Protestantism must instead return to its basic principle —the "Protestant principle." This is the principle of "criticism and protest"[86] directed against all that is wrong with traditional religion.

82. *Protestant*, p. 177.   83. *Protestant*, p. 177.
84. *Protestant*, p. 222.   85. *Protestant*, p. 201.
86. *Boundary*, p. 42.   George Tavard misinterprets Tillich when he says

Protest, however, is not enough. Doubt can drive and has driven man to the "boundary-situation" of despair. He who has ceased to believe, imagines Tillich, gropes for a "meaning" to replace the one that has been lost, for rules of conduct to supplant the divine laws, for courage to accept the "finitude" of human life—and for a new god to take the place of God. This "despair" Tillich would meet with a threefold message. First is the No. The message "must insist upon the radical experience of the boundary-situation; it must destroy the secret reservations harbored by the modern man which prevent him from accepting resolutely the limits of his human existence." By this Tillich means that there can be no compromise with the supernatural. We cannot, for example, continue to believe in a supernatural being subject to the reservations that he is neither vindictive nor anthropomorphic nor spatially localized. Second, the message "must pronounce the 'Yes' that ... declares us whole in the disintegration and cleavage of soul and community; the judgment that affirms our having truth in the very absence of truth (even of religious truth); the judgment that reveals the meaning of our life in the situation in which all the meaning of life has disappeared." Here Tillich alludes to his Yes to humanity and to the "truth" that God is man; this is what overcomes the spiritual "disintegration" that threatens when man pronounces his No to the traditional God. Third, the message "must witness to the 'New Being'" which alone can restore power to the word of Protestantism. This third point is a combination of the first two: it emphasizes that New Being is a *synthesis* of No and Yes.[87]

Here, in three-part formula, is Tillich's redemptive answer for a society that has drifted into doubt. And with the acceptance of this message, pleads Tillich, "may we rather see, through the crumbling

---

that the Protestant principle requires "that every man-made action, formulation or idea must be protested against inasmuch as it tends to undermine God's transcendence" and that the principle "entails an affirmation of the universal power of God." (See Tavard, *Paul Tillich and the Christian Message*, p. 18.) Here is a real object lesson in Tillichian ambiguity. Tavard's description is correct provided one understands that God, salvation, and other supernaturalistic ideas are the man-made ideas to be protested and that humanity's "transcendence" and "universal power" are to be affirmed, but this obviously isn't what Tavard thinks Tillich has in mind.

87. *Protestant*, pp. 203–5.

of a world, the rock of eternity and the salvation which has no end!"[88]

SAYING NO

The Yes—the affirmation that God is man—"is the pith and essence of the Protestant message,"[89] according to Tillich. Thus the bulk of this study will be concerned with the Yes. But the Yes emerges dialectically from the No, which is the new foundation replacing the one which has crumbled. The No denies, unconditionally, the supernatural. Innumerable commentators have completely missed the point of Tillich's Yes because they have not grasped the full meaning of his No. They have blandly assumed that Tillich is in many respects another liberal sharing liberalism's customary rejection of Christianity's more conservative beliefs, for example, belief in the divinity of Jesus and in the cantankerous, Old Testament God. They have also assumed that Tillich, in typical liberal fashion, draws the line somewhere on how much of the supernatural to discard, reserving at least enough room for a supernatural (but not necessarily theistic) God. Anyone who thinks that, contrary to the passage quoted earlier, the No is less than fully "radical" or carries "secret reservations" is not going to understand Tillich. Indeed, part of the secret of interpreting him is to proceed by elimination, taking each ambiguity and setting aside any interpretation which predicates the existence of the supernatural in any degree or form. To accent this point we must pause briefly to inspect Tillich's views on supernaturalism. Under the present heading his attitudes toward biblical mythology generally, divine law, immortality, the divinity of Jesus, and a selection of lesser beliefs and doctrines will be examined. The following division of the chapter will present evidence that, despite the confidence of most supernaturalists and quite a few others that Tillich is ultimately a supernaturalist himself, a supernatural God does not stand as an exception to Tillich's No.

Biblical Mythology

The Bible contains many stories of supernatural events. Among these are the story of paradise, Adam's fall, Noah and the flood, the virgin birth, Jesus' resurrection and ascension to heaven, and

88. *Foundations*, p. 11.   89. *Protestant*, p. 204.

the countless miracle stories. Bible scholars describe these as myth, and liberal Christians (who include most of the scholars) as well as numerous moderates agree; but religious conservatives take them literally. Where does Tillich stand? He declares, "It has been shown that in their narrative parts the Old and the New Testament combine historical, legendary and mythological elements and that in many cases it is impossible to separate these elements from each other with any degree of probability."[90] While conceding that genuine history is often intermingled with mythology, Tillich is quick to recognize supernatural aspects as myth. "It is a disastrous distortion of the meaning of faith to identify it with the belief in the historical validity of the Biblical stories."[91] Such distorted faith, he believes, should be set aside: "We must not preserve or produce artificial stumbling-blocks, miracle-stories, legends, myths, and other sophisticated paradoxical talk."[92]

History as presented in Genesis is a case in point. "It is obvious that a theology which interprets the Biblical story of creation as a scientific description of an event which happened once upon a time interferes with the methodologically controlled scientific work";[93] it simply isn't true. The story of Adam and Eve is "an old myth,"[94] and it is "absurd" to attribute mankind's troubles to Adam's flouting a command of God.[95] As for "the fall," Tillich gives it a symbolic meaning, which will be explained in the next chapter.

Various New Testament tales of the supernatural are similarly given short shrift by Tillich. He terms "idolatrous" the faith of individuals for whom the virgin birth "is understood in biological terms, resurrection and ascension as physical events, the second coming of the Christ as a telluric, or cosmic, catastrophe."[96] The virgin birth, he thinks, is a "most obviously legendary story,"[97] and the other items he also finds unbelievable. It is "fanciful" to think of "dead bodies leaving their graves" or otherwise experiencing resurrection.[98] The miracle stories are "a stumbling block for scholars and preachers and teachers,"[99] and it is "superstitious" to think that the laws of nature can be suspended.[100]

90. *Dynamics*, p. 87.
91. *Dynamics*, p. 87.
92. *Foundations*, p. 129.
93. *Dynamics*, p. 83.
94. *Eternal Now*, p. 16.
95. *ST–2*, p. 130.
96. *Dynamics*, p. 52.
97. *Culture*, p. 66.
98. *New Being*, p. 24.
99. *New Being*, p. 37.
100. *Eternal Now*, p. 116. See also *Dialogue*, p. 158.

31

Divine Law

One of the major assumptions of religion is that there are divine laws governing the conduct of human beings. These are written, so to speak, among the stars; they are supernatural in origin. In Christianity, the source of these laws is God. He has revealed them to man through the Ten Commandments, the prophets, Jesus, religious hierarchies, and preachers and laymen in the grip of the Holy Spirit. The supernatural moral code provides man with ultimate criteria for judging right and wrong.

Tillich doesn't accept this idea. Why, he asks, should anyone obey such commandments if they existed? "How are they distinguished from commands given by a human tyrant?"[101] The divine lawgiver might be stronger than man. He might have the ability to destroy man. But does that make his commands right? Tillich suggests that it would be better to let the giver of arbitrary laws destroy us physically than to accept the psychological destruction that would accompany submission to an alien will.

Those who believe in and champion the divine moral code tacitly assume that might makes right, at least in the divine-human encounter. Tillich argues, however, that injustice occurs whenever, in a struggle between a stronger and a weaker power, the stronger uses its advantage to reduce or destroy the weaker. There is no authority which is just by its very nature. There are, he notes, various authorities which constitute "authority in principle." Examples are the Pope for Catholics, the Bible for Protestants, and the dictator for subjects living under a totalitarian regime. All such authority, avers Tillich, is unjust. "It disregards the intrinsic claim of human beings to become responsible for ultimate decisions."[102] Because it is unjust it should be resisted. "A stranger, even if his name were God, who imposes commands upon us must be resisted or, as Nietzsche has expressed it in his symbol of the 'ugliest man,' he must be killed because nobody can stand him."[103]

In order to drive home his point, Tillich speculates about what might happen if a Christ were to come in power and glory "to impose upon us His power, His wisdom, His morality, and His piety." The Christ could subdue us through his strength, superla-

101. *Love*, p. 76.   102. *Love*, pp. 89–90.
103. *Culture*, p. 136.

32

tive government, absolute wisdom, and general perfection. He would fail, though, to win the hearts of men. "His power would break our freedom; His glory would overwhelm us like a burning, blinding sun; our very humanity would be swallowed in His Divinity." Man longs for divine intervention, but were it to occur we would pay the price in the loss of "our freedom, our humanity, and our spiritual dignity."[104]

Life beyond the Grave

Christianity is and always has been a salvation religion. It derives its name from a divine savior whose death was supposedly necessary in order that man could enjoy eternal life. Although atonement and even the hell from which man was conditionally saved are no longer believed in by millions of modern Christians, life beyond the grave—supernatural immortality—remains a widely accepted doctrine. Indeed, along with creation and divine law, it is one of the chief explanations of what God is all about.

Tillich emphatically rejects the "popular superstition"[105] of immortality. "Man should not boast of having an immortal soul" or assume that he is less mortal than other creatures.[106] "We often hide the seriousness of the 'buried' in the Creed, not only for the Christ, but also for ourselves, by imagining that not *we* shall be buried, but only a comparatively unimportant part of us, the physical body."[107] However, the "assertion that the soul continues to live after the death of the body cannot be proved either by evidence or by trustworthy authority."[108]

Why, then, do people continue to believe in immortality? The answer as Tillich sees it lies in a blend of courage and escapism. The belief in a life beyond the grave "tries to maintain one's self-affirmation even in the face of one's having to die."[109] It does this by continuing life to infinity so that death never takes place. In other words, people don't want to die. "They decide to believe, and make up in this way for the lack of evidence."[110] The belief is then rationalized by calling it faith.

---

104. *Foundations*, pp. 147–48.
106. *Eternal Now*, p. 114.
108. *Dynamics*, p. 36.
110. *Dynamics*, p. 36.

105. *ST–3*, pp. 409–10.
107. *Foundations*, p. 166.
109. *Courage*, p. 169.

To Tillich, faith in the hereafter is a poor substitute for the courage to face life despite the inevitability of death. He would bury once and for all the notion that salvation is "a magic procedure by which we lose our finiteness."[111] His idea of salvation is not "escaping from hell and being received in heaven, in what is badly called 'the life hereafter.' "[112] Rather, Tillichian salvation is a symbol, a symbol for becoming ultimately concerned about humanity. New Being brings salvation in an "eternal" present, not an eternal future.

In case the above evidence isn't sufficiently convincing, there is also some "ear witness" testimony by acquaintances of Tillich to consider. Nels F. S. Ferré records the time he (Ferré) naively recommended Tillich's resurrection doctrine to a student minister seeking funeral advice. "His face fell as he explained that he had had nine courses with Tillich at Union Theological Seminary and that both from his courses and from frequent personal questioning he knew that Tillich did not believe in any life after death." Reluctant to believe this, Ferré went down to Union to hear for himself. Under questioning, Tillich at first treated Ferré as one of the innocent whose abiding faith should not be disturbed. "But by the time I had phrased my questions with depth and seriousness long enough and often enough, I knew that I had to give up my original understanding of what he taught. He actually did not believe in the Christian God who raises the dead and who works personally in human history."[113]

The Divine Christ

Without supernatural salvation there can be no supernatural savior. Thus it should come as no surprise that Tillich disavows the belief that Jesus was the Christ (messiah), Savior, the Son of God, God incarnate, or otherwise divine. Christianity "paints" Jesus in divine colors,[114] but the portrait is not an accurate likeness.

By repeatedly using the phrase, "Jesus as the Christ," Tillich subtly emphasizes the real Jesus' fully human nature. The phrase

111. *Foundations*, p. 172.   112. *Eternal Now*, p. 114.
113. Nels F. S. Ferré, "Tillich and the Nature of Transcendence," *Paul Tillich: Retrospect and Future*, ed. T. A. Kantonen (Nashville: Abingdon Press, 1966), p. 8 (reprinted from *Religion in Life*, Winter, 1966).
114. *New Being*, p. 13.

is used in lieu of "Christ" or "Jesus Christ." It enables Tillich to refer, when necessary, to the fictional Jesus of Christian theology without showing respect for the title "Christ." He points out that "Christ" was originally just that—a title, a word for "messiah," and not Jesus' surname. "Let us at least sometimes remind ourselves and our people that *Jesus Christ* means *Jesus Who is said to be the Christ.*"[115]

Being well versed in the history of religion, Tillich knows that the divine Jesus—Jesus as the Christ—is just one example among many of a certain class of gods which long antedates Christianity. Gods in general, he observes, are sexually differentiated individuals, analogous to human beings, descending from one another, and sharing in the greatness and misery of humanity. Among them are "savior-gods who mediate between the highest gods and man, sometimes sharing the suffering and death of man in spite of their essential immortality."[116] By implication Tillich is linking Jesus with Osiris, Dionysus, Mithras, and other savior-gods of antiquity. Such gods, he says, belong to the world of mythology. With specific regard to the divine Christ, "If the Christ—a transcendent, divine being—appears in the fullness of time, lives, dies and is resurrected, this is an historical myth."[117]

Given such an outlook, it is not hard to anticipate Tillich's view of the notion that Jesus was the Son of God. During a tape-recorded seminar a student once asked Tillich, "Why was it necessary for Jesus to be tempted in the wilderness by God if Jesus was the Son of God?" Tillich's reply, in part, was that the student was "describing the superstitious concept of the Son of God."[118] Elsewhere Tillich stresses that everything said about God must be taken "symbolically," that is, figuratively. "As an example, look at the one small sentence: '*God has sent his son.*'" He states that this, "if taken literally, is absurd."[119] Tillich prefers to view it as a symbolic expression of God's relationship to man. (The symbolism can be taken to refer either to individual men being engendered by humanity or to the "finite" concerns of individuals, insofar as these

115. *Foundations*, p. 145.
117. *Dynamics*, p. 54.
119. *Culture*, pp. 62–63.

116. *Dynamics*, p. 49.
118. *Dialogue*, pp. 136–37.

35

concerns are "true," being fathered by an "infinite" concern for humanity.)

Incarnation fares no better than Christ, Savior, and Son of God. "If the *egeneto* in the Johannine sentence, *Logos sarx egeneto*, the 'Word became flesh,' is pressed, we are in the midst of a mythology of metamorphosis."[120] Incarnation is not metamorphosis but "manifestation in a personal life."[121] (This, as will be explained in Chapter 3, refers to the "incarnation" in individuals of ultimate concern—love—for humanity.) Therefore, while incarnation need not be repudiated, its literal understanding must be replaced by a symbolic one which "removes the pagan connotations and rejects its supranaturalistic interpretation."[122] Plain enough, one would think.

Other Beliefs and Doctrines

We cannot at this point explore Tillich's views on all of the remaining beliefs and doctrines of Christianity, noting how he has purged them of supernatural meaning; this ground must be covered in later chapters. Just to savor the breadth of his antisupernaturalism, however, we can profitably pause to examine a few more of his opinions.

One area not to be omitted is faith, for it encompasses all categories of Christian supernaturalism. Tillich says that the word "faith" has been "abused" by those who use it to mean "the belief in assertions for which there is no evidence."[123] Knowledge about ourselves and our world, he feels, should be reserved for scientific inquiry by us or those we trust. "Almost all the struggles between faith and knowledge are rooted in the wrong understanding of faith as a type of knowledge which has a low degree of evidence but is supported by religious authority."[124] Plainly, Tillich is on the side of knowledge. In turn, the related doctrine of justification by faith "is so strange to the modern man that there is scarcely any way of making it intelligible to him."[125]

The Holy Spirit, the Trinity, and divine providence, three important and interrelated Christian beliefs, also come under attack. "As for the mythology concerning the third person of the Trinity com-

120. *ST–2*, p. 149. 121. *ST–2*, p. 149.
122. *ST–2*, p. 149. 123. *New Being*, p. 38.
124. *Dynamics*, p. 33. 125. *Protestant*, p. 196.

ing down from heaven—forget all about it!"[126] And what about the doctrine that affirms that the Holy Spirit is joined by the Father and the Son in a Trinity, which is the one God of Christian monotheism? This he calls "the logical nonsense that three is one and one is three";[127] he finds it untenable. If God is not a Trinity, does he nevertheless remain the source of providential care? Belief in providence, Tillich argues, is a product of "wishful thinking" and has no basis in fact. "Neither the personal nor the historical belief in providence had depth or a real foundation."[128]

Sin, forgiveness, and grace are other supernatural concepts which Tillich dislikes. Because sin is disobeying divine law and Tillich is unable to discover any such law, he obviously cannot accept the existence of sin in the conventional sense. He declares that we must "realize that sin does *not* mean an immoral act, that 'sin' should never be used in the plural, and that not our sins, but rather our *sin* is the great, all-pervading problem" of the human race.[129] (It will be subsequently explained in detail that our "sin" is the estrangement of man from man—the "plight" that accompanied man when he was "created.") Without sins to be forgiven, the parallel doctrines of divine forgiveness and divine grace are naturally in jeopardy. Tillich has harsh words for the belief in "the willingness of a divine king and father to forgive over and again the foolishness and weakness of his subjects and children." To him this concept is "a merely childish destruction of a human dignity."[130]

THE UNCONDITIONAL NO

Most commentators would acknowledge that Tillich is *generally* antisupernaturalistic in his thought. Where they often go astray is in failing to perceive that Tillich is *absolutely* opposed to supernaturalism. Alexander McKelway seems to think that Tillich is merely trying to refine the anthropomorphic God who some people still believe sits on a throne in heaven into a nobler spirit or, anyhow, some sort of cosmic power which is "not *a* being" yet is still self-conscious and rational (and not too unlike the moderately refined deity in whom—not which—McKelway believes). J. H. Thomas

126. *Dialogue*, p. 77.
128. *New Being*, p. 53.
130. *Foundations*, pp. 155–56.

127. *ST–1*, p. 56.
129. *Foundations*, p. 154.

thinks Tillich espouses a metaphysical God. James Luther Adams can make little sense of Tillich but is convinced that Tillich is not an atheist. And so on. These writers are saying, in effect, that Tillich rejects the supernatural on the condition that he can keep his supernatural God—a God which might be termed panentheistic or pantheistic or metaphysical or mystical but which remains a variation of the supernatural theme. If we are to understand Tillich, however, we must realize that his No is loud and unconditional. The complete evidence on this point must await Chapter 3, where the thesis that Tillich's God is man is developed. Nevertheless, there is abundant preliminary evidence which, by clarifying what God is not, paves the way for a fresh interpretation of what God is.

"All" Supernaturalism Must Go

In describing his own intellectual orientation, Tillich refers to "something . . . that is fundamental to *all* my thinking—the anti-supernaturalistic attitude."[131] Note the word "all." Tillich is allowing no room for exceptions, no room for a supernatural God. The statement is clear and unambiguous. The No is unconditional.

The substance of the above message is restated elsewhere in more detail:

Self-transcending realism requires the criticism of *all* forms of supra-naturalism—supra-naturalism in the sense of a theology that imagines a supra-natural world beside or above the natural one, a world in which the unconditional finds a local habitation, thus making God a transcendent object, the creation an act at the beginning of time, the consummation a future state of things. To criticize such a *conditioning of the unconditional*, even if it leads to atheistic consequences, is more religious, because it is more aware of the *unconditional character of the divine*, than a theism that bans God into the supra-natural realm.[132]

Four comments on this formulation of the No are in order. First, Tillich again opposes "all" types of supernaturalism. There is no reservation to provide for a supernatural God. The clear implication is that God has a nonsupernatural meaning to Tillich. Second, "a conditioning of the unconditional," something Tillich would criticize, refers to making the No subject to the condition that God

131. *Dialogue*, p. 158 (my italics).   132. *Protestant*, p. 82 (my italics).

is excepted. Such conditional antisupernaturalism, he says, must be avoided "even if it leads to atheistic consequences" (which it does). Third, the "self-transcending realism" of which Tillich speaks emphasizes the nonsupernatural nature of his God. Self-realization occurs when man becomes "ultimately concerned" about mankind: man transcends his existential self and realizes his true self. (In a related sense, man also transcends existential concern for himself, his group, or the supernatural self thought to dwell beside or above man's world.) Fourth, the "unconditional character of the divine" means that God includes all of humanity: humanity is not God on the condition that non-Christians or Asians or any other human beings are excluded from the area of concern. God is infinite because it is not limited—not limited to just part of the human race. "God is not God without universal participation."[133]

Now we can begin to comprehend what Tillich is driving at in *The Courage to Be* when he speaks of the "God above God." He is not, as so many have apparently assumed, speaking of an omnipresent, spiritual, yet still rational God who replaces the angry monarch living in heaven. "For facing the God who is really God means facing also the absolute threat of nonbeing."[134] Nonbeing of what? The nonbeing (nonexistence, unreality) of a supernatural God in any form—and of divine law and everything else that such a God implies. The God above God affirms the absolute, unconditional nonbeing of supernaturality.

Let it be perfectly understood that the supernatural God is dead insofar as Tillich's thought is concerned. He is no longer a reality but only a symbol:

God is the basic and universal symbol for what concerns us ultimately.... Everything we say about being-itself, the ground and abyss of being, must be symbolic.... Therefore it cannot be used in its literal sense. To say anything about God in the literal sense of the words used means to say something false about Him. The symbolic ... is the only true way of speaking about God.[135]

Tillich is bluntly asserting that God is a symbol, nothing more. The word "God," in Tillich's thought, cannot be taken literally. "Lit-

---

133. *ST–1*, p. 245.
135. *Love*, p. 109.

134. *Courage*, p. 39.

eralism deprives God of his ultimacy and, religiously speaking, of his majesty."[136] (Caution: do not take "his" literally!)

Belief in a Supreme Being

There is plenty of disagreement among Christians about God's nature, form, temperament, and the like. But whatever else he is or isn't in the eyes of believers, God has always been a being—a supernatural being. He may not occupy finite space but "He" (never "it") has a degree of personality, is endowed with reason, and is aware of his own being. Tillich, however, is notorious for his opinion that God is not a being but being-itself.[137] Now "being-itself" is exceedingly vague, to say the least, but "not a being" is perfectly clear. Tillich does not believe in a Supreme Being, and "being-itself" is not such a being. "If 'existence' refers to something which can be found within the whole of reality, no divine being exists."[138] Tillich repeatedly comes back to this fundamental point, for example when he says that his concept of religion "has little in common with the description of religion as the belief in the existence of a highest being called God, and the theoretical and practical consequences of such a belief."[139]

This outlook is definitely one of atheism, though seemingly contradictory symbolic statements by Tillich lead many to believe otherwise. Those who take Tillich literally when he says "He" or "whose" or otherwise makes personal references to God would do well to review his frequent endorsements of the atheistic viewpoint. The following quotations, each from a different book by Tillich, affirm that atheism is the correct response to belief in a divine being.

Ordinary theism has made God a heavenly, completely perfect person who resides above the world and mankind. The protest of atheism against such a highest person is correct. There is no evidence for his existence, nor is he a matter of ultimate concern.[140]

... the half-blasphemous and mythological concept of the "existence of God" has arisen. And so have the abortive attempts to prove the existence of this "object." To such a concept and to such attempts atheism is the right religious and theological reply.[141]

136. *Dynamics*, p. 52.
138. *Dynamics*, p. 47.
140. *ST–1*, p. 245.

137. See, for example, *ST–1*, p. 237.
139. *Culture*, p. 40.
141. *Culture*, p. 25.

40

... atheism is a correct response to the "objectively" existing God of literalistic thought.[142]

The protest against God, the will that there be no God, and the flight to atheism are all genuine elements of profound religion. . . . In making God an object besides other objects, the existence and nature of which are matters of argument, theology supports the escape to atheism. . . . [The atheist] is perfectly justified in destroying such a phantom and all its ghostly qualities.[143]

Readers bent on finding confirmation of their own "sophisticated" concepts of God will continue to read hidden qualifications into these disclaimers. Many, for instance, will assume that Tillich redefines "being" to mean something approaching the level of humanity, whereas they consider God to be infinitely above man—"wholly other" as McKelway puts it[144]—and therefore not describable in terminology applicable to humans. But Tillich is not in the habit of redefining traditional concepts before attacking them; he redefines only those terms he is preparing to endorse. When he indicates, in the last of the above passages, that the existence of God is not a matter for argument, how can be possibly be talking about a supernatural entity? The existence of *anything* supernatural is *always* subject to argument, and certainly this is true of a rational, self-conscious supernatural entity, whatever we may choose to call it. (Humanity, on the other hand, is beyond argument; it is objectively real.)

The Gods of Metaphysics

The preceding material adequately covers the gods of theism and deism, who are conceived of as rational beings. But what about other supernatural concepts of God? In particular, what about metaphysics, including its pantheistic and mystical variants? Metaphysical concepts are, to be sure, thoroughly contrary to Christian doctrine, but they do qualify as supernaturalism. Could something of this order reflect Tillich's meaning?

The answer is no. In the first place, such concepts still run afoul of Tillich's objections to "all" supernaturalism and his many reminders that his use of the word God should be understood sym-

142. *Boundary*, p. 65.   143. *Foundations*, p. 45.
144. McKelway, *Systematic Theology of Paul Tillich*, p. 140.

bolically. Beyond this, he has expressly repudiated metaphysics in general and pantheism and mysticism in particular. Tillich refuses to apply the "metaphysics" label to his thought, preferring the word "ontology." He does this because metaphysics "conveys the *misconception* that ontology deals with transempirical realities, with a world behind the world, existing only in speculative imagination."[145] Such attempts to establish a hidden reality beyond the level of experience are "speculative-fantastic" in character.[146] These words indicate that, whatever "ontology" means to Tillich, it is not a substitute for "metaphysics" in any genuine sense of that term. Ontology is, in fact, literally "the word" about "being," meaning thought which describes the nature of "being." And if Tillich chooses to give "being" a nonsupernatural meaning, whether it be humanity or chocolate pudding, that takes it out of the realm of metaphysics.

Now let us consider specific types of metaphysical thought sometimes attributed to Tillich. His comments on pantheism merit close attention, for it might be argued that pantheism, if taken to mean nature in the literal sense and not a hidden essence, is by definition natural rather than supernatural and therefore exempt from Tillich's omnibus denial of the supernatural. Supernatural or not, however, pantheism is expressly rejected by Tillich. In volume 1 of *Systematic Theology*, he says this: "God is neither endlessly extended in space nor limited to a definite space; nor is he spaceless. A theology inclined toward pantheistic formulation prefers the first alternative, while a theology with deistic tendencies chooses the second alternative."[147] He elaborates in volume 2. There he identifies three concepts of God, the last being his own. The first, that of a "highest being," he rejects as too finite. The second, pantheism, he also finds overcharged with finitude: "The main argument against naturalism in whatever form is that it denies the infinite distance between the whole of finite things and their infinite ground, with the consequence that the term 'God' becomes interchangeable with the term 'universe' and therefore is semantically superfluous."[148] The important thing here is to recognize what the argument is directed against—pantheism. (In Chapter 3 we

145. *Biblical*, pp. 6–7 (my italics).   146. *ST–1*, p. 20.
147. *ST–1*, pp. 276–77.   148. *ST–2*, pp. 6–7.

42

shall discover that Tillich's symbolism demands that the two-sided, that is, divine-human, God of the Christ myth be analogically preserved. Anything written off as "too finite" or "too concrete" is appropriately analogous to the human side but lacks the counterpoint of abstraction, or divinity.)

In order to be sure we know what it is Tillich denies when he denies pantheism, it is helpful to examine his understanding of what the word means. "Pantheism does not mean, never has meant, and never should mean that everything that is, is God. If God is identified with nature (*deus sive natura*), it is not the totality of natural objects which is called God but rather the creative power and unity of nature, the absolute substance which is present in everything."[149] To paraphrase, a pantheistic God is a universal power, essence, or substance which metaphysically participates in man and everything else that exists. Or, to quote again, "Pantheism is the doctrine that God is the substance or essence of all things, not the meaningless assertion that God is the totality of all things."[150] These statements make it apparent that when he denies pantheism Tillich is not just quibbling about what pantheism means but construes it broadly to include concepts of God as (1) the "power," (2) the "substance," and (3) the "essence" within nature. This broad understanding of pantheism is repeated when Tillich contrasts Spinoza's "naturalistic pantheism," which interprets God as the "substance" of all being, with the "idealistic type," in which God is "the universal essence of being."[151] His willingness to accept "power" in a definition of pantheism has also been repeated by Tillich. Pantheism, "if it means anything at all, ...means that the power of the divine is present in everything, that he is the ground and unity of everything, not that he is the sum of all particulars."[152]

With this understanding of pantheism in mind, let us look again at the second of the three concepts of God identified in volume 2, the first two of which Tillich rejects. "The second way of interpreting the meaning of the term 'God' identifies God with the universe, with its essence or with special powers within it. God is the name

149. *ST–1*, p. 233.   150. *ST–1*, pp. 233–34.
151. *ST–1*, p. 237. Cf. *Perspectives*, p. 74.
152. *Perspectives*, pp. 94–95.

for the power and meaning of reality."[153] This interpretation is broad enough to include the Spinozan concept of a universal "substance," for Tillich goes on to mention Spinoza as an example. When he rejects the "second way" of interpreting God, therefore, Tillich is rejecting the idea that God is the universe, its essence, a metaphysical power, or a metaphysical substance. I submit that these exclusions cover any conceivable metaphysical definition of pantheism, and certainly any form that has been attributed to Tillich. Even mysticism is covered. On what basis, then, can William Rowe (even if he doesn't actually call Tillich a pantheist) and any number of other writers say or imply that Tillich's outlook assumes "the participation [i.e., metaphysical participation] of every being in being-itself"[154] or, what amounts to the same thing, that being-itself "participates in all beings as their ground"?[155]

In case you doubt that the above considerations rule out mysticism, more specific remarks can be quoted. In part, the idea that Tillich is a mystic stems from his assertions that knowledge of God comes through "revelation," the content of which is a "mystery." But those who take these words literally, giving them meanings resembling the traditional ones, miscalculate badly. For Tillich, traditional theological terms, when employed as elements in his system, always carry symbolic meanings. "Revelation" is the value judgment that man is God, nothing more. As for mysticism, it is another of those beliefs which are too one-sided, only this time it is the abstract side—ultimacy—which is overweighted. "Mysticism liberates one from the concrete-sacramental sphere and its demonic distortions, but it pays the price of removing the concrete character of revelation and of making it irrelevant to the actual human situation."[156] This, we are told, "elevates man above everything that concerns him actually, and it implies an ultimate negation of his existence in time and space."[157] Putting it a little differently, "The element of ultimacy swallows the element of concreteness."[158] (The divine side swallows the human.) Tillich has also written that his

---

153. ST–2, p. 6.
154. Rowe, Religious Symbols and God, p. 128; cf. p. 36.
155. Armbruster, Vision of Paul Tillich, p. 140.
156. ST–1, p. 140.   157. ST–1, p. 140.
158. ST–1, p. 226.

"God above God" has been "misunderstood" as being pantheistic or mystical in character.[159]

Psychological Considerations

Because of the increasing tendency of commentators to look upon Tillich as a metaphysician, and because the present interpretation stands or falls on the premise that Tillich is not a supernaturalist in any sense, it is worthwhile to go beyond Tillich's words and introduce a psychological argument. This argument offers no scientifically proven premises; but I suspect that those whose own thinking runs along the channels described will generally find it convincing, although others to whom doubt is an alien experience may regard it as highly conjectural. Briefly, the argument is that a person like Tillich who goes through the process of relinquishing traditional Christian beliefs will reject any other supernaturalistic beliefs for exactly the same reasons. When faith and religious authority become inadequate bases for believing what is otherwise unbelievable, individuals turn to experience, science, and reason for criteria by which to judge hypotheses about reality. By these criteria, however ill-advised their use may be, a metaphysical essence is no more necessary or plausible or empirically substantiated than the God of theism.

Tillich has not recorded the specific considerations which influenced his drift into doubt, but their general nature isn't hard to guess. For a person raised in any religious tradition, doubt generally begins when religious beliefs come into conflict with each other or with nonreligious beliefs and information. The believer may start to wonder how God can be omnipotent and forgiving on the one hand yet somehow powerless or unwilling to forgive errant mortals and admit them to his Kingdom prior to his arranging the death-by-torture of a human scapegoat. Or perhaps there is no devil in the family religious tradition, whereas the Bible and religious instructors affirm the opposite. Books and other literature are encountered which offer scientific explanations of the origins of man and the solar system. Even as mere theories, these become more convincing than the Genesis account. Again, it may be that

---

159. ST–2, p. 12.

the child in Sunday school can't see why a noble person like Jesus would cast demons (entities of dubious reality to begin with) into innocent pigs, causing them to rush into the water and drown, when he could have cast the offending spirits directly into the water. Gradually the conflicts and doubts accumulate, and gradually they are resolved in favor of modern modes of thought. The Bible, tradition, and preachers become highly suspect as sources of wisdom; figurative reinterpretations of the old beliefs and doctrines are viewed as attempts to rationalize myths obviously meant to be taken at face value.

One after another the old beliefs fall, till none save God remains. God is the strongest and most fundamental of the traditional beliefs and usually the last to go. By the time God is left standing alone, the skeptical mind has come around to the position that propositions affirming the supernatural are prima facie unreliable. Plausibility (especially in relation to competing scientific hypotheses), evidence, and freedom from internal contradiction are demanded. God is finally tested against these criteria and found wanting. Skepticism toward the supernatural becomes total.

After reading his many general and specific denials of the supernatural and his accounts of his early years, it is obvious to me that Tillich has gone through this process. He is a thoroughgoing skeptic. And such individuals are not inclined to endorse supernaturalistic viewpoints not supported by logic and evidence, which is to say supernaturalism of any sort. (Granted, there are occasional exceptions, but their rarity only confirms the general rule.) Having no predisposition to look upon Tillich as a supernaturalist, and finding no unambiguous or even hard-to-refute evidence that Tillich has substituted one form of supernaturalism for another, I find the metaphysical hypothesis implausible in the extreme. Why should a man who finds "no evidence" of the God of theism and who regards "attempts to prove" this God's existence as "abortive" be any more convinced that there exists an impersonal, metaphysical God or essence? Why should proof be demanded for one God but not the other? What argument or evidence could be adduced in support of a metaphysical God which could not serve equally well as support for the traditional God? Why should Tillich reject "first cause" in one context yet accept it in another? Or, if Tillich supposedly believes on the basis of ontological intuition which tells him that metaphysics is right and theism wrong, how could he then deny a mystical element in his thought and reject the concept of "supranatural interference in natural processes" (for example, thought)?[160]

In short, why not accept what Tillich says about metaphysics? Why not believe him when he says "the antisupernaturalistic attitude" is basic to "all" his thinking? Why not believe him when he denies that his ontology "deals with transempirical realities," and when he further denies that his system is pantheistic or mystical? Why assume that the No is "conditioned" by "secret reservations" when Tillich pointedly declares otherwise?

The fact is that hardly any atheists "condition" their skepticism with metaphysics. Moreover, indications are that most of the few who do were brainwashed by Tillich at a halfway-house stage of skepticism. Tillich's offer of a metaphysical escape from the contradictions of theism has been accepted not in transition from atheism but as a substitute for liberal Christianity. All of these considerations —Tillich's skeptical mind, the scarcity of metaphysicians, Tillich's many denials of metaphysics—place the burden of proof on those who still wish to classify Tillich as a metaphysician. These analysts must show that statements in Tillich's thought which superficially imply metaphysical if not theistic belief (a) can be reconciled with other statements which deny any "transempirical" or metaphysical reality and (b) cannot be given figurative or symbolic interpretations which belie the overt supernaturalism. Rowe, for example, must show that Tillich's "ontological argument," holding that thought about God presupposes God, can't be interpreted to mean that thoughts about God (in any sense) presuppose humanity ("God"), inasmuch as all thoughts about God obviously come from human beings.[161]

160. *ST–1*, p. 116.
161. See Rowe, *Religious Symbols and God*, pp. 88–92.

CHAPTER 2

He Who Has Ears

Tillich speaks to two audiences, one large and one small. The large one's "questioning power" is weak in varying degrees, while the small one is ready for the full implications of what he has to say. To the large audience Tillich is therefore content to deliver only his No, and just so much of it as particular individuals are prepared to receive. But to the smaller group Tillich offers the Yes which is the "pith and essence" of his message. It is a cryptic Yes, spoken guardedly and with barely enough clues for deciphering, for Tillich does not wish to offend and lose the larger audience. This Yes—the message that God is man—is our principal interest. If we wish to hear it, though, it will be helpful to first confirm that a hidden message actually exists, to understand more fully why it is hidden, and to learn something about the devices Tillich employs to conceal it.

THE HIDDEN MESSAGE

When preaching, Jesus spoke in parables, an ancient form of symbolic language. His deeper message was sufficiently hidden that it had to be explained privately to his disciples. The public, though, had only the benefit of Jesus' warning, "He who has ears, let him hear."[1] Schweitzer theorizes that Jesus was attempting to reach a select few believed predestined for salvation.[2] Schonfield thinks that Jesus was trying to reach his intended listeners without being

1. Matt. 13:9, 43. All Bible citations are from the Revised Standard Version.
2. Albert Schweitzer, *The Quest of the Historical Jesus*, trans. W. Montgomery, (New York: Macmillan, 1966), p. 354.

heard by spies or informers.[3] Whatever the truth, one thing is clear: Jesus offered a hidden meaning and was telling people to search for it. In this respect, Tillich emulates Jesus. He too has a hidden message, cloaked in figurative language. And, like Jesus, he alerts those who can hear that it is there: "I have always felt that there might be a few who are able to register the shaking of the foundations—who are . . . courageous enough to withstand the unavoidable enmity of the many. To those few my words are particularly directed."[4] Significantly, this passage is from the introductory sermon in his collection, *The Shaking of the Foundations*.

Levels of Meaning

Further along in the same book, Tillich drops another hint that his readers should look beneath the surface of his writing. "All visible things have a surface. Surface is that side of things which first appears to us. If we look at it, we know what things *seem* to be." When we try to act according to the superficial we are disappointed. But, he continues, "the truth which does *not* disappoint dwells below the surfaces" and can be found if we make the effort. To reach the full depth of truth, "men have dug through one level after another."[5]

Tillich is indicating that in his own thought there are not just two but several levels of meaning, successively closer approximations to the truth. Those who wish to penetrate the full depth of Tillich's thought must go beyond a number of increasingly less superficial levels of interpretation. However, Tillich does not expect most listeners to reach his deepest meaning, and he is content to let each person seek his own level. He considers it futile to force his more radical ideas on individuals not prepared to accept them; he is satisfied if he can lead someone even part way along the path from superstition to truth.

If this is the case, what are the levels of meaning encountered in Tillich? Because he is deliberately ambiguous, it is possible for careless interpreters—and sometimes even diligent ones—to read almost anything into Tillich's thought. The tendency, therefore, is

3. Hugh J. Schonfield, *The Passover Plot* (New York: Bernard Geis Associates, 1965), p. 81.
4. *Foundations*, p. 9.   5. *Foundations*, p. 53.

for each listener to infer that Tillich rejects only as much of traditional religion as that person has rejected and that he views God
through the same shade of liberal or conservative tinted lenses.
Thus the following levels of meaning, except for the last, are really
benchmarks along a continuum and do not actually signify discrete
stages of understanding. Keeping this in mind, we can identify a
series of increasingly accurate interpretations.

The first, or literal, level of interpretation is one notch above
fundamentalism. (Nobody is going to mistake Tillich for a funda-
mentalist.) An unusually innocent reader of conservative bent can
be led to believe that Tillich is in accord with the conservative outlook. This outlook holds that not quite everything—perhaps not
stories like Adam and Eve—in the Bible can be taken at face value
but that most of it can. There is a very personal God who came to
earth as his son Jesus and whose religion brings salvation. Tillich
gives personal attributes to God, speaks of God's incarnation,
refers frequently to "Jesus as the Christ," and upholds decisions of
ancient councils affirming Jesus' full divinity. If other Tillichian
ideas sometimes seem to conflict with these, one can assume that
the vaguely understood technique of symbolism is interfering with
communications. Meanwhile, Tillich's caveats about literalism may
be viewed as referring to a few parts of the Bible, not to *Systematic Theology*.

Those who are somewhat more advanced can take and have
taken Tillich to be a moderate. Moderates reject the Old Testament
God of anger and vengeance. They also reject hell's fire and brimstone, the devil, and frequently the virgin birth. Outmoded ideas
such as these, many think, are what Tillich wants to get rid of.
References to symbolism and literalism presumably concern such
matters (and who cares exactly what the ancient superstitions are
supposed to symbolize?). At this level of interpretation, people
believe that Tillich simply wants to modernize religion and that his
criticisms of theistic conceptions of God are directed toward the
Old Testament image of a truculent king sitting on a throne in
heaven.

A still deeper level of understanding can be reached by persons
able to recognize liberal ideas when encountered yet lacking ade-

quate perspective to look for new ideas standing beyond religious liberalism. At the liberal level it is accepted that Tillich inveighs against much more than the most primitive aspects of tradition. Tillich is seen as a liberal who objects, as liberals do, to the divinity of Jesus, supernatural salvation, virtually all other supernaturalism save God, and not only excessive personification of God but the whole idea of a manlike God. Tillich's assertion that God is not a being is interpreted to mean that God is a spirit, though still endowed with intelligence and personality.

Quite a few people have penetrated beyond liberalism, the deepest level within Christian tradition, to a depth where Tillich is regarded as a metaphysician. Tillich's complaints about the God of theism are not written off as being directed merely against anthropomorphism; it is understood that when Tillich denies that God is a being he means it. Here Tillich is assumed to be a pantheist or quasi-pantheist, a mystic, or perhaps just a philosopher with metaphysical interests involving a universal essence called being. Christianity in any meaningful sense has departed, but supernaturalism remains.

A tentatively correct level of interpretation is reached when it is realized that Tillich's No to the supernatural is unconditional, i.e., that attempts to condition the unconditional with metaphysical reservations still miss the point. God is no longer a supernatural entity but any human concern ("ultimate concern") which is somehow ultimate to an individual. Beyond the tentative, the full depth of meaning appears when one discovers that Tillichian concerns are two-sided, like theology's Christ. Concrete preliminary concerns, it is understood, can be either "true" or "demonic" depending on whether or not they mirror a deeper, ultimate concern for humanity.

All Things to All Men

Is it reading too much between the lines to infer that Tillich actually wants to convey so many meanings to so many people? Let us again compare Tillich with a biblical figure, this time Paul. Paul traveled widely among Jews and gentiles, spreading the gospel of the emerging Christian sect. Speaking to Jews, he portrayed

Jesus as the long anticipated Jewish messiah who would usher in doomsday, the resurrection of the dead, and an earthly but supernatural Kingdom of God. "To the Jews I became as a Jew, in order to win Jews." But among gentiles, for whom the messianic concept and physical resurrection had no validity, Paul did what was expedient and adapted his preaching to the audience. Sometimes he portrayed Jesus as the divine redeemer of gnostic sects; sometimes Jesus became like the dying and rising gods of the then-contemporary mystery religions. "To those outside the [Jewish religious] law I became as one outside the law . . . that I might win those outside the law." Whatever a group's weakness, Paul sought to exploit it. "To the weak I became weak, that I might win the weak." In short, Paul was a man of many faces: "I have become all things to all men, that I might by all means save some."[6]

In the second of three sermons written (we are told) with students of theology especially in mind, Tillich very pointedly declares that he is doing the same thing as Paul. He quotes the last of the above Pauline statements and then says: "Theological existence demands the same attitude. The theologian, *in his theology*, must become all things to all men." The rest of the sermon elaborates on this theme, finally reaching the part about becoming weak in order to gain the weak. This, asserts Tillich, is the "most profound" of Paul's statements. What he says next is virtually a confession, except that he retains enough ambiguity to hide his full meaning from the larger audience. "We must become *as though weak* . . . We can become weak . . . by participating—not from the outside, but from the inside—in the weakness of all those to whom we speak as theologians." The meaning is clear: the theologian, in his theology, must pretend to participate in the weakness of supernatural belief in order to undermine supernaturalism from within the Church. And if this sounds unnecessarily cautious for an era of "God is dead" theology, remember that Tillich began *Systematic Theology* in 1925, a time of relative conservatism, and through his attacks on the God of theism helped prepare the way for a later generation of theologians.[7]

6. 1 Cor. 9:20–22.   7. *Foundations*, pp. 123–25.

Undermining from Within

Although the evidence of what Tillich is doing is ample, it might initially seem illogical that such an out-and-out skeptic would remain within the Christian fold. Others, of course, have entered the ministry, lost faith, and refused to leave the Church. This happens every now and then to an individual who is too old or ill-equipped to begin a new career or who is unwilling to give up the security and prestige of his position. Tillich, however, was both young and well educated when his faith evaporated. Without significant loss of security or prestige, he could have begun a career teaching philosophy. To grasp Tillich's motives we must look elsewhere.

A related possibility is that Tillich lacked the courage required to face the personal and social implications of renouncing Christianity. In speaking of the "few" to whom his deeper message is directed, Tillich himself observes that most humans are prone to "reject and attack" those who acknowledge that the foundations of their belief have been shaken. The many direct "mockery or fury against those who *know* and dare to say that which they know."[8] Is Tillich therefore afraid to oppose unequivocally the doctrines of Christianity—to say what he really believes in words no one can misunderstand? This is doubtful. Certainly he has been blunt in some of his criticism of religion. Moreover, from what Tillich has written about the unpopularity of the Church among the German masses around the time of World War I, it hardly seems that great courage would have been required to quietly leave.

Other explanations are more convincing. One of these is that Tillich has a very strong emotional commitment to Christianity. The Church, he indicates, has always been his home; he feels he belongs to it:

This feeling grew out of the experiences of my early years—the Christian influence of a Protestant minister's home and the relatively uninterrupted religious customs of a small east-German city at the close of the nineteenth century. My love for church buildings and their mystic atmosphere, for liturgy and music and sermons, and for the great Christian festivals that molded the life of the town for days and even weeks of the

8. *Foundations*, pp. 8–9.

year left an indelible feeling in me for the ecclesiastical and sacramental. ... All this played a crucial part in my decision to become a theologian and to remain one.[9]

A second plausible explanation—this anticipates a point to be developed shortly—is that Tillich has an intellectual commitment to a Grand Synthesis (my term) of theology and philosophy that he is attempting. As an adolescent, Tillich often withdrew into imaginary worlds. Later this romantic imagination became philosophical imagination. The latter remained with him and gave him "the ability to combine categories, to perceive abstractions in concrete terms ... and to experiment with a wide range of conceptual possibilities."[10] This imagination permeates the whole of Tillich's *Systematic Theology* and turns it into far more than the mere theology it purports to be. In line with the preceding quotation, it is a massive effort to combine categories (theological and philosophical), to perceive abstractions in concrete terms (e.g., humanity in terms of concern for polio victims), and to experiment with numerous concepts (e.g., many different ways of symbolizing God and man). This endeavor, which appears to fascinate Tillich as much for its form as for its substance, makes it mandatory for Tillich to win acceptance in both camps, the theological and the philosophical. Were he to renounce Christianity, this would become impossible.

A final explanation, and probably the most basic, has already been suggested. Everyone knows that one of the most effective ways of opposing an organization or ideology can be to undermine it from within. If one wishes to persuade Christians that their beliefs are wrong, one can speak either as a fellow Christian or as an avowed skeptic. The skeptic has little chance of being received with an open mind and usually won't even get many listeners. But when a Christian speaks, he speaks as one of the family and merits respect if not agreement. And if that Christian rises to the station of America's top Protestant theologian, he is in a position to wield considerable influence. Is this not an adequate reason for staying with the Church?

9. *Boundary*, p. 59.   10. *Boundary*, p. 25.

SYMBOLISM: THE NEGATIVE YES

To conceal his message and otherwise facilitate operating "from the inside," Tillich has devised his bewildering "system." It serves to couch radical meanings in language sufficiently ambiguous or recondite that the casual reader and even most theological detectives can read almost anything, or else nothing comprehensible, into it. The system utilizes several tools, the first of which is symbolism. Tillich's is a language of symbols. Indeed, he occasionally seems to imply that everything he says other than the statement that God is being-itself is symbolic. This is hyperbole, for there are may nonsymbolic passages in his writing. Nevertheless, the system is full of symbols and symbolic statements, and he who hopes to discern the hidden message must clearly understand what it is that Tillich calls a symbol and what the significance of symbolism is.

The Concept of a Symbol

What is a symbol? And what is a symbolic statement? A surprising amount of verbiage has flowed back and forth on this subject without really clarifying anything. This is mainly Tillich's fault, because his descriptions of symbols are obviously designed to obscure rather than to illuminate. Tillich is willing to alert people to the presence of symbolism, but he has no intention of making it easy for us to decipher his symbols. One must examine not what he writes about symbolism but the symbols themselves to figure out what he is doing. Actually, this isn't hard to do: the concept of a symbol is a simple one, readily defined. But first, let us oversimplify. A symbol in the Tillichian sense is a familiar theological term, concept, or doctrine (e.g., God, Spirit, sin, or faith) that has been given a new, figurative meaning in place of the old, literal meaning. To use Jesus' metaphor, it is an old wineskin into which new wine has been poured. The new wine, it should be added, is never supernatural.

Now let us refine the definition. Tillich makes a distinction between signs and symbols, although from his discussion one would scarcely know what that distinction is. What he is driving at is that a sign carries an arbitrary meaning—any meaning one cares to assign—whereas the symbolic meaning is always analogous to the symbol. "Symbol" denotes an analogical relationship between the symbol and what it represents. This has always been evident from the new meanings Tillich has given to old doctrines, but only in a few places does Tillich actually mention the word "analogy." One such reference is in volume 1 of *Systematic Theology*: "The phrase 'only a symbol' should be avoided, because nonanalogous or non-symbolic knowledge of God has *less* truth than analogous or symbolic knowledge."[11] In volume 2 Tillich refers again to "the analogous or symbolic knowledge of God."[12] Volume 3 yields this pointer: "As in every symbol, the analogy is limited."[13] Elsewhere, in a letter to Father Gustave Weigel, Tillich says, "I speak of symbolic knowledge and mean with it exactly what St. Thomas means with *analogia entis*."[14]

The symbol of "the fall" provides a good illustration. This expression normally refers mythologically to Adam's fall from God's grace, which fall results from Adam's failure to obey a divine ordinance and eventuates in separation from God. That is the old meaning. The new meaning concocted by Tillich is man's fall from a potential state of *grace* with his fellow man (God), which fall results from man's *disobeying* the "law of love," and leads to *separation* of man from man through selfishness and inter-human strife. Man's "transition from essence to existence" is Tillich's precise definition of the fall.[15] This is the language of philosophy, and it simply indicates that actual man is not what he ideally should be. Creation and the fall coincide. Essence (Eden) is not a state that once was, and the "transition" to existence (sin) is not something that once happened. What happened is that as man evolved from lower beings his potentiality for unity—mutual love and respect—simultaneously evolved but was not realized. More precisely, it was only fragmentarily realized in specific individuals who rose above their "existential predicament": "The essential nature of man is present in all stages of his development, although in existential distortion."[16] The fall, therefore, symbolizes that because man has always been divided against himself the essential unity implied in the concept of humanity is a potentiality

11. *ST–1*, p. 131.   12. *ST–2*, p. 9.
13. *ST–3*, p. 225.
14. Thomas A. O'Meara and Celestin D. Weisser, eds., *Paul Tillich in Catholic Thought* (Dubuque: Priory Press, 1964), p. 146n.
15. *ST–2*, p. 29.   16. *ST–2*, p. 33.

that has failed to materialize. The essence from which man, figuratively, emerged is the goal toward which he must strive.

So far we have spoken only of religious terms as being symbols. Certainly they include some of Tillich's most important symbols. But sometimes Tillich gives symbolic meanings to philosophical jargon and other nonreligious terminology. Estrangement thus becomes a symbol of man's alienation from his fellow man (nationalism, prejudice, selfishness, and so on). Even popular words like relativism and absolutism are employed as symbols: relativism symbolizes man (many, different) and absolutism symbolizes God (one, authority). It should be understood, therefore, that nontheological terms can also carry symbolic meanings, provided of course that analogy is involved.

This brings us to Tillich's own murky discussion of symbols. He tells us that a symbol (a) points beyond itself to something else and (b) participates in that to which it points. His examples are flags and kings, which point to and somehow participate in countries. The pointing to is clear enough, but some critics have made the mistake of assuming that participation means that a symbol is a constituent part of whatever it represents. It is ridiculous, however, to say that Adam's mythological fall is somehow a part of man's fall from potentiality into inter-human strife. No, participation does not mean being a part of in any structural sense. Rather, it means two other things, or perhaps just one, the second being moot. First, it means sharing in the "power and meaning" of what is symbolized.[17] Tillich assumes his symbolic meanings are profound and carry inspirational power (psychological, not supernatural); hence the symbols too can be said to be laden with meaning and filled with power, and a flag can be said to share in its country's power (for if the country lost all power the flag would cease to wave). Second, Tillich may also intend "participates in" as a deceptive way of saying "is analogous to." There are senses in which a flag participates by analogy in its country: a flag being torn down can be the analogue of a country being conquered, and there is also an analogy between adding stars to the American flag and adding states to the union. King and country are analogous in that both are political entities with political power. Whether Tillich intends the analogy interpretation of participation is not worth

17. *Culture*, p. 56.

debating, however. The fact remains that, whether analogy is subsumed under participation or made a separate point, the essence of a Tillichian symbol is analogy.

Now a brief word about symbolic statements. The concept of a symbolic statement is an exceedingly loose one covering just about anything that isn't supposed to be taken literally. A statement might not include a symbol; but if it relates to one, is ambiguous, seems to imply that Tillich accepts something supernatural, or has a pseudo-intellectual ring when taken literally, look out for symbolism.

The Significance of Symbols

One might very well ask what this discussion of symbols is all about. Why must we understand what a symbol is to understand Tillich? Why are symbols so significant? Three points should be made in this respect.

REHABILITATING OLD DOCTRINES. Point number one is that symbolism is ostensibly the device by which Tillich hopes to save Christianity from ultimate rejection by modern man. The word "ostensibly" is carefully chosen. Tillich *says* he wants to breathe new life into Christianity by giving moribund doctrines new meanings, converting them into symbols in the process. This is supposed to enable the old concepts to survive, even if in name only, and with them the Christian religion. An endeavor of this sort is absurd on the face of it—you cannot save something by getting rid of it—and one is strongly inclined to suspect that Tillich knows it. Isn't this attempt to inspire theological metamorphosis really just a cover for subversive activities going on behind symbolic doors?

But let us take Tillich at face value, assuming that his emotional attachment to the Church is so powerful that he really wants to salvage the old doctrines. This is where symbols enter the picture. Tillich argues that the old words must, if possible, be reborn. "This is true of all important terms of our religious language: God and the Christ, the Spirit and the church, sin and forgiveness, faith, love, and hope, Eternal Life, and the Kingdom of God."[18] These

18. *Eternal Now*, p. 113.

words are "vessels and forms" now containing "foolishness" but convertible into symbols that unbar the door to mature thought:

> It is the temptation of the churches in all generations to justify their human foolishness by calling it divine foolishness. This is their defense against becoming mature in thinking. But although Christianity is based on the message of the divine foolishness, it knows that, out of the acceptance of this message, mature thinking can grow courageously and abundantly. What prevents it from growing is that the guardians of the message, churches and individual Christians, imprison the divine foolishness in vessels and forms that are produced by a wisdom that is mixed with foolishness, as is all human wisdom. And if these forms and vessels are declared indestructible and unchangeable, the way to maturity in thinking is barred.[19]

ATTACKING SUPERNATURALISM. Point number two is that symbols are Tillich's way of saying No to the supernatural. That is, they are convenient devices for challenging old theological ideas on the pretense of clarifying their meaning. When he elucidates a symbol, Tillich speaks as though he were simply explaining what the old word or doctrine really means and what it therefore doesn't mean. He seems to be accentuating the positive. But more often than not he is mainly interested in destroying another chunk of traditional theology. Indeed, many of the symbolic meanings are so forced that it is apparent that their main function is to simply get rid of an old meaning, not to replace it. Tillich himself implies as much when he says, in a reply to an essay by Father Weigel, "I believe you are right when you say that my understanding of *analogia* is more negative-protesting than positive-affirming."[20]

Tillich's symbolization of "the wrath of God" is a case in point. He finds objectionable a religion that makes God "a furious tyrant, an individual with passions and desires who committed arbitrary acts."[21] This is wrong because it gives God human attributes in the manner of pagan stories about angry gods. Such a literal understanding of the "wrath of God" is impossible, says Tillich, but understanding is possible through a "metaphorical" symbol. The symbolic meaning is "the inescapable and unavoidable reaction against every distortion of the law of life, and above all against

19. *Eternal Now*, pp. 157–58.
20. O'Meara and Weisser, *Paul Tillich*, p. 24.
21. *Foundations*, p. 71.

human pride and arrogance."[22] Or, as an alternative formulation, it is "the work of love which rejects and leaves to self-destruction what resists it."[23] To paraphrase, anybody who resists the law of love for humanity takes the road to self-destruction (details unspecified). The analogy to destruction by a wrathful God comes from the fact that the "self" who destroys is man and therefore—since man is God—God. Isn't the analogy forced, not to mention vague? From all appearances, Tillich is much more concerned with shooting down a primitive notion than he is in defending the thesis that selfish behavior leads to self-destruction. In effect, "the wrath of God," transformed into a symbol, is a negative Yes.

ENCIPHERING THE MESSAGE. Point number three is that symbols serve to encipher the hidden message. To repeat, Tillich speaks to two groups. Those not ready for fully mature thought are led to believe that Tillich is essentially affirming old beliefs, with or without modification. Only the "few" who have ears to hear are to receive the deepest meaning of his words. Thus Tillich can refer to "something which is perhaps the main function of the symbol—namely, the opening up of levels of reality which otherwise are hidden and cannot be grasped in any other way."[24] However, it isn't really that the hidden reality can't be grasped in any other way; it is just that Tillich can't discuss it in any other way if he wants to retain his credentials as a Christian theologian.

But, since Tillich occasionally reminds us that his words should not be taken literally, isn't everyone led to the hidden meaning? Definitely not. How many of the critics surveyed in Chapter 1 were aware that Tillich's No is unconditional? The fact is that countless individuals have been fooled by Tillich and have in varying degrees taken his symbolic language literally. His reminders that the message is to be understood symbolically rather than literally don't seem to matter. Perhaps this is because many people literally do not know the difference between "literally" and "figuratively." More likely the primary explanation is that Tillich's discussion of symbols is so unclear, and deliberately so, that people can't deduce what he is saying. They therefore tend to assume that minor departures from strictly literal interpretations of the old doctrines will suffice.

22. *Foundations*, p. 71.   23. *ST–1*, p. 284.
24. *Culture*, p. 56.

Is it fair to say that Tillich *deliberately* obscures his meaning? In his book, *Dynamics of Faith*, Tillich describes two stages of literalism—thought that takes the old myths and doctrines literally—in immature individuals. The primitive, or unquestioning, stage "has a full right of its own and *should not be disturbed*, either in individuals or in groups, up to the moment when man's questioning mind breaks the natural acceptance of the mythological visions as literal."[25] Even at the next stage, that of repressed questions, Tillich would not force the truth "if the questioning power is very weak and can easily be answered."[26] It all boils down to this: "It is not meaningless to communicate to children or immature adults objective symbols of faith and with them expressions of the living faith of former generations."[27] In another book, *Theology of Culture*, the same philosophy is repeated: "As long as the pupil lives in a dreaming innocence of critical questions, he should not be awakened."[28]

God as a Symbol

Because God is the symbol that presents the most difficulty, it calls for special explanation. The difficulty arises from passages in which Tillich seems to indicate that God might be something more than a symbol. In volume 1 of *Systematic Theology* Tillich says that the statement, "God is being-itself," is not symbolic but that "nothing else can be said about God as God which is not symbolic."[29] A few pages before this it is implied that "ground of being" and "power of being" can be substituted for "being-itself" in the nonsymbolic statement.[30] The nonsymbolic area is widened a bit more in *Theology of Culture* to include four Tillichian substitutes for God, namely, being-itself, ground of being, power of being, and ultimate reality.[31]

These nonsymbolic statements about God should not be taken to mean that God is more than a symbol. What is really signified is

---

25. *Dynamics*, p. 52 (my italics).   26. *Dynamics*, p. 53.
27. *Dynamics*, p. 102.   28. *Culture*, p. 156.
29. *ST-1*, pp. 238–39. Note the words "as God," which allow Tillich to make nonsymbolic statements about God (humanity) when they refer directly to humanity.
30. *ST-1*, pp. 235–36.   31. *Culture*, p. 61.

that Tillich wishes to correlate the theological concept of God with the philosophical concept of being-itself, both of which concepts stand for humanity in the system. He does the same thing when he correlates the theological concept of sin with the philosophical concept of estrangement, but we must reserve that details of correlation for a later portion of this chapter. What needs to be understood at the moment is that "God is being-itself" is not symbolic because it is a definition,[32] and hardly even a definition but a tautology. Tillich in effect is saying that he is correlating the two concepts, God and being-itself. What he says is literally true and therefore nonsymbolic. The same applies when ground of being, power of being, and ultimate reality are substituted for being-itself. It is literally true that God is a synonym for each of them. The statements therefore are nonsymbolic. But the terms within the statements are symbols just the same.

If this is the case, why does Tillich make such a point of saying that "God is being-itself" is nonsymbolic? Originally the statement was supposedly intended to delimit the symbolic realm with an unsymbolic statement.[33] This is an empty reason: Tillich's writings abound in nonsymbolic statements, and it is reasonably clear where the symbolism begins and ends. Any statement that seems to imply belief in the supernatural, for example, is symbolic; statements attacking supernatural ideas are nonsymbolic. A better explanation is that Tillich wants to create a little confusion as to whether or not God is merely a symbol, and if this is the case he has succeeded admirably. Tillich incurs no risk in discarding (i.e., making symbols of) the Holy Spirit, Christ the Savior, sin, salvation, the resurrection, and other fading stars in the theological firmament. Fosdick and countless others have done the same thing without ceasing to be accepted as Christians. But Tillich cannot bluntly acknowledge that *God* is only a symbol. That would amount to a

32. Cf. Walter Kaufmann, *Critique of Religion and Philosophy* (New York: Harper, 1958), pp. 139–40. Kaufmann's central comment: "But this is surely neither a symbolic statement nor a nonsymbolic statement: it is no statement at all, it is a definition—and as it happens, a definition utterly at odds with the meaning of 'God' in probably more than 95 per cent of our religious tradition" (p. 140).

33. "Answer," in *The Theology of Paul Tillich*, ed. Charles W. Kegley and Robert W. Bretall (New York: Macmillan, 1952), p. 334.

frank admission of atheism. He therefore *must* imply that God has a meaning which is more than symbolic.

Is God then just another symbol? Not exactly, for it is the most important of all the symbols in Tillich's system. But it is a symbol: "God is the basic and universal symbol for what concerns us ultimately."[34] This calls for clarification. Tillich's God is humanity; hence, he often uses God in the narrow sense of humanity or in the related sense of a particular human concern arising from a more general concern for humanity. Nevertheless he also uses God to refer to any other "ultimate concern," good or bad, which a person might have. God can thus mean success, the nation, an imaginary supernatural being, or anything else which is figuratively or literally worshiped by an individual; ultimate concern has the same breadth of meaning. When Tillich refers to being-itself and the ground of being, however, the narrower concept—humanity—is being employed. Beyond this, the important thing to remember about Tillich's statements about God is that they can never be taken as literal references to a supernatural entity. "To say anything about God in the literal sense of the words used means to say something false about Him. The symbolic . . . is the only true way of speaking about God."[35] (Many people read this and immediately make the mistake of taking "Him" literally as a reference to a divine being.)

False Issues

Although critical analysis in this book will generally be reserved for the last chapter, certain criticisms which others have directed at Tillich must be answered now in order to straighten out some serious misconceptions about his symbolic method. Some critics have chosen to take issue with Tillich over how a symbol is conventionally used or should be used. Their position, simply stated, is that Tillich's use of symbols is unorthodox and therefore wrong. Or, from a slightly different point of view, Tillich abuses the concept of a symbol either by providing no connection between the symbol and its referent such as would justify their association or by actually going against the grain of the symbol's characteristics.

34. *Love*, p. 109.   35. *Love*, p. 109.

The point that needs to be made in reply is that the only important issue regarding Tillich's use of symbols concerns how *Tillich* uses them and what his symbols represent.

We begin with the premise that Tillich wishes to disguise his thought. One technique he uses for this purpose is symbolism. Now a person might easily quarrel about the utility or propriety of disguising one's thought, but who will deny that symbolism is a good way to do it? Assuming agreement on this matter, the problem is to learn whatever can be learned about the mechanics of Tillich's symbolism. Our purpose is to understand Tillich. Once we understand him, we can criticize. In the meantime, and recognizing that Tillich must be obscure in order to execute his strategy, it is more pertinent to worry about *what* he is saying than to criticize *how* he says it.

With the foregoing in mind, it is instructive to examine the challenges of William Alston, a representative critic. His misguided attack on Tillich's symbolism seeks (1) to describe how symbols are actually used, (2) to demonstrate that Tillich departs from the "traditional conception" of a symbol, and (3) to show that the result is "disastrous." Alston finds that symbols traditionally rest on "various sorts and degrees" of analogy. Furthermore, "in order to furnish descriptions from which effective identifications can be made," religious symbols must refer to something that can be experienced. If the referent can't be experienced, it can't be described. And if it can't be described, there can be no analogy. Tillich uses the metaphysical concept of being-itself as the referent not only of the symbol God but of all his other symbols. Yet, Alston continues, Tillich holds that nothing can be said about being-itself, and neither can it be experienced, so "it is not susceptible of any characterization." Hence there is no analogy in Tillich's symbolism, and all of Tillich's symbols are meaningless and worthless.[36]

Alston's analysis has so many flaws that one hardly knows where to begin. As a preliminary comment, the critic is presumptuous in telling Tillich what rules he must follow in using symbols. I like to think that symbolism allows complete freedom to the imagination

36. William P. Alston, "Tillich's Conception of a Religious Symbol," *Religious Experience and Truth: A Symposium*, ed. Sidney Hook (New York: New York University Press, 1961), pp. 12–26.

and that analogy isn't absolutely necessary. Where is the analogy between the swastika and the Nazi party? But this is beside the point, because Tillich's symbols do in fact rest on analogy—always. (Numerous symbolic analogies are identified in this study.) Alston overlooks a very good analogy between God and being-itself, and this analogy would obtain even if being-itself held for Tillich the metaphysical meaning Alston thinks it holds. Both God and being-itself are absolutes, in the sense of items of paramount concern or significance for those who believe. God is the absolute of theology and being is the absolute of metaphysical philosophy.

Actually, though, this is not the best example, because Alston is also wrong in suggesting that God symbolizes being-itself. As said before, God *is* being-itself by definition (really by correlation) in Tillich's system; it isn't a symbol for being. What God (and being) symbolizes is humanity, which can certainly be characterized. Now there are lots of analogies. In addition to being the respective absolutes of Christianity and humanism, for example, both God and humanity might be regarded as the source of human beings, or as in some sense living, or as influencing the course of history. Another serious defect in Alston's analysis is that he assumes that by debunking God as a symbol, he has established a general rule that disintegrates all of Tillich's symbols. This assumption arises from still another misconception, namely, that all of Tillich's symbols refer to the same thing, being-itself. (Here Alston is thinking mainly of ultimate concerns, which he misconstrues as always "pointing to" being-itself; but he even mentions Jesus Christ as a symbol for being-itself,[37] whereas Tillich is quite specific that the Christ symbolizes New Being.) It is true that some of Tillich's symbols share the same referent, but otherwise Alston is wrong: many different things are symbolized.

Other objections could be raised to Alston's critique, but the above are sufficient to show the hazards of (a) telling Tillich how to play the game and (b) assuming that Tillich's symbols cannot be given specific, meaningful, discoverable interpretations. Those who raise these points miss the point, which is that Tillich uses symbols to convey a hidden message. This, by the way, is the only point

37. William P. Alston, "Paul Tillich," *The Encyclopedia of Philosophy*, ed. Paul Edwards (New York: Macmillan and the Free Press, 1967), 8: 125.

Tillich really has to offer in his many essays on symbolism. Everything else is designed to raise false issues and divert attention. It would be extremely difficult to grasp the expository aspects of these essays without first having discerned by other means Tillich's rather orthodox rule of analogy.

A DIALECTICAL APPROACH

A second device for concealing the hidden message is dialectics. Tillich is at heart a German philosopher following the dialectical tradition that dominated nineteenth-century German philosophy from the time of Hegel. Before publication of the first volume of *Systematic Theology* he suggested that "neo-dialectical" would be a good description of his projected work.[38] The label he uses in *Systematic Theology* is "dialectical realism."[39] This term contrasts with the "dialectical idealism" of Hegel and the "dialectical materialism" of Karl Marx. "Realism" is about as close to "humanism" as Tillich can come without giving himself away, although I suspect for reasons that will become increasingly apparent in later chapters that Tillich's preference would be "dialectical humanism."

The Dialectical Tradition

The central idea of dialectics, namely, that processes are governed by opposing tendencies, goes back to early Greek speculations about nature: cosmic activity was seen as controlled by opposites, e.g., day and night. The idea resembles that of compromise: the view that both of two sides are partly right and partly wrong and that a third position incorporating the best from each can be reached. Plato first used the term "dialectic." Later philosophers believed that his dialogues reflected the insight that one tendency generates an opposing tendency which destroys the first. There emerged the notion that every idea or *thesis* breeds its opposite or *antithesis* which leads to a *synthesis*. Hegel called the thesis-antithesis-synthesis formula the "dialectic triad"; he took the word "dialectic" from Kant, who had reintroduced it in discussing "theses" and "antitheses." However, Hegel labeled the three steps "affirmation," "negation," and "negation of the negation"—terms which Tillich also prefers. Kant, Hegel, and later Marx applied the

38. *Protestant*, p. xxiv.   39. *ST–1*, p. 234.

dialectical principle to man; Hegel and Marx also applied it to history; and Hegel used it for ontology as well. In the process, some sort of identity between man and God became a virtual corollary of dialectics.

SELF-ALIENATED MAN. As applied to man, dialectics is closely bound to the concept of alienation. Beginning with Kant, German philosophy nurtured a pattern of thought which, as Tucker puts it, "revolved in a fundamental sense around the idea of man's self-realization as a godlike being or, alternatively, as God."[40] This thought regards man as alienated from his true self; there is a struggle between the actual and the ideal. Only by reconciling himself with himself can man realize his essential divinity. Man's quest for reconciliation, or self-realization, is an embryonic form of dialectics. It displays (a) the conflict of opposites—divine and human—and at least looks toward (b) the union of these opposites but downplays (c) the sequential movement from thesis to antithesis. In their later thought, where Hegel and Marx shift the alienation theme from man to a self-alienated "God" marching through history, dialectics reaches its full development.

Although it was Hegel who popularized the term "dialectical" and used it to elevate man to divinity, Immanuel Kant was the first to apply the term to the idea of opposing forces within man. Kant described man as having a dual personality, half human and half godlike. The human half, *homo phenomenon*, fails to conform to man's idealized image of his virtuous "real self," *homo noumenon*. Consequently, noumenal self rejects phenomenal self as an alien or stranger. From within man is torn by a "natural dialectic": the one self tries unsuccessfully to drive the other to perfection. Kant didn't think the conflict could be resolved short of a life hereafter.

As a young theology student, Hegel predicted that Kant's philosophy would yield a new movement based on the idea of the absolute and infinite self. (These adjectives are prominent in Tillich's vocabulary.) In a subsequent essay he found in Kant a "virtue religion" pointing to man's self-realization as a divine being. Hegel believed Jesus had been distorted by Christianity and

---

40. Robert Tucker, *Philosophy and Myth in Karl Marx* (Cambridge: Cambridge University Press, 1961), p. 31. The material in this section draws heavily on Tucker's excellent and highly relevant analysis.

had actually taught that God is within man, a doctrine Hegel found to his liking. Despotism and misery had turned man from himself and made him seek the divine in heaven, where a deity was objectified as real. But Jesus refused to deny his own selfhood (divinity). Four years later Hegel wrote another essay in which he contrasted God and man with a hill and the eye that sees it. Hill and eye are object and subject, but God and man are one, separated only by one's failure to recognize the other as itself. Hegel proceeded to identify Kant's *homo noumenon* with God. Still another essay followed wherein Hegel declared, "This self-elevation of man . . . from finite life to infinite life, is religion."[41] The meaning here is that God's self-recognition of himself through man is the essence of religion. Man is alienated from himself (from his essential self) because he does not recognize the divine—the infinite—within himself. Self-realization overcomes self-alienation; man reaches beyond the limits of his own finitude and grasps infinity.

By placing God within man, holding at the same time that man was divided against himself through obedience to external religious and political authority (Tillich's heteronomy), Hegel set the stage for a synthesis in which man realized himself as God. The dialectical character of this synthesis is at least implied in Hegel's *Logic*, where he comments on the myth of the fall. Man's drive for knowledge destroyed his original harmony with God; man must achieve new harmony by seeking absolute knowledge. In effect, belief in God becomes thesis, unbelief combined with self-unawareness the antithesis, and new belief in the form of self-recognition the synthesis. (Tillich employs the very same pattern in his formulation of "the divine life.") Young Hegel was vague as to the precise nature of the God within man. However, in the second of the aforementioned essays ("The Spirit of Christianity") he questions whether the divine should be placed *entirely* outside man. This sets the pattern for a concept of God, developed in Hegel's later writings, which is essentially metaphysical with strong pantheistic overtones: the world-self, or Spirit, comes to know itself as God through that part of itself which is man.

Toward the middle of the nineteenth century Ludwig Feuerbach

41. Georg Wilhelm Friedrich Hegel, *Early Theological Writings*, trans. T. M. Knox and Richard Kroner (Chicago: University of Chicago Press, 1948), p. 311.

took aim at Hegel's metaphysics and, denying that God is *in* man, announced that God *is* man. Man is not the manifestation of divine substance; God is the manifestation of human substance. Christianity, according to Feuerbach, is a case of man's being alienated from himself, that is, of man's turning to a false God. True religion requires that man learn to direct his love toward man—to cease deprecating himself as weak and sinful and instead seek reconciliation with his own humanity.

Though not himself a dialectician, Feuerbach strongly influenced Karl Marx, who was. He convinced Marx that there is but one world, the material world, and that both the Christian world of sinful man and the Hegelian world of metaphysical self struggling to conquer self-alienation were fantasy. Thus Marx, in his early writings, defines man's goal as the realization of his own humanity. "Man, who has found in the fantastic reality of heaven, where he sought a supernatural being, only his own reflection, will no longer be tempted to find only the *semblance* of himself—a non-human being—where he seeks and must seek his true reality."[42] This true reality will be found "with the idea that man is the supreme being for man."[43]

In statements like these, Marx builds a new doctrine of self-alienated man based on the human self-alienation ideas of Hegel and Feuerbach. But for Marx, man becomes the proletariat. Living in misery, proletarian man stands separated from his materially satisfied self, hence "*the estrangement of man* from *man*."[44] This estrangement is to be overcome "through the annulment of private property, through *communism*."[45] Borrowing from Hegel, Marx describes as "the negation of the negation" the world revolution which will bring the communist paradise to fruition.[46]

SELF-ALIENATION IN HISTORY: HEGEL. Both Hegel and Marx expand their philosophies of alienated man into systems concerning alien-

---

42. Karl Marx, *Early Writings*, trans. and ed. T. B. Bottomore (London: C. A. Watts, 1963), p. 43.

43. Karl Marx, *Economic and Philosophical Manuscripts*, trans. T. B. Bottomore, in Erich Fromm, *Marx's Concept of Man* (New York: Frederick Ungar, 1961), p. 220. An improved translation suggested by Tucker, *Philosophy and Myth*, p. 11, is used above.

44. Karl Marx, *Economic and Philosophic Manuscripts of 1844*, ed. Dirk J. Struik, trans. Martin Milligan (New York: International Publishers, 1964), p. 114.

45. *Ibid.*, p. 146.   46. *Ibid.*

ated worlds evolving dialectically through history. The dialectical aspects of Hegel's thought are often subtle, so much so that some competent scholars have questioned the "legend" that Hegel was dialectical in the sense of thesis, antithesis, and synthesis. These scholars have failed to recognize that the historical stages discussed in Hegel's thought must be reduced to abstractions—ideas—before the dialectic becomes evident. We can avoid this mistake by first getting acquainted with some of the more important abstractions. Tillich adopts these (along with others), and only by grasping them can we fully decipher his thought and see its links with Hegel's. Here is an illustrative list:

	THESIS	ANTITHESIS	SYNTHESIS
(1)	One	Many	One comprised of many parts
(2)	General	Particular	General comprised of particulars
(3)	Absolute	Relative	Absolute embodied in related parts
(4)	Essence	Existence (appearance)	Realized (apparent) essence
(5)	Union	Separation	Reunion (union of separate parts)

To see the relationships, think of a forest. Seen from above it is one, the general category embracing the unseen particulars (trees), the absolute which stands alone (assume there are no competing forests). It is the essence embodied in the trees; potentially, for we do not yet see it as such, it is a union of trees. But if we descend from the clouds to the forest shadows, to the realm of antithesis, our perspective changes. We see not one but many—many trees. Each tree is a particular, standing in relation to all the others. Each appears to exist as a separate individual, competing with others for moisture and sunshine, rather than as part of the invisible whole. The opposing viewpoints seem to conflict. But there is a synthesis. The forest is one *and* many, general *and* particular, the absolute *reflected* in participating relatives. When this is realized, existence appears to us in its essential form, and there is a "reunion" (alluding to the potential but conceptually unrealized union of step one) of the separated.

Now for Hegel's system. Hegel describes "God"—an abuse of the term—as absolute and infinite being, the World Spirit, or simply Spirit. By this Hegel means the Spirit is a metaphysical self comprising all reality, both nature (God's spatial dimension) and history (God's temporal dimension); the world and Spirit are one. But the Spirit is not fully itself until it knows itself as Spirit. History is the process of the Spirit's self-realization: the movement from an unconscious primal state of nature through self-alienation to an ultimate self-conscious state in which philosophical man (the seat of consciousness) recognizes that he and the rest of the world are one.

In becoming conscious of itself, the Spirit passes through a condition of *selbstenfremdung*, which can be translated either as "self-alienation" or as "self-estrangement." Nature, which is unconscious of itself as Spirit, is perceived as alien by man, who is becoming conscious of himself as Spirit. Thus the alienation found in man by young Hegel repeats itself in the metaphysical world-self (Spirit) of Hegel's later thought. While estranged, Spirit knows "finitude" (a favorite Tillichian expression); man sees himself as a finite being, failing to recognize that he is *all* being. Estrangement is overcome and Spirit breaks through to "infinity" when it, through the mind of the philosopher (Hegel), becomes aware of its totality. The dialectic: union, separation, reunion. *Re*-union, incidentally, does include the antithesis: "re" stands for the separation on which the new union is based.[47]

The historical manifestation of this process is the unfolding of successive civilizations. History moves from one society to another under dialectical compulsion. Change emanates from the realm of ideas. Each national culture, in its art, philosophy, ethics, and reli-

47. Because Tillich's agreement with the present interpretation of Hegel could conceivably become an issue, and because the crucial role of Hegelian concepts in Tillich's system makes further clarification desirable, Tillich's own summary of Hegel is worth consulting. It comes from a 1963 classroom lecture: "The absolute Spirit of which Hegel speaks is . . . . [based on a] vision of the world as a process of the self-actualization of the divine essences in time [history] and space [nature] . . . . God . . . comes to himself, to what he essentially is, through the world process, and finally through man and through man's consciousness of God. . . . God in himself is the essence of every species of plants and animals, of the structures of the atoms and stars, of the nature of man in which his [God's] innermost center is manifest. . . . Hegel cannot, therefore, conceive of God as a person beside other persons. Then he would be less than God. Then the world process, the structure of being, would be more than he, would be above him. . . . There is a point of identity between God and man insofar as God comes to self-consciousness in man, . . . [producing] the synthesis of the divine and the human spirit." (*Perspectives*, pp. 121–22.) In a later lecture Tillich accuses Hegel of "metaphysical arrogance" for "sitting on the throne of God as Hegel implied he was doing when he construed world history as coming to an end in principle in his philosophy." (*Perspectives*, p. 245.)

71

gion, reflects a "spirit." The spirit goes through a "natural" period (analogous to primal nature), representing the thesis. Then it is "turned inward" in antithetical reaction. Finally it "returns to itself" at a higher level of synthesis. Separation and return—the Spirit's movement echoes in each national spirit.

The details are all quite obscure. Hegel was prepared to read affirmation and negation into anything that fitted his preconceived conclusions. Nevertheless, he presumed that each historical synthesis brought a closer approximation to complete self-realization by the world-self. A crucial facet of the Spirit's coming into its own is the emergence of the national state, which Hegel, an ardent nationalist, viewed as the highest form of social organization and the ultimate manifestation of Spirit on earth. To Hegel, the state was the equivalent of the Kingdom of God.

Within the historical process, dialectics operates at several levels. The Spirit's metaphysical advance from union to separation to reunion is the most general. Next is a sociological dialectic wherein thesis is family (one, closely knit, unified), antithesis is society (many), and synthesis the national state (one composed of many). The state, in turn, embodies a political dialectic. Here the three stages are Oriental despotism, Greco-Roman democracy and aristocracy, and Germanic monarchy. Since it has been said that no one could possibly construe this triad as thesis, antithesis, and synthesis,[48] elaboration is demanded. There are actually two dialectics in one. The first dialectic is one, many, and one composed of many. Under Oriental despotism, the state consisted of *one*, the ruler; the people were not free, hence not (in Hegel's eyes) participants in the state. Greek and Roman polity, despite slavery, had *many* free citizens—many rulers (democracy). This was an advance, for some rather than one were now free, yet the fragmented authority of democracy (distasteful to Hegel) deprived the state of its essential oneness. With the emergence of national monarchies, especially the Germanic monarchies, and more especially Hegel's Prussia, all became free (Hegel's concept of freedom). This culmination freedom was effected by a synthesis of *one and many*: many free citizens participating in the state under the unifying rule of the one,

48. Walter Kaufmann, *Hegel: Reinterpretation, Texts, and Commentary* (Garden City: Doubleday, 1965), p. 254.

the monarch. The one and many dialectic can also be phrased as union (one ruler), separation (divided rule), and reunion (one ruler). This first political dialectic provides glimpses of the second: authority, freedom, and freedom under authority. Oriental despotism abstracts into authority; the ancient democracies depict freedom—but without authority, something Hegel felt only an absolute ruler could provide. The Germanic nations presented a synthesis of authority and freedom.[49]

SELF-ALIENATION IN HISTORY: MARX. Marx was thoroughly intrigued by Hegel's dialectics but thought Hegel had turned reality upside down by claiming that change originates in the world of ideas and involves the self-realization of God. According to Marx, change comes from forces in the material world of socioeconomic activity—hence "dialectical materialism"—and is directed towards the self-realization of man. Similarly, alienation is not a matter of the psychological dynamics of a divided world but the economic dynamics of a divided society.

With this recasting of Hegelian premises Marx moved from his own early thought about self-alienated man to his mature thought wherein self becomes society, or rather, the proletariat. Although he rarely took pains to explain precisely what he meant by thesis and antithesis, he described the flow of history as a "dialectical" process punctuated with change-producing "contradictions" within society. At any stage of history men enter into certain social relations for meeting their economic needs. These "relations of production" form a material base on which there arises a legal and political superstructure of ideas: the material world shapes the world of

49. Predictably, the Germanic period also subdivides into three stages: Reformation, post-Reformation, and a "Modern" period beginning around 1800. A dialectical interpretation now becomes speculative, however—needed for consistency but not obvious as to content—and there are no specific parallels in Tillich; hence the final triad is of dubious illustrative value. For what it may be worth, though, the Reformation, with its break from the papacy, seems to represent potential German unity. The post-Reformation era, with its proliferation of tiny German states, would then stand for separation—the antithesis of union. "Modern Times" is the period of Hegel's sponsor, Frederick William III of Prussia (1797–1840), and the inference to be drawn is that Hegel saw in Prussia a balance between union and separation: Prussia had grown to include a number of formerly independent states and was thus a union of separate elements. The dialectic could also be construed as separation (from the authority of the Pope) and return (to the authority of the monarch).

73

ideas, not the reverse. But the material world is in constant flux. As productive relations change, for example, with the replacement of the hand mill by the steam mill, conflicts arise between the class structure and the relations of production, as well as within the class structure. Classes that have been hurt fight classes that have been helped.

As Marx sees things, history moves through five social orders, or stages of production: primitive communism, ancient slavery, feudalism, capitalism, and final communism. Underlying this movement is a superdialectic with the thesis of communal property in the primitive state, the antithesis of private property in the next three stages, and the synthesis of renewed common ownership in a classless society. Separation and return—proletarian man is separated from and returns to his labor (represented by the master, the lord, and the capitalist in exploitative systems). We are now entering the final stage: the death knell of private property is sounding. A class upheaval will lead to a transitional "dictatorship of the proletariat"; then the state will "wither away." When this happens the Marxian Kingdom of God—world communism—will reign as "the negation of the negation."

SELF-ALIENATION IN ONTOLOGY. Hegel's history, in contrast to that of Marx, fits into the broader context of ontology. Ontology is the branch of metaphysics concerned with "being" in the sense of a presumed essential nature of reality. Philosophers used to think, and apparently some still do, that an invisible supernatural "essence" is the true substance of everything that is. This ultimate reality has been regarded as something beyond sensory perception, hence as knowable only through ontological intuition. For Hegel ultimate reality is the Spirit, which he describes as "the inner being of the world," "the supersensible beyond," and "the fluent self-identical essential reality."

Hegel's ontology, at the highest level of abstraction and divorced from its historical applications, could be termed semidialectical. It has thesis and antithesis standing in opposition to each other even though essentially united in synthesis, but the dynamic characteristic of sequence is missing. The analysis revolves around the concepts of general and particular, that is, around "the opposition of universal and particular."[50] In brief, the Spirit is a universal, one (thesis), but one built of particulars (antithesis), making it a union of general and particular (synthesis). The particulars are everything comprising reality, as manifest in both nature and history.

Once dynamics enters the discussion, ontology describes the Spirit's self-realization as a three-stage movement from "potentiality" to "appearance" to "actuality." The Spirit, which is potentially *one*, a union of all particulars, goes out from its potential essence to the world of human experience. There it appears as *many* to man, the subuniverse of particulars in which consciousness and ultimately self-consciousness materialize; everything in man's world is differentiated from himself—particulars galore. When consciousness (specifically Hegel) eventually realizes that the many seemingly external particulars are really itself and that it and its world are both essentially Spirit, potentiality and appearance are united as actuality. "Hence the third stage is the return of self thus alienated [from itself] . . . into its first primal simplicity."[51] Any resemblance between this process and either the Eden-sin-salvation saga or the Christ myth—wherein the absolute, God, goes out from himself as his son (becomes physically alienated from himself) and is then reunited with himself through the Holy Spirit (the dove)—is purely intentional. To quote Tillich: "Obviously—and it was so intended by Hegel—his dialectics are the religious symbols of estrangement and reconciliation conceptualized and reduced to empirical descriptions."[52]

The next facets of Hegel's ontology should prove familiar to persons closely acquainted with Tillich's. Stage one, potentiality, has two "elements." Referring back to our initial abstract description, these are the general ("universal") and the particular, one and many. Potentially, but not yet actually, they are united. In stage two, appearance, the one and the many are separated. This is the self-alienation mentioned earlier in relation to Hegel's concepts of man and history. The Spirit, as consciousness, goes out into man and becomes "subject." Subject is the Spirit's ego, the Spirit manifest in a person conscious of himself as a person but not yet con-

---

50. G. W. F. Hegel, *The Phenomenology of Mind*, trans. J. B. Baillie (New York: Harper Torchbooks, 1967), p. 261.

51. *Ibid.*, p. 555. 52. *ST–3*, p. 329.

scious of his true identity as Spirit. Anything external to subject, including other subjects, appears to subject as a separate "object." Existentially, the Spirit is divided within itself; one and many are separated; thesis has become antithesis. The Spirit attains self-realization, or true self-consciousness, when subject recognizes object (i.e., all objects) as itself. *Potential* becomes *actual* when it *appears* to (is recognized by) consciousness as the actual. In this synthesis, "the spirit has made its existence equal to its essence; . . . and . . . the separation of knowledge and truth is overcome."[53] Thus: "With this inner truth, this absolute universal which has got rid of the opposition between universal and particular, and become the object of understanding, is a supersensible world which henceforth opens up as the true world, lying beyond the sensuous world . . . of appearance."[54]

In his much-cited discussion of "the unhappy consciousness," Hegel in effect uses the three members of the Christian Trinity as symbols for the three stages of the ontological dialectic. It would be more accurate, though, to say they become Spirit's emerging self-consciousness' clouded vision of its own inner life. God, Christ, and Holy Spirit are not mentioned by name, but the allusions to them are unmistakable. In the first instance the unhappy consciousness (self-alienated Spirit manifest in human thought) perceives itself as God, "the alien, external Being, which passes sentence on particular existence"; next it perceives itself as another man, the Christ, a "mode of particularity like itself," who stands in antithesis to the Heavenly Father as the symbol of existential particularity. Consciousness "becomes in the third place spirit (*Geist*)," which is to say—subtly—that man's image of a Holy Spirit presages the Hegelian Absolute Spirit's actualization upon the no-longer-unhappy consciousness' recognition of itself and its world as Spirit. Stage three reconciles the "two elements" labeled "one" (essence, God) and "the manifold" (existence, the Christ), just as theology's Holy Spirit joined God and Jesus. Thus, referring to his system's Spirit, Hegel says "it discovers *itself* . . . and becomes

53. G. W. F. Hegel, Preface to the *Phenomenology*, trans. Walter Kaufmann in *Hegel: Reinterpretation, Texts, and Commentary*, p. 412. Kaufmann's translation is used here because it is sharper and more lucid than Baillie's. Cf. Baillie's translation, p. 97.
54. Hegel, *The Phenomenology of Mind*, p. 191.

aware within itself that its particularity has been reconciled with the universal."[55]

Tillichian Dialectics

Most people who have read Tillich realize that his thought is, in some sense, "dialectical": he says it is, repeatedly. What "dialectical" means, however, is another matter. Some interpreters, basing their views on Tillich's talk about existential questions and revelatory answers, assume that Tillichian dialectics is more or less a literary format relating to Plato's dialogues.[56] Others, schooled in theology and thinking of the non-Hegelian theological "dialectics" of Karl Barth, believe that certain nonsequential "polarities" Tillich discusses are his dialectics.[57] But anyone with more than a casual knowledge of Hegel and Marx will, with just a little probing, recognize in Tillich the familiar pattern of thesis, antithesis, and synthesis. (It may also be recognized that much of what passes for existentialism in Tillich's thought—the seeming pessimism and the preoccupation with estrangement—is simply dialectical symbolism involving antitheses.) There are, in fact, extremely close parallels between Tillich's doctrines of man, history, and ultimate reality and the German dialectical tradition after which they are modeled.

THE DIALECTICS OF MAN. Tillich's description of a mature attitude toward life is presented dialectically in his parable of "life." The "divine life" of which Tillich so often speaks is the life of Yes (thesis), No (antithesis), Yes (synthesis). The primitive Yes is uttered in man's youthful state of "dreaming innocence"; it affirms that there is a God and an accompanying realm of supernatural existence. Then man awakens to reality and voices his No; it is the negation of God in particular and supernaturalism in general. This disorients man, creates a vacuum in his life, and leads to "despair."

---

55. Ibid., pp. 251–67, esp. p. 253.
56. For the view that Tillichian dialectics involves question-and-answer style dialogue, see Guyton B. Hammond, The Power of Self-Transcendence (St. Louis: Bethany Press, 1966), pp. 27, 53–54.
57. The opinion that Tillich builds his dialectics largely on the principle of "coincidence of opposites" is expressed by David Hopper in Tillich: A Theological Portrait (New York: Lippincott, 1967), pp. 41, 133–34. Hopper expressly indicates that "the idea of polarity" is something other than the Hegelian dialectic, which he says is also involved but in a manner not explained by Tillich.

Man is now estranged not only from humanity, which has been the case all along, but from the imaginary God who once filled his life with meaning. In time this plight is overcome. Man experiences "revelation"—really nothing more than a value judgment—in which he apprehends that God is man and undergoes "salvation." There really is a God after all! It is, quoting Tillich (and Hegel, and Marx), "the negation of the negation."[58] The Yes to God has been joined with the No to supernaturalism to form the synthetic Yes to the God above the God of supernaturalism.

The "divine life" introduces a key feature of Tillich's dialectics and of his thought generally. Many efforts to interpret Tillich have foundered because, among other reasons, they have not recognized the identification of thesis and antithesis in Tillichian dialectics with theology's divine-human dichotomy. The divine life is Tillich's analogue of the Son going out from and returning to God: the Johannine Son initially is with *God* (thesis), then he goes out to *man* (antithesis), and finally he returns to *God*, uniting God and man in the process (synthesis). God "goes out and returns."[59] This movement of separation and return symbolizes the movement of the human intellect in initially accepting God, later going out into atheism, and finally "returning" to God—a higher God. In the antithesis, No and man are equivalent, for in saying No to God the intellect substitutes human reason (man) for divine revelation (God). The Yes-No-Yes dialectic is thus equivalent to a movement from God to man to the synthesis, God = man.

There are many hidden applications of this dialectic in Tillich's thought. In each instance the thesis is analogous to God and the antithesis to man. God and man translate into such antinomies as one and many, supernatural and nonsupernatural, faith and doubt, revelation and reason, and authority and autonomy. The divine side of each pair symbolizes the Yes to the one (one God), to the supernatural, to faith, and so on. The human side of the pair symbolizes the No, the stage where man denies God and turns to himself—to

58. *Courage*, p. 179.
59. *Perspectives*, p. 112. Tillich has also drawn a theological analogy between man's "divine life" and the idea of a human soul going out from and returning to God. See *History*, p. 202. The basic concept of union, separation, and reunion in relation to God is unchanged.

78

personal autonomy in moral matters and to the life of reason. By grasping these associations, one can draw an important conclusion. A dialectic must always culminate in a synthesis that unites thesis and antithesis. Therefore, there must be a synthesis of God and man. God and man must become one—the hidden message.

THE DIALECTICS OF HISTORY. Like Hegel and Marx, Tillich formulates an interpretation of history based on his picture of man. Tillich's history, also like its prototypes, is dialectical and shifts the alienation theme from man to society. Again like the earlier histories, Tillich's involves progress towards the self-realization of a corporate God, which self-realization becomes a substitute for Christianity's Kingdom of God. Finally, Tillichian history repeats the Hegel-Marx pattern of having dialectical movements at more than one level.

The overall historical dialectic—the top level—is that of separation and return. Here we encounter Tillich's equivalent of (a) Hegel's metaphysical world-self, or Spirit, passing from nature to self-alienation to self-realization, and (b) Marxian society's movement from primitive communism to private property back to communism (final communism). Tillich's God, of course, is neither Hegel's Spirit nor Marx's proletariat. It is humanity—all humanity. Tillichian history therefore becomes the story of the self-realization of humanity as God. At the hypothetical moment in history when man evolved from lower orders, there materialized the thesis of the *potential* unity and godhood of mankind. Call this union or, alternatively, essence—the essential humanity and divinity of all men. Man's essential unity, Tillich notes, has never been realized: human existence has been from the beginning a condition of strife and alienation among men. This gives us the antithesis: the separation of man from man, otherwise called existential estrangement (existence). Man, like Hegel's Spirit, stands alienated from himself because he does not see himself as he essentially is, that is, as one and as God. The answer to man's predicament lies in the realization by individual men that all men are essentially one and that the one is God. This self-realization, or self-recognition, is a "return" to union: potential becomes actual. The return is a synthesis, a synthesis of essence and existence. Essence, in this case, means one,

God, or humanity; existence indicates many, man, or individual men.

Certain aspects of Tillich's version of separation and return as applied to history need clarification. The opposition between essence and existence is "the fall," which we discussed earlier as an illustration of symbolism. To repeat, the fall in Tillich's vernacular is the transition from essence to existence. Because Tillich is forced to maintain that creation and the fall coincide—there never was a period of harmony among men—this is distinctly third-rate dialectics; the "transition" with which Tillich struggles to provide the element of sequence between thesis and antithesis is sham. Just the same, human unity and human separation are intended as thesis and antithesis, and the matter of sequence becomes less debatable as they move toward a synthesis. The return movement is what Tillich calls "salvation" (in the historical rather than the personal sense). And the synthesis is existential essence. Alternatively it is actualized potentiality, reunion of the estranged, or, for the religious touch, the Kingdom of God.

Tillich's second dialectical level compares with Hegel's political dialectic of despotism (authority without freedom), democracy (freedom without authority), and monarchy (freedom under authority). Tillich's counterparts are "heteronomy," "autonomy," and "theonomy," terms that can be used in either a personal or a historical sense. Heteronomy, the thesis, is authoritarian rule by church or state; it is to be identified primarily with religion. Autonomy, the antithesis, reacts against authority by stressing the rule of reason. Think of autonomy in terms of antireligious, antiauthoritarian attitudes (free thought). Theonomy, the synthesis, also involves the rule of reason, but this time guided by authority. The authority is love for humanity. Referring back to the dialectics of man, theonomy is the sociohistorical equivalent of an individual's simultaneously embracing the No and the Yes; it is a period of humanism. History does not end with the theonomous synthesis but repeats itself in never-ending cycles. Periods of heteronomy lead to autonomy and then theonomy, but theonomy generates a new antithesis that renews the progression. The goal of history—Tillich's Kingdom of God—is a state of brotherly love by all toward all. Tillich has no illusions that it will ever materialize, but he is confident that it can be approached via successively closer theonomous approximations.

THE DIALECTICS OF ONTOLOGY. Continuing in the dialectical mode, Tillich again follows Hegel in setting his interpretation of history within an ontological framework. Tillich's "ontology," which is pure fabrication, closely follows Hegel's but employs the opposing assumption—definition, that is—that the ultimate reality of the universe is humanity. The Tillichian model adopts Hegel's concepts of subject (the ego, particular) and object (externality, general). These are recast as subjective and objective *reason*, analogous to the Spirit as subject and as object. The term "reason," adapted from Baillie's translation of *Geist* (Spirit) as "mind," allows Tillich to conceptualize his version of ultimate reality in terms of ultimate concern. Subjective reason relates to particular men and to their preliminary concerns; objective reason concerns humanity, the ultimate concern to which all "true" preliminary concerns are transparent. Humanity, of course, is the "world" to which individual humans belong and, as ultimate concern, is also the "world" to which true preliminary concerns belong. Essentially—here is the thesis—subjective and objective reason are united as ontological reason, that is, as humanity in its twofold character of particular and universal. But subjective and objective reason form an antithesis when reflected in three "conflicts in reason." "Revelation" resolves each conflict by showing that subjective reason and objective reason form a synthesis: each holds as its inner essence the "depth of reason" (analogous to Hegel's Spirit), which is another code phrase for humanity. The clash between relativism and absolutism ends, for instance, when we see that relativism describes man (many related particulars), that absolutism describes God (one, absolute), and that man and God are identical. The revelation of the "depth of reason" is the counterpart of Hegel's ontological synthesis, which Hegel once called "the revelation of the depth of spiritual life."[60]

Tillich's treatment of reason and revelation is a preface to an expanded ontology. This ontology simply repeats the Hegelian story of self and world: their potential unity, their existential sepa-

60. Hegel, *The Phenomenology of Mind*, p. 808.

ration, their essential realization as God. Hegel's two "elements," particular and general, reappear clearly labeled as "elements" but otherwise dressed up in such terminology as "dynamics and form" (Tillich's equivalent of Hegel's "changeable" and "unchangeable"). Whatever their names, one element is always analogous to humanity (one, form) and the other to particular men (many, dynamic). Potentially humanity and the persons of which it consists are the infinite; existentially they are finite, separated by subject's (man's) failure to recognize object (humanity) as God. By performing a pseudo-analysis of traditional philosophical "categories" of knowledge (time, space, and so on), Tillich suggests that the elements can be united (for example, by occupying the same "social space" of a humanistic value structure). All this semantic hocus-pocus enables Tillich to reach into the depths of Hegel's metaphysical hat and pull out humanity, disguised as a rabbit named "being-itself."

CORRELATION: A REINTERPRETATION

Symbolism, Tillich's first device for encoding the hidden message, deals primarily with theological ideas. Dialectics, the second cryptographic tool, turns to philosophy. A third basic instrument employed in the construction of Tillich's system combines theological and philosophical concepts. Tillich calls this instrument the method of correlation. What does this mean? Writers attempting to explain Tillich customarily take him at his word concerning what he means by correlation. This is risky business, for we know that Tillich delights in leading people astray. And in this particular instance, correlation is something substantially different from what he says it is.

Tillich's Explanation

Let us begin with Tillich's explanation. Correlation, he indicates, is a process whereby philosophical questions are correlated with theological answers derived from the traditional Christian message. He identifies five types of questions pertaining to human existence and five general answers derived from theology: (1) questions implied in the conflicting paths of reason, to which the answer is "revelation," (2) questions implied in finite man's quest for meaning, to which the answer is "God," (3) questions implied in the despair characterizing man's estrangement from God, man, and self, to which the answer is "the Christ," (4) questions implied in the uncertainties and ambiguities of life, to which the answer is "the Spirit," and (5) questions implied in the ambiguous course of history, to which the answer is "the Kingdom of God." These five set of questions and answers correspond to parts I through V of Tillich's *Systematic Theology*.

If the method of correlation were no more than what is described above, we could ignore it as insignificant and largely irrelevant to the content of Tillich's thought. For all this description amounts to is a presentation of the first two levels of an outline, a kind of introductory overview—and a rather cloudy one at that. "Correlating" question and answer becomes the time-honored technique of expressing each new point or heading as a question. We see this done from time to time in magazine articles wherein an author develops each topic beneath a heading consisting of a question printed in bold face or colored ink.

The fact is, however, that there is more to correlation than Tillich spells out. When we examine his thought carefully it is evident that he is attempting something far more ambitious than correlating philosophical questions with theological answers. Indeed, in their orientation the questions are as much theological as philosophical. And Tillich's answers, once understood, are as much philosophical as theological. In fact, the answers are 100 percent philosophical; only the language belongs to theology.

Correlation of Concepts

Some remarks about God and being, the respective absolutes of theology and philosophy, provide a clue to what correlation really means. These competitors pose what Tillich calls *"the problem of the two Absolutes."* The problem is for man to decide between them. The solution: "The religious and the philosophical Absolutes, *Deus* and *esse* cannot be unconnected!"[61] And what is the connection? Tillich avoids any useful explanation, but both absolutes happen to be symbols for the humanistic absolute—man. Or, to

---

61. *Culture*, p. 12.

rephrase, God and being, theological concept and philosophical, are *correlated* so that they jointly symbolize a humanistic concept.

This interpretation, suggested by the analogical relationship between being and God, is confirmed by a reference elsewhere to "the correlation of . . . being and God" and a companion reference to "the correlation of reason and revelation."[62] Both correlations pair a philosophical concept with an analogous theological one. Thus reason and revelation are analogous in that reason is the basic tool of philosophy and revelation the basic tool of theology. We have discovered the real meaning of correlation: the use of pairs of analogous theological and philosophical concepts to jointly symbolize humanistic concepts.

Once the existence of correlative pairs is recognized, they can be found everywhere in Tillich's thought. The five "answers" Tillich gives in his "question and answer" pseudo-explanation of correlation illustrate things. The answers are (1) revelation, (2) God, (3) the Christ, (4) the Spirit, and (5) the Kingdom of God. Each of these is the theology member of a theology-philosophy pair. Revelation, as just observed, correlates with reason: Tillich is going to make Christian revelation rational by giving it a nonsupernatural interpretation. God is correlated with the concepts of being and being-itself, taken from Greek and scholastic philosophy. The Christ has two philosophical correlates, essence and existence, which link together to form realized (rather than potential) essence —essence under the conditions of existence. The Spirit, which is as close as Tillich ordinarily comes to saying Holy Spirit (he chokes on Holy Ghost), enters into correlation with dialectical synthesis. The Kingdom of God is the correlate of philosophy's utopias, particularly Germanic monarchy (Hegel) and world communism (Marx).

Other theology-philosophy correlates permeate Tillich's thought. Eden correlates with essence, both symbolizing the potential essence of human unity. The fall, we have seen, is the transition from essence to existence. Existence is a Tillichian synonym for estrangement, and estrangement correlates with sin: both describe separation. The cure for separation is salvation, and here the theological concept is correlated with a return to essence, or for reunit-

62. *ST–1*, p. 163.

ing of the estranged. Man's fall and resurrection occur in the context of history, where Christianity's eschatological narrative merges with the dialectical philosophies of history to produce Tillich's humanistic interpretation of history. To repeat another earlier observation, the divine-human dichotomy emphasized by theology becomes the correlate of philosophy's clash between thesis and antithesis. Not all of the correlative analogies may be immediately apparent, but they will unfold as we proceed.

The method of correlation, then, involves the creation of triangular analogies. Three concepts—theological, philosophical, and humanistic—are joined by a three-way analogy. The theological and philosophical concepts form a synthesis providing dual symbolization of the humanistic one. Both symbols contribute nuances of meaning. To use Tillich's words: "Philosophy and theology are not separated, and they are not identical, but they are correlated, and their correlation is the methodological problem of a Protestant theology."[63] Translation: If you want to understand the system of my systematic theology, look for a correlation of philosophy and theology.

We begin to see how subtle Tillich can be. When he professes to correlate questions and answers he is speaking symbolically. "Questions" symbolizes philosophy; "answers" symbolizes theology. This being the case, symbolic analogies must be present. Where are they? Man, the philosopher, asks questions, and God, the omniscient, has the answers, to be found in theology. Looking at it another way, reason, the instrument of philosophers, leads to questions for which authority (or revelation), the instrument of theologians, provides answers. The analogies tell us that correlation of question and answer actually means correlation of philosophical and theological concepts.

Broad and Narrow Meanings

A qualification must now be added. Strictly speaking, correlation has a more general meaning with several connotations. The general meaning is synthesis: the combining of opposites into a single item. These opposites should be understood as divine and human. The divine member of any pair of correlates always comes from this list

63. *Protestant*, p. xxii.

of related categories: theology, God, general (one God), symbol, thesis. The human member is drawn from a corresponding list: philosophy, man, particular (many men), symbolic meaning, antithesis. Tillich can therefore speak of "correlation in the sense of correspondence between religious symbols and that which is symbolized by them."[64] Since Tillich's symbols mean roughly the opposite of what they seem to mean (God means man), opposites are being correlated. As an illustration of correlation between general and particular, Tillich finds correlations "between man's ultimate concern and that about which he is ultimately concerned."[65] This refers to the connection between a particular, humanistic concern (preliminary concern) and the general, divine concern (humanity) which it reflects. Similarly, in the dialectics of man, thesis and antithesis are correlated, becoming a synthesis: life moves from revelation to reason to humanism, or from God to man to God = man.

But correlation has one connotation that overrides all the others, distinguishing it as a unique methodological tool standing apart from symbolism and dialectics. This is the correlation of theology and philosophy. Hereafter, therefore, except where otherwise indicated, correlation will be used exclusively in reference to conceptual exercises that seek to relate theological concepts to philosophical ones.

The practical significance of correlation in this narrower sense, and the reason it will be referred to frequently, is that it helps us to interpret symbols. We can find the meaning of one symbol, say a philosophical one, by turning to another that has already been deciphered. Or, if we are having trouble with both members of a correlative pair but recognize them as correlates, interpretation can be approached from two directions. The process will be demonstrated shortly when we consider Tillich's concept of estrangement and examine it in relation to its correlate, sin.

The Grand Synthesis

The far-reaching nature of correlation introduces the next point, namely, that Tillich's thought is considerably more than the blend of antisupernaturalism and reverence for man that gives it substance. It is a monumental exercise in form and structure, an

64. ST–1, p. 60.   65. ST–1, p. 60.

artistic work to be appreciated. Earlier it was said that one reason Tillich is unwilling to openly disavow religion is that he must be accepted as a theologian in order to formulate and gain acceptance of an imaginative Grand Synthesis of theology and philosophy. This enterprise, Tillich's *Systematic Theology*, is an elaborate effort to bring together major concepts of theological and philosophical thought in a compendious synthesis.

Synthesis—this is the challenge that fires Tillich's imagination. His response, one which could only come from a prodigious imagination, is a four-level synthesis: (1) disciplinary, (2) ontological, (3) historical, and (4) personal life. The foundation level is the broad disciplinary synthesis of theology and philosophy. This supports what might loosely be termed an ontological synthesis, which combines the two absolutes, God and being. The ontological synthesis leads to a historical one. It is a merger of theology's eschatological history—Eden, sin, and the Kingdom of God (or salvation) —and the dialectical histories of Hegel and Marx. On this same level are subsidiary syntheses of Eden and essence, sin and estrangement (existence), and the Kingdom of God and utopia (Hegel's Germanic monarchy, Marx's world communism, and so on). The top level is a "life" synthesis, in the sense of a personal life. Here the theological story of the Son's going out from and returning to the Father ("separation and return") is correlated with philosophy's dialectical movement of affirmation, negation, and negation of the negation (Yes-No-Yes).

No matter what the theological and philosophical inputs at each level, the output—Tillich's synthesis—is always humanism. T + P = H is the rigid formula. On the first level, theology plus philosophy yields Tillich's own peculiar brand of humanism. Next, the synthesis of absolutes correlates God and being (or being-itself), giving us humanity as the humanistic absolute. History, the third level, becomes a dialectical uphill-and-downhill trek toward the goal of universal humanism, wherein all human beings are ultimately concerned about all mankind. Finally, at the level of personal history, the Son's separation and return link up with dialectics' movement from Yes to No back to Yes (a higher Yes) to form a humanistic parable. It is the symbolic story of man's separation from the supernatural God and ultimate "reunion" with a higher God named mankind.

Tillich has explained all this: he has said in his own way that he wants to unite theology and philosophy. The trouble is, he likes to bury his explanations in remote corners and keep them more than a little blurred so that the hidden message does not become too obvious. In this case he has written in his autobiographical volume that Schelling's philosophy (the subject of Tillich's doctoral dissertation) prepared the way for "a unification of theology and philosophy." But due to the post-World War I reaction against idealistic thought, "not even he was able to achieve a unity of theology and philosophy." The war in turn convinced Tillich that any such union could not ignore the "abyss in human existence" that accompanies doubt. "If a reunion of theology and philosophy is ever to be possible it will be achieved only in a *synthesis* that does justice to this experience of the abyss in our lives." A synthesis that fills the abyss with love for humanity is Tillich's answer.[66]

Philosophical Theology

A word must now be said about some remarks in *Systematic Theology* that seem to contradict the point just advanced. Tillich states that a synthesis between philosophy and theology is not possible.[67] Scrutinizing this statement, we find that it refers to "the dream of a 'Christian philosophy.' "[68] Tillich argues that *if* these words are used in the sense of a philosophy that bends to the demands of theology, the philosophical element is lost. This contention ties in with an earlier one that lack of common ground has barred the way to synthesis. The philosopher proceeds from reason, the theologian from revealed authority; and if the philosopher accepts the constraints of religious authority he is no longer a philosopher.

Note that the possibility Tillich rebuts is not the type of synthesis he is attempting. He is not writing a Christian philosophy or any other kind of theological philosophy. Rather, he is writing what he calls "philosophical theology."[69] The word "systematic" in

66. *Boundary,* pp. 51–52 (my italics).
67. *ST–1,* p. 26.   68. *ST–1,* p. 27.
69. *Protestant,* pp. 92, 93.

"systematic theology" is an allusion to philosophical systems, a code word for "philosophical"; systematic theology means philosophical theology. This is no petty distinction, not as Tillich sees it anyway. It is one that goes to the very heart of his thought and determines his interpretation of God; it is a distinction between a philosophy based on revelation and a theology based on reason. Tillich originally tried the former approach: he explored a "theonomous metaphysics" (metaphysics represents philosophy) as "a first and rather insufficient step toward what I now call the 'method of correlation.'"[70] Even before this he admired Schelling's approach, one Tillich describes with the terms "Christian philosophy" and "theonomous philosophy."[71] But he eventually decided that the philosophical route was inadequate and turned to philosophical theology. For Tillich, a theology based on reason is one that uses biblical "revelation" as a starting point but, instead of taking it literally, gives it a rational interpretation. Rational means nonsupernatural. As opposed to a Christian philosophy, the result is a humanistic theology.

Those who believe that Tillich wants to base his system on logic —and who proceed to cavil at this supposed logic—err badly. Tillich isn't trying to prove anything. His propositions are not rational (in the sense of being logical) but dogmatic; they are rooted in the authority of the revealed "Word of God," as manifested in the Bible and theological tradition. But this is authority with a difference. Instead of using the traditional meanings he often pretends to accept, Tillich adopts private interpretations with humanistic content. He thus operates like a typical neo-orthodox theologian, finding in the Bible deeper meanings that aren't really there; but he does this with full awareness of what he is doing. The interpretations that result are rational insofar as they reject supernaturalism; they are also rational in a stricter sense to be explained later in connection with the symbol, Jesus as the Christ. It is this loosely defined rationality and not reasoned argumentation that makes Tillich's so-called theology philosophical. There is no point in engaging in semantic disputation over whether this is really "synthesis" in some appropriate sense of the word. What-

70. *Protestant*, p. xxii.   71. *Boundary*, pp. 51–52.

ever we call it, correlation is intended as a broad-scale bringing together of theology and philosophy. "Both philosophy and theology become poor and distorted when they are separated from each other."[72]

ESTRANGEMENT: A DOCTRINE OF MAN

We have just examined three devices Tillich uses to conceal his message: symbolism, dialectics, and correlation. One other subject relating to concealment must now be discussed to round out the picture. That subject is estrangement. Estrangement is not a tool or device in the same sense as the three mentioned above; it is a joint application of them. It is a symbol describing the separation of man from God, though not a supernatural God as is usually assumed; it is part of a dialectic, the antithesis standing between union and reunion in relation to God; and it is a correlate, the philosophical correlate of theology's doctrine of sin. In this triple role, estrangement gets so much exercise that it demands special attention.

The Plight of Man

No theology would be Christian without a doctrine of man, one that elaborates the plight of man. Tillich, of course, thinks the plight outlined by traditional theology is blasphemous nonsense, so he does what for him is routine: he invents a new to replace the old. The new plight revolves around the synonymous ideas of existence and estrangement, often combined as "existential estrangement." Existence, a term from existentialist philosophy, signifies man's previously described state of unrealized potentiality, or unfulfillment; it stands opposed to the essence that defines the essential state. Estrangement is the Hegelian term for dialectical separation of actual self from ideal self.[73] For Tillich, the ideal self (or the essential state) involves, like two sides of a coin, union of man with God and the self-realization of man as God.

---

72. *Protestant*, p. 89.
73. Acknowledging his conceptual debt to Hegel, Tillich points out that Hegel's Spirit is "alienated or estranged" from itself. "In my opinion the two words mean the same thing, but I know that some philosophers prefer the word 'alienation,' perhaps because it is a bit more abstract. I myself have preferred to use the word 'estrangement' because it contains the imagery of the stranger and the separation of people who once loved each other and belong essentially to each other." (*Perspectives*, p. 124.)

What puzzles many readers is what passes as extreme pessimism about this "existential predicament" of man. Everybody, it seems, falls into "universal estrangement"[74] simply by existing. We start our lives born into estrangement. God—humanity—"creates" the newborn babe; "but, if created, it falls into the state of existential estrangement."[75] This sounds bad enough, but to make matters worse the estrangement, we are told, can be "only fragmentarily" overcome, and the New Being which gives us one foot in the door of essence remains "under the condition of man's existential predicament" in all cases.[76] (Note the dialectical flavor of New Being, which absorbs estrangement into the synthesis rather than conquers it.)

This much may not sound crucial. The trouble is that estrangement is hopelessly entangled with "despair" in Tillich's thought. Despair is, indeed, the trademark of Tillichian estrangement. "It is not an exaggeration to say that today man experiences his present situation in terms of disruption, conflict, self-destruction, meaninglessness, and despair in all realms of life."[77] Everywhere there prevails "cynicism and despair" which are "driving the masses into the hands of agitators, driving the strong to the glorification of heroic self-destruction and the weak to the loss of all meaning of life and to suicide."[78] We are overpowered by insecurity which "drives toward a despair about the possibility of being at all."[79] An "anxiety of meaninglessness" has become a "vivid and threatening" reality for twentieth-century man.[80] This sort of talk has puzzled many individuals, who probably wonder if they and Tillich are members of the same society. Yet it is a constant theme in Tillich's discussions of man.

A Formalistic Pessimism

We can begin to comprehend the estrangement theme if we first realize what it is not. It is not an expression of pessimism regarding the situation of man. For example, Tillich is not worrying out loud about the poverty, starvation, filth, and disease in the world.

74. ST–2, p. 44.
75. ST–2, p. 44.
76. ST–2, p. 118; cf. ST–3, p. 282.
77. ST–1, p. 49.
78. Protestant, p. 187.
79. ST–2, p. 73.
80. Courage, p. 139.

That is material despair, whereas Tillich is referring to what might be called spiritual despair. Moreover, this spiritual despair is conceptual rather than genuinely psychological. The discussion is *symbolic*; it is not meant to be taken literally. To be sure, Tillich's words often make it sound as though he thinks the whole world is neurotic, just as they often make it sound as though he believes in a supernatural being. But this gloomy outlook is philosophic license employed to conjure up a bit of concreteness for what is essentially an abstraction. Tillich has lived on college campuses and otherwise circulated in society; it is hard to believe he fails to recognize that people are generally cheerful and often as not buoyed up with supernaturalistic confidence that their lives are meaningful. At any rate, he can see "the gracious beauty which we encounter again and again in the stars and mountains, in flowers and animals, in children and mature personalities."[81] And he cautions that existential elements are not only combined with essential ones in man's "predicament" but that both elements "are always abstractions" from life rather than life itself.[82] "For the sake of analysis, however, abstractions are necessary, even if they have a strongly negative sound."[83]

"Meaninglessness" and "despair" are thus reduced to abstractions employed for the sake of analysis. As a theological pretender, Tillich feels obligated to come up with some sort of doctrine of man; and his method of correlation dictates that this doctrine correlate the traditional theological doctrine with an analogous philosophical concept. Sin must have its mate, and existence and estrangement are the obvious (if bigamous) choices. Call this the game of correlation. Existence and estrangement, meanwhile, happen to fit in very nicely with the dialectical game Tillich is simultaneously playing: yes-no-yes equals essence-existence-essence and union-separation-reunion, which in turn correlate with innocence-sin-salvation. In this context of games, despair and estrangement assume perspective. What initially registered as an ultrapessimistic variety of existentialism can now be seen as little more than a philosophical ploy. Tillich's constant harping on the subject, in

81. *Foundations*, p. 48. 82. *ST–2*, p. 28.
83. *ST–2*, p. 28.

turn, mirrors the central position the doctrine of sin holds in traditional theology.

The Substance of Estrangement

Granting all this, it would be a mistake to write off estrangement as all form and no substance: ploy or not, there is a strong element of seriousness in the concept. But just what is it Tillich is trying to say? Let us look more closely at his formulation which, as it happens, provides useful preliminary evidence supporting the proposition, developed at length in the next chapter, that Tillich's God is man. Tillich asserts in various places that man is estranged from the ground of being, life's source and aim, the infinite, others, other men, his essential being, his true being, his own being, and self. These objects fall into three categories—God, other men, and man's self—and Tillich's basic formulation covers all three: "Man is estranged from the ground of his being, from other beings, and from himself."[84] Now God, the first object, can mean anything one chooses to call God, be it a Supreme Being, man, truth, or something else. However, when Tillich mentions other men, specific concepts of the deity begin to materialize. Either Tillich is talking about several different types of estrangement, which doesn't quite fit the contexts of his remarks, or other men are a part of God, which is certainly true if God is humanity. The third category, estrangement from himself, also allows two interpretations, though they don't necessarily conflict. The first, which clearly holds whether or not the second does too, posits separation between states rather than persons: "Man as he exists is not what he essentially is and ought to be."[85] The other interpretation is that man is the God from whom man is estranged.

So far two hints but nothing conclusive. Can "God is man" be the hidden message buried in Tillich's concept of estrangement? To find out we must manipulate the three main tools of the system: symbolism, correlation, and dialectics. Symbolism and correlation are closely related: both are based on analogy. This means that the symbolic meaning of estrangement, whatever it is, must be analogous to the original meanings of both the philosophical symbol

---

84. ST–2, p. 44.   85. ST–2, p. 45.

(estrangement) and the correlated theological symbol (sin). Looking first at the philosophical side, Tillichian estrangement follows the Hegelian and Marxian models. Hegel and Marx both visualized estrangement, or alienation, as the condition of a divided self. This self is identical with the divine. For Hegel the divided self is the world-self, or Spirit. It overcomes estrangement by becoming aware of itself (through man) as God. For Marx the divided self is downtrodden proletarian man, who will overcome self-estrangement by realizing his materially satisfied essential self through world revolution. Neither Hegel nor Marx introduces an outside party; self is estranged from itself. The same holds true for Tillich, for to introduce a second party as God would violate the analogy, which would be contrary to the rules of symbolism. A reference to "man's existential *self*-estrangement"[86] drives home the point.

Turning to the theological perspective, the technique of correlation provides further evidence that Tillich is dealing with just one form of estrangement, not two or three. Sin, we have seen, is the theological correlate of estrangement: sin is theology's plight of man, estrangement is philosophy's. In the doctrine of sin, as with philosophy's theories of estrangement, there is just one type of estrangement. Sin is the estrangement of man from God and from no one else. Granted, the two analogies—estrangement and sin—together add up to two types of estrangement—from man and from God. But in correlation you don't add things together to get two ideas: you form a *synthesis*, a single idea with two aspects. In the case at hand, estrangement and sin are being correlated, which means they are the same: estrangement from self *is* estrangement from God. Man and God become two aspects of the same reality. Man and God become one.

The answer provided by symbolism and correlation is amplified and confirmed by an application of the third systematic tool, dialectics. This application is hinted at in *On the Boundary*. There Tillich emphasizes his penchant for synthesis under a dozen headings, each starting with "Between" (theology and philosophy, church and society, and so on). The penultimate "Between" concerns Hegelian idealism and Marxism. Tillich says he stands on the

86. *ST–2*, p. 39 (my italics).

boundary between them. Since Hegel and Marx are the Big Two of dialectics, this suggests a dialectical movement running from Hegel to Marx to Tillich. Hegel and Marx each conceptualize individual man as an element of a collective God, but otherwise they take opposing positions. Hegel's God goes beyond humanity to include the whole world—thesis. Marx's God appears as a reaction to Hegel's and goes in the opposite direction, eliminating from humanity all but the proletariat—antithesis. Tillich's God negates Marx's negation of Hegel by taking the compromise position, the view that God is neither more nor less than humanity but human being itself—synthesis. Therefore Tillich can avow, in pointedly rejecting the interpretation that God is a stranger, that "man discovers *himself* when he discovers God; he discovers something that is identical with himself although it transcends him infinitely, something from which he is estranged, but from which he never has been and never can be separated."[87]

If that last phrase sounds familiar, it is because the initial words, right down to the italics, imitate Hegel's "it discovers *itself*" dictum, appearing within the terminal quotation in our review of Hegel's ontology. Hegel means it quite literally, and so does Tillich. Hegel is referring to the dialectical synthesis wherein Spirit, embodied in human consciousness, discovers its true identity as Spirit —as the infinite—and thus overcomes the estrangement of self and world. This is our clue to a further application of dialectics. Tillichian estrangement, like Hegelian estrangement, is the antithesis of a dialectic. Hegel's is the prototype dialectic: (1) thesis: the world-self in unconscious primordial union with itself, (2) antithesis: world-conscious man estranged from world, perceived as a hostile "object," and (3) synthesis: self-conscious man reunited with world, now recognized as essentially identical with himself. In Tillich's analogical system, the world-self is replaced by humanity. The "dreaming [unconscious] innocence" of potential human unity becomes estrangement (the fall) when human existence materializes as a state of conscious hostility among men. This estrangement of man from humanity is overcome (salvation) when "man discovers *himself*" by realizing the identity of himself and the infinite.

87. *Culture*, p. 10.

We need no longer ponder what Tillich means in saying man is born into estrangement and can only hope for fragmentary reunion with God. Unrequited love is the answer. Individual men may learn the "law of love" for humanity, but humanity as a whole does not reciprocate. Nation remains divided against nation, faith against faith (and, especially, against nonfaith), race against race, and individual against individual. Men shoot people, cheat people, lie, and steal. Some individuals are selfish; not everyone has been "grasped" (as Tillich would say) by humanity. Yet only when *all* men accept man as their God will the love of individual men for humanity be fully requited. "Only universal healing is total healing—salvation beyond ambiguities and fragments."[88]

Why God Does Not "Exist"

The point that reunion can only be fragmentary leads to an explanation of an apparent inconsistency which has troubled some of Tillich's critics. Tillich claims that God does not exist, yet he constantly speaks of God in a manner implying that "he" does exist. As Rowe puts it: "on the one hand he holds that the concept of existence and the concept of God are incompatible; whereas, on the other hand he makes statements about God and formulates arguments about God which imply or presuppose that there *is* a God, that God *exists*. Clearly, he cannot have it both ways."[89] Rowe is referring to Tillichian statements like this: "God does not exist. He is being-itself beyond essence and existence. Therefore, to argue that God exists is to deny him."[90]

It should be quite obvious from the fact that, as Rowe points out, Tillich discusses and characterizes God that "God" or "exist" is being used in a special sense when God's existence is denied. Actually, both words are used in special senses, although these senses are not combined. First, Tillich sometimes uses "God" to mean the God of theism, conceived as an intelligent, self-conscious being. When Tillich remarks that God "cannot be found within the totality of beings,"[91] a statement appearing shortly before the "God

88. *ST–3*, p. 282.
89. William L. Rowe, *Religious Symbols and God: A Philosophical Study of Tillich's Theology* (Chicago: University of Chicago Press, 1968), p. 95.
90. *ST–1*, p. 205. Cf. pp. 236, 237; *Culture*, pp. 4–5.
91. *ST–1*, p. 205.

does not exist" one, this is in part a denial of the existence of the God of theism; the remark does not deny the existence (in the conventional sense of existence) of the Tillichian God. Second, and here we get back to estrangement, Tillich is using the word "exist" in a special Hegelian sense when he further indicates that his own God "does not exist." Hegel's metaphysical God, the world-self or Spirit, goes through a process of "becoming" before its potential being becomes actual. Spirit does not become Absolute Spirit until self-recognition takes place, until it comes to know itself as Spirit. History "is the process of becoming in terms of knowledge," says Hegel, and its goal "is Absolute Knowledge or Spirit knowing itself as Spirit."[92] God becomes God when it recognizes itself as God. In the movement from thesis (potential unity) to antithesis (man estranged from nature, and essence from existence) to synthesis (self-realization), Spirit exists in several senses. At the outset it has potential existence; there is an embryonic reality which, however, has "not yet" materialized in its mature form of Absolute Spirit. At stage two, "existence" becomes a synonym for estrangement: Spirit "exists" in a self-divided state which contradicts its essential unity. In the third stage, what had been "becoming" becomes, and Spirit truly comes into existence as Absolute Spirit.

Now we can understand what Tillich means when he indicates that his own God, being-itself, does not exist. His God is humanity, dialectically conceived. Humanity is in a state of "becoming." At the moment humanity is estranged, divided against itself. It cannot become *fully* God until *all* human beings recognize humanity as God. Fragmentary self-realization is not enough: humanity will not come into existence *as God* until complete self-realization comes about. When Tillich asserts that God is "beyond" essence and existence, therefore, he is simply saying that synthesis is beyond thesis and antithesis. The "beyond" will never materialize, because "fragmentary" reunion is the best we can hope for. In terms of the three dialectical stages, then, God has potential existence; God also exists actually (existentially), estranged from itself; and God even exists as actualized potentiality, but only in a fragmentary sense, in particular individuals. God will not truly exist as God until *all* indi-

92. Hegel, *The Phenomenology of Mind*, pp. 807, 808.

viduals ("all in all") adopt humanity as their God. Tillich means this when he describes "the fulfilled Kingdom of God" as being characterized by "universality" and by *the negation of the negative* in everything that has being [i.e., in all human beings]."[93] The italicized expression is, of course, the Hegelian-Marxian term for dialectical synthesis; it refers to progressing "beyond" estrangement (the antithesis) to the ultimate union of essence and existence. When humanity is conceived as a dialectical God in a state of "becoming," therefore, "to argue that God exists is to deny him." For to argue that God exists is to be speaking of the traditional God and thereby denying "him," in the dialectical sense of humanity.

93. *ST–3*, pp. 405, 406 (my italics). Here a minor difference between Hegel and Tillich requires explanation. For Hegel's Spirit finally to come into existence as Absolute Spirit it was necessary for just one person, Hegel, to recognize that he and everything else real were essentially Spirit. Tillich, on the other hand, demands that all human beings recognize humanity as God before humanity can realize its essential divinity. Why? The Hegelian synthesis unites essence and existence, where essence is what is really real and existence is what things appear or are understood to be. Tillich also wants to unite essence and existence, but his concept of existence—strife and selfishness among men—requires different treatment. Estrangement of this variety is not overcome simply by one person's recognizing and declaring an identity between essence and existence. Therefore Tillich provides a different type of synthesis: essence (the divinity of man) and existence (the human predicament) are united in particular individuals who embrace humanity as their God. Similarly, humanity becomes a synthesis of fragments (persons) which have realized their essential divinity and other fragments representing the existential state.

CHAPTER 3

The God above God

Anyone seeking incontrovertible proof that Tillich's God above God is humanity will not find it. Tillich is willing enough to say what his God is not—that it is not a being and not the God of theism, for example. But he is not about to enlighten the larger of his two audiences with an unambiguous statement about what God is. God's identity must be deduced. One must interpret, draw inferences, and test hypotheses against various assertions and doctrines. This isn't as hard as it sounds, because Tillich has scattered many hints and clues throughout his works. As foundation information, he has told us never to give him a supernatural or metaphysical interpretation, and this much he has said in words no careful, open-minded reader could misunderstand. (Part of the problem is that most analysts, though usually careful, have closed their minds by taking it for granted that Tillich holds at least a qualified belief in the supernatural.) Tillich has also indicated, now in words more difficult to interpret, that we should look for his meaning in analogies and dialectical triads and that some of the analogies will involve the correlation of philosophical and theological concepts. Quite openly he has employed the Hegelian theme of estrangement, and one can only express amazement that the very obvious analogical relationship between Hegelian and Tillichian estrangement has not been adequately explored heretofore. Another of Tillich's techniques is to plant one premise in one book and another somewhere else, leaving it to the reader to find them and put them together to arrive at a conclusion. We shall even run into the crude device of contriving special initials to serve as hints (Chapter 5). All this gives us ample means of verifying the identity of the higher God. In this chapter I shall start with the conclusion from the analysis of Tillichian estrangement—the conclusion that humanity is the God from whom man is estranged—and treat it initially as just a hypothesis. The hypothesis, it will become evident, not only fits some surprisingly explicit clues ensconced in obscure places but is systematically verified through analogical and dialectical formulations constituting the formal structure of Tillich's "systematic theology." In the ultimate test, which comprehends interpretations presented in this and the next two chapters, and also the interpretation of estrangement, the vagueness and seeming contradictions in Tillich become clear and coherent. Indeed, precise meanings emerge for all of Tillich's basic concepts and doctrines, and these meanings are fully consonant from one interpretation to the next.

FIVE BASIC CLUES

Outside the mainstream of Tillich's doctrinal formulations, one encounters five especially significant clues as to the identity of the God above God. The first clue is theoretically derived; the other four come from scattered passages in Tillich's works, with some of these clues materializing only when separate passages from different sources are put together. The clues deal with (1) Tillich's philosophical background, (2) the apologetic method, (3) self-transcendence, (4) the Ugliest Man, and (5) love.

Theory: Tillich's Philosophical Background

The first clue comes not from Tillich's writing, except insofar as antisupernaturalism is the ultimate premise, but from theoretical analysis. The analysis begins with the point that Tillich totally rejects supernaturalism (see Chapter 1). Therefore the God of the system is nonsupernatural. Or, as Tillich puts it, being includes nonbeing. Now place yourself in the position of a philosopher wishing to attack Christianity by writing an atheistic "theology" about a nonsupernatural God. Who or what would you pick to be this God? The most obvious alternatives are idealistic or moralistic abstractions which men have long upheld—abstractions such as freedom, honesty, love, nature, . . . and humanity.

Any of these might suffice. The idealistic abstraction becomes "God," shaped as the analogue of Hegel's Spirit, and any concrete example of this God is equivalent to the numerous manifestations of the Spirit in men and their world. Estrangement is still the separation of the actual from the ideal, and self-realization is still the attainment of the ideal. Of course, most of the available abstractions make poor substitutes for humanity in this construct. If God is honesty, for instance, estrangement loses the idea of conflict among the particulars, and the "self" in self-realization becomes impersonal to the point of meaninglessness. But these problems digress, because at the moment we are trying to go beyond Tillich's writing and approach his God from a theoretical angle. Is there any a priori basis for assuming that Tillich might be more receptive to humanity as a deity than to some other idealistic abstraction?

There is such a reason. That reason is that the concept of humanity as God is deeply rooted in the German philosophy in which Tillich was educated. In Chapter 2 this point was introduced in connection with the concept of self-alienated man. We saw that Kant, Hegel, Feuerbach, and Marx all spoke of man's alienation from himself, as opposed to the God in heaven. They looked upon man as a quasi-divine being or else actually as God. Kant described man as having a godlike side, *homo noumenon*, engaged in psychological conflict with a human side, *homo phenomenon*. Hegel posited the metaphysical Spirit as "God," and man became not only a part of God but the most important part—the conscious element in which the Spirit's ultimate self-realization takes place. Feuerbach went all the way and, throwing out Hegel's metaphysics, defined God as man. Marx did likewise, declaring that "man is the supreme being for man."

Two other German philosophers inclined toward deifying man must now be added to the preceding four. The first is Schelling. Significantly, he was Tillich's first love in philosophy: Tillich read Schelling's collected works through several times as a student and wrote two dissertations (1910 and 1912) dealing with Schelling's thought. A contemporary of Hegel, Schelling formulated a philosophy of nature from which Hegel drew heavily for his own philosophy of nature. As in Hegel, there is a pantheistic quality: the divine materializes in nature and achieves self-consciousness through man. Tillich can thus characterize Schelling as a romantic philosopher who "wanted to show . . . that in nature spirit is struggling for its full actualization in man."[1] Amplifying: "His whole philosophy of nature was an attempt to show the indwelling of the potential spirit in all natural objects and how it comes to its fulfillment in man."[2] Man, in turn, is dependent on the "ground of being" (here is where Tillich's terminology originates) through nature. Once more there is a point of identity between man and God. Schelling could therefore write, in a passage quoted in Tillich's 1912 dissertation, that "God must become man, in order that man comes again to God."[3] Schelling added (and Tillich duly notes) that communion with God depends on God's becoming individual personality: man communes with God through communion with his fellow man.

The remaining German philosopher with tendencies toward deifying man is Nietzsche. Although Tillich acknowledges the "tremendous impression" made on him by Nietzsche, it would be a mistake to infer that Nietzsche directly influenced Tillich's choice of a god: Tillich was thirty before he read Nietzsche (in 1916) and had already formulated the basic principles of his system. Yet Nietzsche remains an important contributor to the quasi-humanistic tone of Tillich's philosophical tradition. Nietzsche's brand of humanism is expressed in two related concepts, "will to power" and the "overman" (*übermensch*). Will to power does not refer to power in a social or physical sense but to the psychological power to affirm and transcend life. Man wants to improve and develop himself, to triumph over the stultifying forces of existence, and to become creative. Life "must ever surpass itself." (Tillich's concept of self-transcendence, to be reviewed shortly, has noticeable similarities but can also be found in Hegel, who even uses the word "self-transcendence.") The higher life to which man aspires is that of the overman, or superior man. The overman is passionate but

1. *Perspectives*, p. 125.   2. *Perspectives*, p. 145.
3. Paul Tillich, *Gesammelte Werke* (Stuttgart: Evangelisches Verlagswerk, 1959), I, 96. Quoted in David Hopper, *Tillich: A Theological Portrait* (Philadelphia: Lippincott, 1968), p. 124 (my italics).

governs his passions, knows fear but vanquishes it, sees the "abyss" of human existence but grasps and overcomes it. Above all, he is creative, rejects traditional values, and substitutes his own aims and rules. By becoming creator rather than created and by establishing his own values, the overman in effect assumes the role of God; he becomes a godlike being who is nevertheless human. Therefore, in a symbolic story we shall examine as one of the five basic clues, Nietzsche can tell of the Ugliest Man finding God in man after the death of God.

This analysis hardly proves anything, but it does suggest that humanity is a more plausible hypothesis as to the identity of being-itself than is any other hypothesis. And if we add to the God-can-be-found-in-man theme in Tillich's philosophical background the fact that humanism (God is man) is the dominant philosophy among those who have forsaken religion, it becomes even more plausible that the God above God is humanity. Then if we further consider that the humanity hypothesis has already met the test of rendering intelligible Tillich's doctrine of estrangement, including the point that estrangement can be overcome only "fragmentarily" and the point that God "does not exist," we have more than a hypothesis; we have an extremely promising theory. To this theoretical clue, derived largely without help from Tillich, can now be added four other clues found in widely dispersed places within Tillich's works.

The Apologetic Method

Tillich likes to describe his so-called theology as "apologetic." This description is not to be taken casually: it offers fundamental insight into what he is trying to do. A close look at apologetics shows that to Tillich it means using the tools of theology to construct a synthesis of Christianity and humanism, in the process giving humanistic meanings to Christian concepts. Tillichian apologetics takes the focus of humanism, man, and presents it as the focus of Christianity, God.

CHRISTIANITY AND HUMANISM. In his essay, "Autobiographical Reflections," Tillich refers to the "basic spiritual conflict" in Europe between the religious and humanistic traditions. This he contrasts with the conflict between religion and scientific naturalism in

America. Tension arising from the opposing pulls of European secular education in the German humanistic *gymnasium* and religious education at home, church, and school, he contends, drove many individuals to one pole or the other. But some sought to reconcile the conflict through synthesis. The "way of synthesis" Tillich identifies as "my own way."[4]

As a student at Halle (1905–7) Tillich shared the hope of his friends "that the great synthesis between Christianity and humanism could be achieved with the tools of German classical philosophy." But this hope was a remnant of the nineteenth-century spirit and was not to be realized. As Tillich matured, he gravitated to the view that the "great synthesis" would have to be achieved through theology, not philosophy. (Because Tillich pre-empts the phrase "great synthesis" to describe a desired union of theology and humanism, I have adopted a different phrase, "Grand Synthesis," to describe the union of theology and philosophy which Tillich seeks to effect through his method of correlation. Grand Synthesis is a broader term which includes "great synthesis"; the Grand Synthesis is Tillich's means of achieving the great synthesis.) Speaking of "the way of synthesis," Tillich writes, "It has found its final form in my *Systematic Theology*."[5]

What led Tillich to this shift in emphasis from the philosophical approach to the theological was a supposed conviction that humanism embodies the substance of Christianity. "My contact with the Labor Movement, with the so-called dechristianized masses, showed me clearly that here too, within a humanistic framework, the Christian substance was hidden, even though this humanism looked like a materialistic philosophy that had long since been discredited by art and science."[6] Living among the masses, Tillich found "an absolute devotion to justice and love," evidence of "the latent Church" among the unchurched.[7] Tillich need not be taken too seriously on what he says *is* the substance of Christianity; he is really referring to what he would like to substitute

4. "Autobiographical Reflections," in *The Theology of Paul Tillich*, ed. Charles W. Kegley and Robert W. Bretall (New York: Macmillan, 1952), pp. 9–10. Elsewhere Tillich reiterates: "The way of synthesis alone is genuine and legitimate" (*Religion*, p. 30).
5. Kegley and Bretall, *The Theology of Paul Tillich*, pp. 10–11.
6. *Boundary*, p. 62.　　　　　　　7. *Boundary*, p. 67.

for supernaturalism as the new substance of Christianity. The point is that Tillich is paving the way, however equivocally, for a theology that synthesizes Christianity and humanism. "An apologetic message to the masses" seemed necessary.[8]

These passages are Tillich's way of telling "those who have ears" that his theology is to be understood as a synthesis of Christianity and humanism. Its words are the words of the Church, but its "Christian substance" is to be found in humanism. Anyone who doubts this should read Tillich's 1963 University of Chicago lectures on nineteenth- and twentieth-century Protestant theology. The binding theme of these lectures is that there is a need to unite the traditions of Christian orthodoxy and humanism. Tillich discovers many efforts to culminate "the great synthesis," the most notable being Schleiermacher's theology and—especially—Hegel's philosophy.[9] These earlier efforts Tillich considers to be failures, which explains his expressed determination to try again.[10] Once this orientation toward "the great synthesis" is understood, Tillich's claim to be speaking an apologetic message becomes radically meaningful.

APOLOGETICS AS SYNTHESIS. An apologetic message would ordinarily be taken as meaning one that defends a certain viewpoint being regarded with skepticism. This is generally what Tillich has in mind, but what he particularly means is a defense that tries to show that the skeptic's position is in substance the same as that of the apologist, the real conflict being semantic. If a Christian tells a Moslem that God and Allah are really the same, that's the sort of thing Tillich has in mind. "To be apologetic means to defend oneself before an opponent with a common criterion in view."[11]

Tillich uses the early Christian evangelists to illustrate what he means. We recall that Paul became "all things to all men" in order to speak to all men: to Jewish audiences he described Jesus as the messiah, to certain pagans as a mystery savior akin to Adonis or Dionysus, to gnostics as a redeemer from the realm of light, and to

8. *Boundary*, p. 62.
9. *Perspectives*. See esp. pp. 4–5, 63, 75, 91–92, 114, 136, and 215.
10. *Perspectives*, p. 91. Cf. *History*, pp. 292–93.
11. *Boundary*, p. 60.

those steeped in hellenistic thought as the Logos become man.[12] "In order to be received, the church had to use the forms of life and thought which were created by the various sources of Hellenism and which coalesced at the end of the ancient world."[13] Widespread acceptance made the Logos (translated "Word" in the Bible) especially suitable for apologetic debate. Hence:

In the beginning was the Word [Logos], and the Word was with God, and the Word was God. . . . And the Word became flesh and dwelt among us, full of grace and truth; we have beheld his glory, glory as of the only Son from the Father.[14]

"Because the apologists equated Christ with the Logos, and the divine commands with the rational law of nature, they could plead the cause of Christian doctrine and practice before their pagan opponents."[15]

Apologetics, then, becomes a matter of finding a common criterion. Now let us relate this to the problem of Christianity and humanism. This problem "is the drama of the rise of a humanism in the midst of Christianity which is critical of the Christian tradition, departs from it and produces a vast world of secular existence and thought."[16] To effect reconciliation, an apologetic message is needed, and it in turn requires a common criterion. But what? The humanists certainly aren't going to accept God or any other supernaturalistic criterion as common ground. However, Tillich thinks—or pretends to think—that the real substance of Christianity is a humanistic attitude of love for and justice toward man. (If this were really the case, apologists for every religion and for irreligion could with equal validity make the same claim, and Christianity could no longer be distinguished by its substance from Judaism, Buddhism, or atheism.) Thus he asserts that "the distinctive factor in modern apologetics is its confrontation with a humanism that is Christian in substance."[17] The common denominator—the twentieth-century Logos—becomes love for mankind. It takes little

12. For further development of this point, see A. Powell Davies, *The First Christian: A Study of St. Paul and Christian Origins* (New York: Farrar, Straus, and Cudahy, 1957), pp. 128–29, 135–44, 190–91.
13. *ST–2*, p. 141.   14. John 1:1, 14.
15. *Boundary*, p. 60.   16. *Perspectives*, p. 5.
17. *Boundary*, p. 61.

imagination to get from this premise to the proposition that "God is man" is Tillich's apologetic message to a humanistic society.

With this deduction, some remarks about the relationship of apologetics to the method of correlation suddenly assume meaning. Tillich argues that systematic theology must use the method of correlation, "especially if the apologetic point of view is to prevail."[18] Correlation "gives pointed expression to the decisive character of the apologetic element in systematic theology."[19] In line with the interpretation of correlation given in the last chapter, these statements refer to the fact that apologetics correlates God with man. (Here Tillich is using correlation in the broad sense of synthesis, including in this instance the synthesis of a symbol and "that to which it points"; the theology-philosophy correlation of God and being is not contradicted.) The Christian absolute and the humanistic absolute are synthesized into one concept. Therefore: "When Calvin . . . correlates our knowledge of God with our knowledge of man, he . . . expresses the essence of the method of correlation."[20]

One point must be clarified. Tillich seems to be saying that he is offering an apologetic Christian message to humanists. He claims to speak as a Christian. But relatively few humanists read Tillich's books. They are written for and read by Christians, many of them deeply involved in theology. And they are written by a humanist. Just as Hegel, in Marx's view, had turned things upside down, so has Tillich turned his explanation upside down. Tillich is actually directing an apologetic humanistic message to a Christian audience. He is telling those Christians who can hear that they can accept humanism without relinquishing Christianity if they will accept man as the true meaning of God.

A Self-Transcending God

A third clue to the identity of God comes from the concept of a "self-transcendent" God. This idea of God is offered by Tillich as his answer to two alternative views, the idea that God is a highest being (theism) and the idea that God is the universe, its essence,

18. ST-1, p. 60.
19. ST-1, p. 31. Cf. ST-2, p. 16.
20. ST-1, p. 63.

or a special power within it (pantheism-metaphysics-mysticism). Something that immediately arouses curiosity is that "self-transcendence" in relation to God first appears in the introduction to volume 2 of *Systematic Theology* as a purported restatement of a basic concept from volume 1. But volume 1 discusses self-transcendence only in relation to man. Tillich stresses that the substance of his earlier thought has not changed. "In none of these cases [of points being restated] has the substance of my earlier thought changed," he states.[21] It follows that a self-transcending God is the same as self-transcending man: God is man.

This interpretation certainly agrees with the "earlier thought" in volume 1. There man is said to exhibit dynamic creativity: man's creations constantly change. We can infer that the creations Tillich wishes to emphasize are the many gods man creates. (The inference is supported by the fact that Tillich is writing what claims to be a theology, not a cultural commentary, and the fact that translating "creations" as "gods" dissolves the verbal fog which clouds the discussion.) With self-transcendence, the contents of man's creations become "meaningful." And what makes them meaningful? The tendency of everything "to conserve its own form" is "the basis of" self-transcendence.[22] Therefore, man's creations—his gods—become meaningful when based on the form of man. When man transcends himself he conserves man as the meaningful contents of the god he creates. Slowly, the evidence accumulates that "God is man" is the hidden message.

And there is more to consider. Who is the "self" that the "self-transcendent" God transcends? "God as the ground of being infinitely transcends that of which he is the ground."[23] In Tillich's thought, God is the ground of man's being, and man is said to be estranged from the ground of his being. Therefore, the transcended "self" of which God is the ground would appear to be man. When God transcends himself he transcends man. Again there is a strong implication that God is man. One might, it is true, assume the pantheistic viewpoint and contend that man is but one element of a broader realm which is transcended. However, this position is

21. *ST–2*, p. 5.   22. *ST–1*, p. 181.
23. *ST–2*, p. 7.

vitiated by Tillich's pointed rejection of pantheism, which is the second of the two broad theological alternatives for which he offers a "self-transcendent" God as a substitute.

The evidence gains weight when we probe behind Tillich's words to get at the concept itself. In Tillich's system, God can be viewed as man in two states or dimensions: selfish man and selfless man. Selfish man is estranged man, discussed in the previous chapter. Existential man, as a collective entity, is filled with selfish concern for self, group, nation, and the like; the human race is divided against itself. Essential man (man in essence) transcends selfish concerns and grasps all humanity as a selfless concern; the estrangement of man from man is overcome. This happens only fragmentarily as individual members of the collective being rise above their existential situation. But to the extent that it does happen, man in his infinite dimension of unlimited concern for others transcends man in his finite dimension of concern for only part of the human race. This is what Tillich means when he says, "the one reality which we encounter is experienced in different dimensions which point to one another."[24] Man is the "finite" which "goes beyond itself in order to return to itself in a new dimension."[25] Man is God.

A significant aspect of Tillich's self-transcending God is its relationship to similar ideas in Hegel and Marx. Young Hegel and young Marx, we recall, both spoke of alienated man. Hegel's man was alienated from his essential self in which there would be self-recognition of God; Marx's exploited man was alienated from his materially fulfilled self, that is, from his labor. For both, self-realization was the goal. Tillich's self-transcending man of volume 1 repeats the "early" orientation toward man. In their mature thought, Hegel and Marx switched to self-alienated gods moving toward self-realization, although with Marx the conceptualization of the proletariat as God is merely implicit. The same sort of metamorphosis takes place in Tillich's volume 2 switch to a self-transcending God. This reformulation has all the earmarks of a calculated effort to plant a clue. Tillich even calls attention to his reworking of Hegel by taking the term "self-transcending" from

24. ST–2, p. 8.   25. ST–2, p. 8.

Hegel's vocabulary.[26] In offering two versions of the same concept Tillich allows those "who have ears" to detect the analogy between his own transition from "early" (volume 1) to "mature" (volume 2) thought and the prototype transitions in Hegel and Marx. The models involved no change in substance; God transcended his existential self when man did so, because man in essence was God. In Tillich there is again no substantive change. Self-transcending man *is* self-transcending God.

Zarathustra and the Ugliest Man

The boldest clue from Tillich as to the identity of God lies in his retelling of Nietzsche's story of the Ugliest Man's encounter with Zarathustra. Introducing the story, Tillich credits Nietzsche, whom he describes as "the famous atheist and ardent enemy of religion and Christianity," with more knowledge "about the power of the idea of God than many faithful Christians."[27] This is the story and Tillich's explanation of its symbolism:

In a symbolic story, when Zarathustra, the prophet of a higher humanity, says to the Ugliest Man, the murderer of God, "You could not bear him to see you, always to see you through and through. . . . You took revenge on the witness. . . . You are the murderer of God", the Ugliest Man agrees with Zarathustra and replies, "He *had* to die." For God, according to the Ugliest Man, looks with eyes that see everything; He peers into man's ground and depth, into his hidden shame and ugliness. The God Who sees everything, and man also, is the God Who has to die.[28]

Tillich asks if it is possible to overcome our hatred for the God who strips away all privacy and pries into our innermost secrets. Then he answers:

Nietzsche offers a solution which shows the utter impossibility of atheism. The Ugliest Man, the murderer of God, subjects himself to Zarathustra, because Zarathustra has recognized him, and looked into his depth with divine understanding. The murderer of God *finds God in man*. He has not succeeded in killing God at all. God has returned in Zarathustra . . .[29]

26. See G. W. F. Hegel, *The Phenomenology of Mind*, trans. J. B. Baillie (New York: Harper Torchbooks, 1967), p. 797.
27. *Foundations*, p. 42.   28. *Foundations*, pp. 42–43.
29. *Foundations*, p. 47 (my italics).

Here is Tillich's thought in a nutshell. He who frees himself from the tyranny of the false God, the God of theism, finds God in man. Lest there be doubt about this interpretation, Tillich has provided further comment on Nietzsche's "death of God" elsewhere. What Nietzsche meant, he says, is that something else dies and must be replaced when the traditional idea of God dies. "The idea that God in himself is dead would be absurd. The idea is rather that in man the consciousness of an ultimate in the traditional sense has died." Therefore, "*somebody else must replace God* as the bearer of the system of traditional values. *This is man.*" In place of the God who said "thou shalt" and "thou shalt not" to us, "Nietzsche put man who says 'I will.' " Man decides what is good and evil: man plays the role of God.[30]

One can doubt that Nietzsche's overman philosophy is sufficiently broad in its appreciation of man to qualify as humanism, but it is clear enough that Tillich, in his customary manner of interpreting others as thinking Tillichian thoughts, intends to interpret Nietzsche humanistically on the point in question. Tillich's favorite epithets are "absurd" and "nonsense," so when "absurd" appears in the interpretation, we can recognize Tillich speaking. Tillich is saying that the traditional idea of a divine being telling us what and what not to do must be replaced by the view that man is God and must decide for himself what is right and wrong.

In one of his many paradoxes Tillich has said, "We have God through *not* having Him."[31] The story of Zarathustra and the Ugliest Man explains what Tillich means.

God as Love

The fifth clue about God arises from Tillich's discussion of love in relation to God. Like numerous other members of the theological profession, Tillich has employed the popular theme that God is love. When the man in the pulpit says this he is speaking figuratively, not literally (Bishop Robinson is an exception), and the same is true of Tillich. He is saying that the concept of love is important to an understanding of God. Love and God come to grips through what Tillich calls ultimate concern. Along with being-itself

30. *Perspectives*, pp. 201–2 (my italics).
31. *Foundations*, p. 151.

and ground of being, ultimate concern is a synonym for God; God is that which concerns us ultimately. How does this relate to love? "Ultimate concern is the abstract translation of the great commandment: 'The Lord, our God, the Lord is one; and you shall love the Lord your God with all your heart, and with all your soul and with all your mind, and with all your strength.' "[32]

This much tells us nothing; it could be said of any God, e.g., nature. We have only part of a clue. Elsewhere, however, Tillich observes that some people attempt to develop attitudes of total unconcern. But, he says, "since man is that being who is *essentially concerned* about his being, such an escape finally breaks down."[33] The word "essentially" is the key to this statement. It refers to man in essence, to existence transcended. We know from other parts of Tillich's thought that essential man has overcome separation from God through becoming concerned about God. Essential man has faith, and faith "is the state of being ultimately concerned."[34] Being essentially concerned is therefore synonymous with being ultimately concerned. This allows us to paraphrase the earlier statement as follows: man is that being who is ultimately concerned about his own being. Or: man is ultimately concerned about man. We are led ineluctably to the conclusion that the ultimate concern we are commanded to love with all our heart, soul, mind, and strength is man.

Confirmation of this interpretation comes from a sermon by Tillich on "The Power of Love." He begins by quoting 1 John 4:16: "God is love, and he who abides in love abides in God, and God abides in him." He then defines love by means of a lengthy example. His example is Elsa Brandström who, says Tillich, rarely if ever used God's name and would have been surprised to be counted as belonging to God. The implication is that devotion to a divine being has nothing to do with love of God. Elsa Brandström devoted her life to helping others—first World War I prisoners in Siberia, later the orphans of Russian and German war prisoners, and still later refugees from Nazi Germany. We are not told whom she loved, but the inference is easily drawn. Elsa Brandström loved

32. ST–1, p. 11.
33. *Dynamics*, p. 20 (my italics).
34. *Dynamics*, p. 4.

mankind, and mankind abided in her heart. Without realizing it, she loved God with all her heart, soul, mind, and strength.[35]

REASON AND REVELATION

We have seen that Tillich is attempting to formulate a philosophical theology, which is to say a rational theology. It is to be rational in the sense that supernaturalism—including metaphysics —is nonrational and that a rational, nonsupernatural interpretation is to be given to each supernatural concept or doctrine encountered in traditional theology. By rationalizing the supernatural, Tillich is bringing reason and revelation together. The introduction and Part I ("Reason and Revelation") of the first volume of *Systematic Theology* tell us what is going on; they are designed to help anyone who can decode them to understand the more substantive parts which follow. The message that God is man begins to unfold here in propositions about "the norm," ultimate concern, reason, revelation, and the unity of reason and revelation.

The Christ Norm

In the introduction to *Systematic Theology* Tillich lays the groundwork for everything that follows: he says that "Jesus as the Christ" must be the norm for using theological sources. A full discussion of what this means must be reserved for the next chapter, dealing with Jesus. However, because Tillich's Christ norm is an outstanding clue as to what he means by "God" and because it shapes his discussion of reason and revelation, a preview is necessary.

What does Tillich mean in calling "Jesus as the Christ" a norm? The answer has something to do with theology's Christ being not half God and half man but fully God and fully man. This is an essential concept for Tillich: even though he completely rejects the supernatural and does not believe that Jesus was in any sense supernatural, he insists that "the full humanity of Jesus must be maintained beside his whole divinity."[36] Why? In order to make revelation rational. Suppose one were to meet a person who claimed that his canine pet was 100 percent wolf and 100 percent collie. It

35. *New Being*, pp. 25–29.   36. *Culture*, p. 66.

could reasonably be assumed that the man was an idiot, a liar, or a theologian. Half wolf and half collie is believable but not fully wolf and fully collie. That adds up to two wolf-dogs. By playing word games, though, one could make arithmetic sense out of the claim. Figuring out how to do this provides Tillich's answer to how theology can be made rational.

There is another aspect of theology's Christ which is also basic to understanding Tillich's concept of God. Jesus, pictured as the divine Christ, is said to have been God incarnate. The Christ concept describes a two-sided God, the transcendent God living in heaven and the immanent God walking the earth as a man. To be true to the Christ model, Tillich must create his own two-sided God. This brings us to the subject of ultimate concern.

God as Ultimate Concern

More than one critic has made the wrong turn through a mere half-way understanding of Tillich's well-known concept of ultimate concern. Ultimate concern has been casually identified with God and then totally ignored while the critic expounded on the emptiness of phrases like "being-itself" and "ground of being," as if they had never been linked by Tillich to ultimate concern. We can avoid this mistake, learning at the same time about the two-sided nature of Tillich's God, by looking very carefully at Tillich's description of ultimate concern and the examples he provides.

ULTIMATE CONCERN DEFINED. When Tillich refers to an ultimate concern, he means something that concerns a person to the extent that it dominates that person's life. It "unites man's mental life and gives it a dominating center."[37] With typical exaggeration, Tillich calls it "a matter of infinite passion."[38] This simply means that any other concern or group of concerns will always be subordinated— sacrificed if necessary—to that which is called "ultimate."

God is the content of an ultimate concern, and "ultimate concern" is one of Tillich's basic synonyms for "God." As such it can be substituted for "being-itself," "ground of being," "power of being," and "God." When this is done, however, it should be recognized that the variants of "being" refer narrowly to humanity

37. *Dynamics*, p. 107.   38. *Dynamics*, p. 106.

114

and that "God" (upper case) is either humanity or the traditional God, whereas "ultimate concern" describes any "god," for example, money.

Tillich has identified ultimate concern with the deity in numerous passages. For example: "The fundamental symbol of our ultimate concern is God."[39] Referring again to ultimate concern, he states: "The predominant religious name for the content of such concern is God—a god or gods."[40] Defining faith as "the state of being grasped by an ultimate concern," he declares that "God is the name for the content of the concern."[41] (In this instance he is referring to humanity; hence he draws a distinction between what *he* calls faith and "the belief in the existence of a highest being" known as God.) In still another place Tillich indicates that what men call "God" *may* be the content of an ultimate concern but that "everything which is a matter of unconditional concern is made into a god."[42]

SOME EXAMPLES. In *Dynamics of Faith*, which is the best place to turn for enlightenment on ultimate concern, and in other works Tillich supplies numerous examples of what constitutes an ultimate concern. These examples involve both religious and secular interests. The religious ultimate concerns, generally speaking, are various deities or their manifestations. "Faith, for the men of the Old Testament, is the state of being ultimately and unconditionally concerned about Jahweh [Yahweh] and about what he represents in demand, threat and promise."[43] In modern times, many Christians still have Yahweh as their ultimate concern, though he has been refined, remade into more of a spirit, and renamed "God." For Islam, "the revelation given by Mohammed" is of ultimate concern.[44] Among the nontheistic religions, the ultimate concern is "a sacred object or an all-pervading power or a highest principle such as the Brahma or the One."[45]

On the secular front, Tillich's favorite example—and favorite whipping boy—is the nation. "If the nation is someone's ultimate concern, the name of the nation becomes a sacred name and the

39. *Dynamics*, p. 45.   40. *World*, p. 5.
41. *Culture*, p. 40.   42. *Dynamics*, p. 44.
43. *Dynamics*, p. 3.   44. *Dynamics*, p. 65.
45. *World*, p. 5.

nation receives divine qualities which far surpass the reality of the being and functioning of the nation."[46] Other people are ultimately concerned "with 'success' and with social standing and economic power."[47] In a similar vein, some individuals embrace pleasure as their ultimate concern.[48] Russia's Bolsheviks were concerned "about the transformation of reality,"[49] and present-day Communists are concerned about the realization of the final stage of society.[50] Scientists may be ultimately concerned about science, "and they are ready to sacrifice everything, including their lives, for this ultimate."[51] Among existentialist philosophers, the human predicament is of ultimate concern.[52] Finally, but really foremost, there are the humanists: "For humanism the divine is manifest in the human; the ultimate concern of man is man."[53]

HUMAN AND DIVINE. A refinement in the concept of ultimate concern must now be introduced. Tillich sometimes makes a distinction between preliminary concerns and ultimate concerns.[54] In related fashion, he also talks about concerns being either "transparent" or "opaque" to God. These dichotomies arise from the analogy Tillich builds between the God he calls ultimate concern and the two-sided God of Christian tradition who, through his incarnation in Jesus as the Christ, acquired a human nature to go with the divine. The analogy works like this: If your deepest concern, the one for which you would (to beg the question) sacrifice all else combined, is helping the poor, then fighting poverty is your preliminary ultimate concern. But anyone who takes a good hard look can see that your concern for the poor rests on a deeper, or ultimately ultimate, concern for humanity: your preliminary concern is "transparent to" humanity. The transparency metaphor treats the preliminary concern as a window through which the more abstract concern for humanity can be seen or, to vary the metaphor, through which the light of humanity can shine.

Ultimate concern thus has two meanings, one concrete and the other abstract, and these are analogous to the human side of the

46. *Dynamics*, p. 44.
47. *Dynamics*, p. 3.
48. *New Being*, p. 158.
49. *Culture*, pp. 183–84.
50. *World*, p. 5.
51. *Dynamics*, p. 82.
52. *Culture*, pp. 186–87.
53. *Dynamics*, p. 63.
54. See *ST–1*, pp. 12–13.

Christ and to the divine side. In line with his policy of being obscure, Tillich usually avoids the term "preliminary concern," preferring to use "ultimate concern" ambiguously. This has apparently led some observers to doubt that he really means it when he says that ultimate concern is another name for God. The fact is, however, that ultimate concern can refer to either the human or the divine. For example, when Tillich suggests that only a person "who experiences the Christian message as his ultimate concern is able to be a theologian,"[55] he is speaking of a preliminary concern. Only humanity, which stands amidst many "false ultimacies," is truly ultimate in Tillich's system; the theologian's (Tillich's) ultimate concern with spreading the "Christian message" (the message of humanism) is ultimate in a loose sense of ultimate concern, but in a stricter sense the message is a preliminary concern transparent to the theologian's ultimate concern for God (humanity).

Reason

Using the Christ—the mythological Jesus of Christian theology —as the norm for interpreting biblical and other source material, Tillich is going to rationalize revelation. Every concept and doctrine of traditional theology is to be made rational by relating it to a two-sided concept of God wherein God is both humanity in the abstract and a multitude of incarnations, the latter being concrete human concerns which are "transparent to" humanity. "The more transcendent the gods become, the more incarnations of personal or sacramental character are needed in order to overcome the remoteness of the divine which develops with the strengthening of the transcendent element."[56] The point is developed by Tillich in his Part I discussion of reason.

ONTOLOGICAL AND TECHNICAL REASON. Two types of reason are initially distinguished, ontological and technical. The description of ontological reason is rather fuzzy. It identifies ontological reason with metaphysical thought generally and the metaphysical Logos in particular. This gives the false impression, intended to mislead the larger audience, that there is a mystical cosmic reason which every now and then creeps into the human mind and to which

55. *History*, p. 281.   56. *Culture*, p. 64.

117

Tillich thinks he has access. What Tillich actually has in mind, however, is a complex structure of conceptual categories which is *analogous* to metaphysical concepts about the Logos. Oversimplified, ontological reason refers to value judgments about what is "God," that is, what is important and to be sought in life. It concerns ends—ultimate concerns—rather than means. (This meaning we shall find buried in the middle of the discussion of technical reason.) As for the Logos, it is used in this context as an abstract term for reason (but has other meanings elsewhere): in Greek philosophy the Logos was a sort of rational natural law, universal reason, in which the human *logos*—human reason—participated. Tillich is establishing an analogy between the Logos, with its universal and human sides, and ontological reason. Ontological reason also has a universal and a human side, general and particular. And no wonder: hidden in its depths will be found Tillich's counterpart of Hegel's Spirit (sometimes translated "mind").

The discussion of technical reason is much easier to follow but not very important. Tillich's chief purpose is to differentiate ontological reason from what men ordinarily call reason. The latter, technical reason, is a mixture of good old-fashioned logic and common sense. It takes us from premises to a conclusion. Alternatively, it accepts a goal as given and tells us how to get there. Technical reason "determines the means while accepting the ends from 'somewhere else.' "[57] This is all right, believes Tillich, if technical reason is used in conjunction with ontological reason; hence we can infer that ontological reason concerns our ends. It involves the value judgments—their content, that is—which tell us what we seek in life.

In this discussion of ontological and technical reason Tillich has given us a preliminary glimpse of his picture of the dialectical life of man. Life begins under the guidance of revelation (akin to ontological reason), then rejects divine authority in favor of reason (technical reason), and finally combines revelation and reason (synthesis: reason in the broadest sense). This dialectic leads us to an inner one focusing on ontological reason and describing it as consisting of two elements which are (1) potentially united by

57. ST-1, p. 73.

something essential within their depths but (2) existentially in conflict and waiting to be (3) united in synthesis through revelation. This is Tillich's version of Hegel's ontology.

OBJECTIVE AND SUBJECTIVE REASON. Tillich proceeds with his ontological inquiry by subdividing ontological reason into two categories, objective and subjective. Objective reason and subjective reason are best understood by ignoring the word reason. Its main function is to deceive. We aren't dealing with rationality but with value judgments. Aside from an intentional resemblance between "mind" (Hegel's Spirit) and "reason," the only link between ontological reason and rationality is that (a) objective and subjective reason are analogous to the Greek Logos as participated in by human minds and (b) the Logos was viewed as a rational force. Tillich can therefore suggest that objective and subjective reason are like the universal Logos and the human *logos*. (Again note the effort to create the impression that he is dealing with metaphysics.) These were assumed by ancient philosophers to be related: the objective reality which was the Logos entered the human *logos*, the seat of subjectivity. By analogy, objective reason is defined as "the rational structure of reality" and subjective reason as "the rational structure of the mind."[58] This cryptic phraseology refers to the following conceptual structure:

A. Objective Reason = Humanity (Logos, universal)
   1. Physical: humanity per se
   2. Mental: humanity as ultimate concern
B. Subjective Reason = Individuals (*logos*, particular)
   1. Physical: concrete individuals
   2. Mental: preliminary concerns

Note that both elements—universal and particular—have a physical aspect and a mental aspect, matter and mind: Tillich is constantly shifting from one viewpoint to the other.

Logos and *logos* compared to humanity and the individuals it consists of are not the only analogies, or even the most important. It isn't hard to see that Hegel's subject-object split provides the parent terminology. (Hegel, in turn, borrowed concepts from

58. ST–1, p. 75.

ancient Logos philosophy, thereby making things easy for Tillich.) In Hegel's thought man, in terms of an individual consciousness or ego, is subject. Everything in his external world, including both nature and other egos, is misinterpreted as an object, apart from himself. Actually, both—the self and its world—are Spirit. Meanwhile, both subject and object have a physical side and a mental side. For subject, the physical is the man who houses the mental, the ego. For object, nature is the physical side of the world and all the other egos are its mental side. Tillich uses exactly the same scheme. He states that objective reason has a "corresponding structure" relative to subjective reason.[59] We aren't told what this correspondence is, but the above outline shows that both have a physical and a mental side. Objective reason, man's "world," can be viewed as either physical humanity (nature) or humanity as a concern (other egos). Subjective reason breaks down into individuals and preliminary concerns. Either way, the particulars add up to the corresponding general subdivision under objective reason. The point is, then, that Tillich must be understood through analogy to Hegel.

Elsewhere in the analysis, objective reason is said to be "grasped" and "shaped" by subjective reason. One easily infers that grasping corresponds to something general and shaping to the particular. Ultimate concern for mankind is like an amorphous blob of clay which is grasped and shaped into a particular figure: subjective reason shapes concern for humanity into a particular, preliminary concern. This concern can be seen by the discerning eye to consist of humanistic substance. The mind has created a god which, because it is divine and human at the same time, is true to the Christ norm.

THE DEPTH OF REASON. In describing the two elements of ontological reason, Tillich prepares to unveil the thesis of an ontological dialectic. Here we must recall that, in Hegel's ontology, the thesis is the potential unity of universal and particular as two aspects of Spirit: Spirit is their inner reality. Is there a comparable inner reality in objective and subjective reason? We are informed that both elements point to "something which appears in these struc-

59. ST–1, p. 76.

tures but which transcends them in power and meaning."[60] This something is the "depth of reason." Besides being the analogue of Hegel's Spirit, the depth of reason is clearly God: Tillich says it might be called "being-itself"—a dead giveaway—or the creative "ground" of all rational creations. Now if depth of reason is God and God is the deeper meaning of objective and subjective reason, a point begins to emerge. That point is that objective and subjective reason are substantially identical and describe two aspects of God. As to the nature of this identity and these aspects, we have three clues: the Hegelian object-subject terminology, the Logos-*logos* obfuscations, and the references to grasping and shaping. All point to a general-particular relationship. Tillich is indicating that he is describing God and that God is a universal made up of particulars.

Other clues follow. Anticipating his later comments on the dialectic's antithesis and synthesis, Tillich contrasts the depth of reason's status under the opposing conditions of existence and essence. In his existential predicament, man is tied to superstition. The depth of reason is present but hidden. Reason's transparency toward its depth "is opaque and is replaced by myth and cult." But in man's state of essence, the depth of reason manifests itself in human reason: "Essentially reason is transparent toward its depth [humanity] in each of its acts and processes." This transparency is a sign that "rational knowledge" and "rational morals" have vanquished myth and cult. Rational morals plainly stand in opposition to revealed morals and at least hint of humanism. Essential man's actions are transparent to humanity.[61]

Revelation and the Logos

A new interpretation of revelation flows from Tillich's discussion of reason. Tillich has convinced many critics that his idea of revelation resembles conventional belief in divine inspiration, in either a theistic or a metaphysical sense. He achieves this effect by dragging "mystery," "ecstasy," and "Logos" into the discussion. But again the implications of supernaturalism are there only to mislead the larger audience: insiders will believe Tillich when he says that

60. *ST–1*, p. 79.   61. *ST–1*, p. 80.

revelation "cannot be interpreted in terms of a supranatural interference in natural processes."[62] In fact, knowing that Tillich's method of correlation calls for the pairing of analogous philosophical and theological concepts, we should immediately suspect that revelation will turn out to be nothing more mystical than the theological correlate of reason: reason is the philosopher's source of wisdom, revelation is the theologian's.

Going on this hypothesis, we owe ourselves a quick restatement of the character of Tillichian reason. Although Tillich's treatment of reason was somewhat discursive, the central idea that emerged was that of a human being (subjective reason) "grasping" humanity (objective reason) and "shaping" it into a preliminary concern transparent to the ultimate. The mind grasps God—the rational God. Assuming that revelation and reason are correlates, revelation should mean about the same thing. Hence it is no surprise to find that in revelation "the mind is grasped by . . . the ground of being and meaning."[63] Don't be misled by the passive phraseology: it is purely figurative. It is really the mind that grasps the ground of being, and the ground of being is God, our ultimate concern. Tillich can therefore say in an alternative formulation that revelation is "the manifestation of what concerns us ultimately."[64] Since what concerns us ultimately is humanity, revelation is simply the process of deciding or becoming aware that humanity is one's ultimate concern. Revelation is a value judgment.

Then why all this metaphysical-sounding talk about the Logos in connection with revelation? Tillich declares that "the divine discloses its *logos* quality without ceasing to be the divine *mystery*."[65] Similarly, expressions like "the principle of the divine self-revelation"[66] and "God manifest"[67]—terms that describe traditional revelation—are applied to the Logos. It sounds very much as though revelation has something to do with the supernatural. Supernaturalism is, indeed, exactly the impression Tillich wants to give the larger audience. But we know that supernaturalistic interpretations must be ruled out. What we are looking for is not supernatural but something analogous to the supernatural concept.

62. *ST–1*, p. 116. The quotation refers directly to miracles, but Tillich uses the word miracle as a synonym for revelation.

63. *ST–1*, p. 112.

64. *ST–1*, p. 110. Cf. *Dynamics*, p. 78.

65. *ST–1*, p. 119.

66. *ST–1*, p. 16.

67. *ST–1*, p. 159.

When it comes to the Logos, Tillich finds many analogies and invents many meanings. He does this partly to muddy the waters, but principally it is a matter of remaining true to a variety of meanings attached to Logos by philosophy and theology. To understand Tillich, we must find these meanings. They can be found among four pairs of opposites, one member of each pair falling under the heading "God" and the other listed under "man":

	GOD	MAN
(1)	Universal Logos	Man's *logos*
(2)	Logos-God	Logos-Son (incarnation)
(3)	Word of God	Logos
(4)	Revelation	Reason

The analysis which follows serves as an introduction to what will become a familiar Tillichian process of effecting a coincidence of opposites. Each member on the divine side of the equation relates to God in one of three ways: it represents the one or the general category, it is directly identified with God, or it is a theological concept. The items listed under man, in turn, are variously representative of the many or the particular, are directly identified with man, or are philosophical concepts. By making the two members of each pair identical in substance, Tillich states his hidden message that God and man are identical.

The relationships are as follows: (1) The first pair, universal Logos and human *logos*, takes us back to ancient metaphysics. The original Logos speculations postulated an intelligent but impersonal cosmic force, the universal Logos, by which all change was regulated and in which human reason—man's *logos*—metaphysically participated. God's philosophical analogue is found in the universal Logos, and the human *logos* expressly relates to man. From another viewpoint, there is one Logos but the *logos* is manifold, just as there is one God but manifold human beings. (2) Early Christian apologists carried their message to a hellenistic society by equating God with the Logos, a concept more in tune with the Greek way of thinking. Through the gospel of John, the Logos insinuated itself into the Christian religion. John treats the Logos as both God ("the Logos was God") and Jesus ("the Logos became flesh"), permitting us to directly identify the Logos with both God and man. (3) English translations of the Bible—the Moffatt translation is an exception—do not use the Greek word "Logos"; they substitute the grossly inaccurate term, "Word." Thus: "In the beginning was the Word, and the Word was with God, and the Word was God." Through misunderstanding, "Word" has come to mean "Word of God." Logos stands opposite Word of God in the third pair because the two correlate by analogy: Word of God is theology's version of what goes out from the ultimate to man, and Logos is the philosophical version of the same thing. (4) Revelation and reason, the final pair of opposites, become synonyms for, respectively, Word of God and Logos. Revelation and Word of God are often used interchangeably, especially in reference to the Bible, while the Logos *is* reason in a loose sense of the word. We have already seen that revelation and reason correlate as the opposing theological and philosophical sources of wisdom.

This analysis stands as a warning that when Tillich speaks of the Logos (or *logos*) he may mean reason in the abstract, human reason, revelation in the Tillichian sense, the Christ, God, or the universal Logos of the Greeks. By analogy to the Greek Logos he may also mean something general or universal (specifically, humanity), something particular or finite (men), or the general and the particular in combination. But never, never does Logos mean a genuine metaphysical entity. On the contrary, it is a many-faceted symbol used to state the absence of metaphysical and other supernatural entities. For when we look at the four pairs of opposites we see that both members of each pair are in substance the same. Man's *logos* is a manifestation of the universal Logos. The Logos Incarnate—the Christ—is God. In biblical usage, the Logos is the Word of God. And, as Tillich's definitions indicate, reason and revelation are the same: both describe man's recognition of God. No matter which pair of opposites we examine, the message is the same: God and man are identical.

Conflict and Resolution

Reason and revelation are brought together by Tillich in a highly pretentious discussion, actually symbolic, of what he calls conflicts in reason.[68] He sets up several pairs of opposing categories of

68. *ST–1*, pp. 81–94, 147–55.

"reason" and then uses "revelation" to unite the opposites. For this purpose, the "final revelation" of God in Jesus sets the standard: God becomes man. When God incarnated himself as man the two opposites, divine (one) and human (many), became identical. Revelation—incarnation—works in resolving the conflicts because reason has been carefully structured to represent God and man. Simultaneously, it has been structured to represent objective (universal) and subjective (particular) reason. In bringing revelation and reason together, Tillich is completing his ontological dialectic. It began with the thesis of potential unity, represented by the depth of reason, which potentially unites objective and subjective reason under the heading of ontological reason. Potential unity leads to its antithesis, "conflicts in reason," where object and subject clash. Finally, revelation produces the synthesis in which the hidden identity of the two elements is revealed.

CONFLICTS IN REASON. Tillich begins by mentioning what Cusanus called the "coincidence of opposites." These opposites he describes in general terms as the finite side and the infinite side of reason. They obviously correspond to the subjective and objective sides of ontological reason, discussed a few pages back. The thrust of the analysis is toward establishing artificial categories of "reason" which are analogous to the human and the divine sides of the Christ, as "final revelation." If the resulting association of certain concepts with reason seems forced or even arbitrary, the thing to remember is that the discussion is symbolic and does not deal with what *we* call reason.

Three conflicts within reason—finite vs. infinite—are explored. The first is between autonomy and heteronomy. Autonomy refers to independence in decision and action; heteronomy signifies submission to authority. In autonomous situations the individual obeys the law of reason which he finds in himself as a rational person. This means his ultimate concern (assuming he has one) is not dictated from without. Under heteronomy, the individual responds to commands from an outside source which speaks in an "ultimate" manner. Typically this outside source is expressed in terms of "myth and cult," in which case it is apt to be a supernatural being called God. In order to establish the desired conflict within reason,

Tillich gives the outside authority the title, "depth of reason." This is, of course, a synonym for God. God, the authoritarian being of theological tradition, is being placed in opposition to man, the rational being of philosophical tradition. Tillich thinks that reason without God (autonomy) is bad and that God without reason (heteronomy) is bad. He therefore resolves the conflict within reason by introducing theonomy. Theonomy combines the authority of one's own reason with the authority of God. This union spells a rational God, and for Tillich the only rational God is man. "Final revelation" establishes the "essential unity" of autonomy and heteronomy. What this means is that, in the theonomous situation, the individual has an autonomous concern (many options) which is transparent to the heteronomous ultimate concern (humanity) dictated by the revelation of God as man.

The second conflict within reason opposes relativism and absolutism. Relativism can mean simply that there are a number of items, related as members of a group or class, or it can mean that the priority of something is relative to a person, group, or society. For example, moral relativism holds that what is right depends on the group or society in which an act is judged. Absolutism can denote the existence of a single item, or it can mean that something has priority—is absolute—among whatever competes with it. A good illustration is divine law, which is customarily regarded as absolute in relation to competing moral codes. In order to force relativism and absolutism into the context of reason, Tillich calls relativism the dynamic side of reason and absolutism the static side. Where there are many (e.g., concerns) there can be change; where there is one (e.g., humanity) change is absent. The dynamic and static sides of reason conflict. "Only that which is absolute and concrete at the same time can overcome this conflict."[69] We have yet to inquire what absolute and concrete mean but, in line with "final revelation," they obviously relate to God and man. What Tillich is saying is that God is absolute only when God is concrete man. When God is man, men are individuals relative to each other but collectively they are God, the absolute. Or, in the language of ultimate concern, concerns can be different and changing relative to

69. ST–1, p. 89.

126

one another, but true concerns stay transparent to humanity, the absolute that never changes.

The third conflict is between formalism and emotionalism. Formalism implies a structured approach to something, whether it be logic or art: there is a fixed form. Emotionalism puts man's poetic soul into an endeavor: the product expresses feeling rather than conformity to a set approach. Translating these concepts into reason, formalism can be expressed in formal logic while emotionalism describes the irrational, nonlogical workings of the mind. Once again there is a conflict within the house of reason. To resolve the conflict, the ultimate concern must be "as radically rational as it is radically emotional,"[70] meaning that it must be human (only man is rational) yet must command the emotional respect of what men call God.

SYNTHESIS THROUGH REVELATION. Reviewing the three conflicts, one sees that the general or unitary side always bears an analogy to God. God stands for (1) heteronomy, or authoritarian rule, (2) absolutism, the single immutable standard, and (3) emotionalism, describing man's attitude toward God. The particular or multiple side of each conflict is analogous to man. Man represents (1) autonomy, or the exercise of one's own reason, (2) relativism, whether it be many related persons or many courses of action, and (3) formalism, as represented in rational—loosely, formally logical —thought patterns which revolt against God. Tillich says the conflicts within reason must be overcome by something wherein the opposing elements coincide. This something is final revelation. "Final revelation does not destroy reason; it fulfils reason."[71] Since Jesus as the Christ is what Tillich calls final revelation, "incarnation" is the basic solution. Humanity is incarnated in men, both biologically and as transparent concerns. Each incarnation is not only rational but unique; hence there is no loss of autonomy, relativism, and formalism. Yet the particulars remain circumscribed by the general. The range of autonomy, for example, is limited to those autonomous concerns which are consistent with humanity's heteronomous authority.

This analysis spotlights some misconceptions about what Tillich

70. ST–1, p. 154.   71. ST–1, p. 150.

is doing when he manipulates "polarities." David Hopper has suggested that eliminating conflicts and uniting disparate elements "is clearly *a* major, if not *the* major, purpose and goal of the *Systematic Theology*—depending upon how one also weighs the closely related and long-standing apologetic concern which Tillich sets forth in the Introduction to the *Systematic Theology*."[72] The implication seems to be that reconciling opposites is not only an important end in itself but the real substance of Tillich's system. Actually, Tillich isn't at all concerned about uniting opposing concepts taken at anything approximating face value. To be sure, words like relativism and absolutism have connotations that point up specific facets of Tillich's conceptual structure, but ultimately the concepts are merely symbols for what Tillich does want to unite, namely, God and man. One member of each polar set is a symbol for God (one, general, authoritarian) and the other a symbol for man (many, particular, rational). When you recognize this and the fact that Tillich wishes to merge the two into one, you needn't even understand the mechanics of reconciliation (though it helps). You will still get the message: God and man are one.

The mechanics, nevertheless, are simple enough. There are several ways of viewing the solution, although it is basically the same in each case. The first perspective, in line with Tillich's practice of giving words many connotations centering around a controlling meaning, gives revelation a brand new connotation. The controlling meaning of revelation, remember, pertains to God becoming man. Since there is only one God but many particular individuals, we get this connotation: general becomes particular. When God is defined as humanity, each man is a particular element of the deity. Needless to say, this sort of reconciliation does not work for any other definition of God. The christological connotation of revelation points to a second solution. Here we have the mythological picture of incarnation. To fit Tillich's symbolism, this picture can be given either a mental or a physical interpretation—mind or matter. From the standpoint of mind, we can visualize ultimate concern for humanity incarnated in preliminary concerns transparent to the divine; from the standpoint of matter, we have humanity incarnated as individual men. The solution to the conflicts in reason can also be handled dialectically. In this case the general pole, sym-

72. Hopper, *Tillich: A Theological Portrait*, p. 129.

bolizing God, is the thesis; the particular pole, symbolizing man, is its antithesis; and the dialectical clash is resolved through a synthesis of God and man into a single concept. The movement is from God to man to God = man. An alternative formulation treats God and man as the Hegelian "elements" (universal and particular): the thesis is God and man potentially united as "ontological reason," the antithesis is God and man existentially separated through "conflicts in reason," and the synthesis is God and man reunited through the "revelation" that humanity is the "depth of reason" found in both.

From any of the above viewpoints, Hopper is more correct than he realizes in saying that apologetics is closely related to reconciling disparate elements. Reconciling disparate gods is the very essence of apologetics, whether it involves reconciling God and the Logos or God and Allah or some other pair. Reconciling the God of Christianity with the God of humanism is Tillich's apologetic mission.

BEING AND GOD

Part II of *Systematic Theology*, entitled "Being and God," contains the most direct discussion—though still thoroughly oblique—Tillich has to offer on the subject of God. Being and God, the philosophical and theological absolutes, are correlates, and Tillich's God is their synthesis; hence what is said about the one applies also to the other. And what Tillich says continues the theme that man and God, he who questions and he who answers, are identical. On the philosophical side (being), this identity is spoken dialectically, with being portrayed as a dialectical synthesis of God and man. On the theological side (God), other dialectical formulations appear but emphasis shifts to the Christ analogy with its picture of incarnational unity between concreteness and ultimacy. The two sides jointly portray the God Tillich calls being-itself, the ground of being, and the power of being.

A Dialectical Ontology

Tillich first erects a so-called ontology, which is to say that Tillich calls it ontology and others refer to "Tillich's ontology" whereas the product is strictly bogus. Ontology, once more, is the branch of metaphysics that deals with a supposed essential nature of reality called being. The term occasionally connotes mystical intuition. But Tillich is deeply opposed to metaphysics and mysticism, as his statement that thought "is wrong if it establishes a second reality behind empirical reality" plainly indicates.[73] What Tillich labels ontology is nothing more than a coded message (and statements praising the "richness" of his analysis are inappropriate). With this in mind we can fruitfully investigate the four conceptual levels of Tillich's ontological construct. These are (1) the "basic ontological structure" of self and world, (2) the three pairs of polar "elements" constituting the structure, (3) the "characteristics" of existential being, as opposed to essential being, and (4) the "categories" which unite essence and existence, or being and nonbeing. Although predictably obscure, the four labels in fact relate to the hard-worked dialectic of union, separation, and reunion. "Basic ontological structure" refers to this Hegelian dialectical structure. The "elements," in turn, are Hegel's universal and particular, but with the concepts now referring to God and man (i.e., to the divine and human sides of humanity) and disguised by other names. The "characteristics" of existence describe the state of separation, wherein man and God (like Hegel's subject and object) are separated through lack of self-awareness. Lastly, the "categories" portray the synthesis wherein the two elements are reunited: man becomes God by realizing himself as God.

SELF AND WORLD. Tillich's exploration of being begins with remarks about his ontology's basic structure. Because ontology deals with being and Tillich openly acknowledges the correlation of being and God, "basic ontological structure" should be understood as referring to God. This structure is the familiar Hegelian one of self and world. Self and world are described as "the basic articulation of being."[74] In other words, self and world jointly describe God (being), and the description seems to imply a need for reconciliation between two aspects of God.

The self-world polarity is based on Hegel's God, the Spirit or world-self. The clue to Hegel emerges when Tillich says "this highly dialectical structure" in reference to a self with a world to which it belongs.[75] In Hegel's philosophy the world was literally the

73. *ST–1*, p. 178. 74. *ST–1*, p. 164.
75. *ST–1*, p. 164.

world. Man, as the world's center of consciousness, was alienated from himself because he lacked self-awareness of his essential unity with the world. He saw nature as something alien, something apart from himself. The emergence of self-awareness (self-realization) marked the conquest of alienation and the overcoming of the split between self and world. The Spirit's coming into its own, that is, its self-recognition as God, culminated a dialectical movement from unconscious primeval essence to world-conscious estrangement to self-conscious essence.

Back to Tillich: The chief characteristic of selfhood, we are told, is self-awareness, meaning consciousness of being related to one's environment. This environment is the self's "world." But: " 'World' is not the sum total of all beings—an inconceivable concept."[76] Much less, we can infer, is it the universe or nature, for they include all beings. Rather, by analogy to Hegel, world is the whole to which the self belongs as a part. Man alone qualifies as a self opposed to a world: "Only man has a completely centered self and a structured universe [world] to which he belongs and at which he is able to look at the same time. All other beings . . . are only partly centered and consequently bound to their environment."[77] (Observe how the word "universe," which Tillich uses in the statistical sense, is presented in a manner calculated to suggest that he is a pantheist speaking of the physical universe.)

Let us review the logic. Proposition: World means the whole or universe to which man belongs as a part. Proposition: *Only* man has a world to which he belongs. Deduction: Any universe which includes other beings besides man is not the "world." Now man belongs to many universes: humanity, mammals, carnivorous beings, self-conscious beings, all beings, living organisms (plant and animal), nature, the earth, our solar system, and so on. But of these, only humanity excludes other beings. Conclusion: Humanity is the world to which man belongs as a self, or part. "*Humanity, of which each individual is a special and unique mirror, is the key to the universe.*"[78]

Here is another statement confirming the conclusion: "Man occupies a pre-eminent position . . . as that being . . . in whose self-

76. ST-1, p. 170. 77. ST-2, p. 60.
78. *Perspectives*, p. 101 (my italics).

awareness the ontological answer can be found."[79] To those of us who think that apes and aardvarks, among other creatures, are sufficiently intelligent to enjoy self-awareness—consciousness of self in relation to environment—this sounds nonsensical. At first. But the nonsensical tenor of a straightforward interpretation points to a hidden one. In what sense of the term "self-awareness" might man be called the only being with self-awareness? Tillich's unspoken answer is that, because only humanity is God, man is the only being with the capacity to recognize itself *as God*. "Capacity" implies that some men, in fact most, never attain self-awareness. "There is no self-consciousness without world-consciousness," Tillich asserts.[80] Self-awareness materializes, in other words, when man becomes conscious that man is God. For this reason Tillich can state, referring to his neo-Hegelian dialectical synthesis, that "with the presence of the infinite [humanity] in ourselves we can *re*-cognize (I purposely underline the first syllable) in the universe the infinite which is within us."[81] The italics Tillich gives to the "re" in "*re*-cognize" are his cryptic way of saying that self-recognition is a *reunion* with God, occurring within the context of a dialectic moving from potential *union* of man and humanity to existential *separation* of man and humanity to *reunion* (actual union) of man and humanity.

Once the analogy between Tillich and Hegel is recognized, with Tillich's substitution of humanity for Hegel's world, the solution to the polar split between self and world is evident: man must develop an awareness (self-awareness) that humanity is God. The concept of self and world, their opposition and their unity, is simply another version of the estrangement-reunion story, reviewed in the previous chapter. It is also the story of self-transcending man and self-transcending God, discussed at the beginning of this chapter. It is the story of an existential self which at first does not recognize its essential nature but later does, the story of man becoming God.

ONTOLOGICAL ELEMENTS. Self and world constitute an introduction to the general "problem of the one and the many." The problem, as developed in one of Tillich's lectures, is how to reconcile con-

79. *ST–1*, p. 168.
80. *ST–1*, p. 171.
81. *Perspectives*, p. 101.

cepts fitting these opposing descriptions. The solution is to make the one the general category which many particulars form. World, or universe, is the "one" side of the self and world picture: "Even in the word 'universe' the word 'one' is contained." Tillich asks, "How is it possible that the many are diverse, but nevertheless form the unity of a cosmos, of a *world*, of a universe?" His answer is that "there must be an original unity of the one and the many." Unity? Identity. "The *principle of identity* says that the one substance . . . makes togetherness possible in the same time and the same space." These words are as applicable to the ontological elements, the next level of Tillich's "ontology," as they are to self and world.[82]

As indicated in the preliminary synopsis of the four ontological levels, what Tillich calls the "elements" comprising the basic ontological structure of self and world are God and man as two facets of humanity. God and man are the building blocks for two distinguishable dialectics which are easy to confuse. The first treats God and man as thesis and antithesis in a dialectical movement from God (revelation) to man (reason) to God = man. This describes the self's life within the world's life. The second dialectic, conceptually very similar, is Tillich's retelling of Hegel's ontological tale of the life of the world. Now the three steps are the essential unity of the elements (potential essence), their existential separation from each other (existence, appearance), and their ultimate reunion (actual essence: potentiality = appearance). Man and God—the elements—appear behind different masks in three more polarities: (1) individualization and participation, also called individuality and universality, (2) dynamics and form, and (3) freedom and destiny. The elements can be united if, and only if, God is made the general category which particular men constitute. In the first polarity we meet the idea that God consists of individuals who, by participating in humanity, overcome individuality and achieve universality. The second polarity contrasts the dynamic nature of individual men (their changing appearances, personalities, interests, and so on) with the fixed form of humanity (that which *forms* or molds men to fit the species called man). The third polarity is based on

---

82. *Perspectives*, p. 144 (my italics).

theological controversy pitting free will against predestination. The debate opposes man's will to God's—man and God.

Beyond the basic symbolism of man and God and their substantive identity, each polarity has special connotations illuminating some facet of the divine-human relationship. These connotations stress the basic contrast between self-estrangement and self-awareness. In the individualization-participation polarity, individualization describes the situation of a society divided against itself, a society of individuals looking out for their own interests and the interests of the groups (church, nation) to which they belong. Estranged man sees himself as an individual, struggling against others, but with self-awareness man sees himself as God. The dynamics-form polarity focuses on man's creativity, an important aspect of human dynamics. When Tillich speaks of creativity, he is thinking especially of the gods man creates. "Man's dynamics, his creative vitality, . . . transcends itself toward meaningful contents."[83] This means that self-estranged man creates selfish gods, for example, fame, but that with self-transcendence (self-awareness) a meaningful God appears as the general form which gives a unifying meaning to the diverse gods which are man's dynamic concerns. As for freedom and destiny, man is free to choose his gods. At the same time, man is destined to be human, so destiny establishes the "conditions and limits"[84] of human freedom. Man's destiny can be realized existentially or essentially. Freedom is the medium through which man can choose humanity as God, thereby fulfilling his essential destiny.

This marriage of general and particular which attends self-realization carries us beyond the polarities to an interpretation of Tillich's best-known formulation on God, to wit: "God is being-itself, not *a* being."[85] The formulation closely parallels Tillich's description of the Hegelian God. "The absolute Spirit of which Hegel speaks is not a being beside the finite spirit [man],"[86] explains Tillich. In Hegel's case, God is not *a* being because the Spirit embraces all being, including all human *beings*. Tillich's God is analogous, but world has been condensed to humanity. God

83. *ST–1*, pp. 180–81.
84. *ST–1*, p. 185.
85. *ST–1*, p. 237.
86. *Perspectives*, p. 121.

is not *a* being because God is billions of beings—human being itself.

SEPARATION. After finishing with the ontological "elements," Tillich turns to the existential aspect of being. We have seen that the basic ontological structure of self and world, as reflected in the three God-man (or thesis-antithesis) polarities, can display either separation or union (i.e., estrangement or self-awareness): separation is the existential state, union the essential. Man exists under conditions of estrangement from his fellow man, yet man in essence is one and can realize his essential unity to the extent that he recognizes himself as God and treats himself accordingly. Tillich's third ontological level is concerned with the existential side of the separation-union dichotomy, the side where man and God are separated. Three concepts describe the state of separation: nonbeing, finitude, and existence.

Hegelian dialectics pervades the discussion: "The mystery of nonbeing demands a dialectical approach."[87] Thus we encounter sentences like this: "Nonbeing appears as the 'not yet' of being and as the 'no more' of being."[88] (Nonbeing precedes the synthesis and follows the thesis of a dialectic; it is the antithesis.) And this: "The potential presence of the infinite (as unlimited self-transcendence) is the negation of the negative element in finitude."[89] (Infinity is the "negation of the negation," which is Hegel's alternate term for synthesis, and finitude is the antithesis that infinity negates.) Also: "Whatever exists, that is, 'stands out' of mere potentiality, is more than it is in the state of mere potentiality and less than it could be in the power of its essential nature."[90] (The existential state is an antithesis, standing opposed to the thesis of potential unity and leading toward the synthesis in which the potential becomes realized as the actual.)

A full-blown discussion of Tillich's dialectics must be reserved for Chapter 5. For present purposes it will suffice to refer to the introductory description provided in the previous chapter, briefly identify the three existential concepts, and relate these concepts to

87. *ST–1*, p. 187.
88. *ST–1*, p. 189. The words "not yet" in reference to antithesis preceding synthesis come straight from Hegel. See Hegel, *The Phenomenology of Mind*, pp. 180, 191, 251, 625, 785, 790, 794, 799.
89. *ST–1*, p. 191.   90. *ST–1*, p. 203.

man and God. As indicated above, nonbeing, finitude, and existence are alternative names for the antithesis in a dialectical situation. The thesis is potentiality (the analogue of Eden), a concept explained in Chapter 2 in connection with the symbol of the Fall. Because men have not realized their potential for living in harmonious union with one another, man exists in the antithetical state of estrangement (the analogue of sin). Man is unaware of his own godhood. When and to the extent that men turn to man as God, self-awareness materializes and the synthesis in which man transcends himself is reached (salvation).

As to the three variants of the antithesis—nonbeing, finitude, and existence—nonbeing has several meanings in Tillich's thought but refers generally to the absence of being. In the present context, being is the situation in which God emerges from potentiality into actuality. It is the state of self-transcendence which eventuates when self recognizes world as itself—when man recognizes humanity as God. Being means God *is*: there is mutual love among men. Nonbeing, therefore, means God is *not*. Tillich's second name for the antithesis in his social dialectic is finitude. Finite means limited. Finitude is a state of limited love, limited concern. Man's attention is diverted toward himself, special groups to which he belongs, and a finite supernatural being he imagines to exist as God. Regarding the latter: "Infinity is a demand, not a thing"[91] (infinity demands unlimited love for humanity). Existence, the third variation of the antithesis, is the familiar philosophical term for an actual state of affairs, as opposed to the ideal. The ideal is essence, which refers both to the potentiality from which man has "fallen" and to the state of humanistic synthesis toward which man should strive.

THE CATEGORIES. The fourth level of Tillich's ontological analysis deals with his point that existential separation can be overcome. To put things in the proper ontological mode, Tillich employs what philosophers have called the categories of being and knowing. Four are identified as significant: time, space, causality, and substance. Separation and union are again the focal points of the discussion. The categories tell us that what is separated can be united. Time

91. *ST–1*, p. 190.

separates; space separates; cause is separated from effect; and items differing in substance are separate. But if properly manipulated, the categories can unite.

The task is to use the categories to unite God and man. "The categories . . . unite an affirmative and a negative element."[92] This is dialectical speech, referring to thesis and antithesis. The thesis is God, whose undivided character symbolizes a state in which God and man are (potentially) united. The antithesis is man, whose separateness (multiple identity) symbolizes a state of separation between God and man. In the synthesis, God and man merge in two senses: God and man become identical, and—regarding the two states—man embraces humanity under conditions of continued estrangement within humanity. How do the categories unite thesis and antithesis? Time, says Tillich, unites anxiety with courage. Anxiety, we know, relates to the antithetical state of separation from God; and courage ("the courage to be") is a term used to describe the humanistic synthesis. Time carries man from anxiety to courage; courage includes anxiety—synthesis includes antithesis —but enables man to accept it. Space, the second category, is a concept Tillich is hard pressed to employ. But he manages to stretch it to cover "social space," meaning a place within a humanistic value structure. When a preliminary concern finds a place within a humanistic value structure (i.e., when human creations and antisupernatural interests become humanistic), God and man are united. Causality is easy to employ: humanity is the "cause" or matrix which gives rise to human beings. God engenders man. Substance likewise presents no difficulty: humanity and man are one in substance.

The last two categories, causality and substance, help to clarify what Tillich means when he calls God the "ground of our being." Humanity is both cause and the substance (effect) which is caused. Accordingly, Tillich can assert that "ground" means neither cause nor substance but that "the difference between substance and causality disappears, for if God is the cause of the entire series of causes and effects, he is the substance underlying the whole process of becoming."[93]

92. ST–1, pp. 192–93.   93. ST–1, p. 238.

God as Concreteness and Ultimacy

Tillich's discussion of God is termed an answer to a question implied in the discussion of being. People have found limitless questions in Tillich's ontology, questions which the ontology itself answers if you read between the lines, but one question is fundamental: Who or what is this God Tillich calls being and from which man is said to be estranged? The heart of Tillich's answer lies in descriptive remarks about concreteness and ultimacy, two characteristics Tillich claims are combined in God. This strongly recurrent theme is phrased in a number of ways: concrete and universal, finite and infinite, conditional and unconditional, immanent and transcendent, and so on. Always, however, the point registers that God is very tangible, specific, and close to man yet somehow intangible, abstract, or far beyond man. Such talk has led George Thomas and probably others to assume that Tillich embraces a form of panentheism. He doesn't, but the paired opposites do illuminate the God above God. Close observation of Tillich's usage of "concrete" and "ultimate" makes vivid the two-sided character which the normative picture of Jesus as the Christ imparts to his God.

A TYPOLOGY OF RELIGION. The basic statement of what he means by concrete and absolute is provided by Tillich in a comparative analysis of different types of religion. It should be clearly understood that the typology discussion, like that of ontology, is not a scholarly inquiry, much less a "brilliantly concise analysis"[94] dealing with religious evolution; it is a symbolic discussion serving to define the terms "concrete" and "ultimate" and to state the need to combine them in a synthetic concept of God. To achieve this end Tillich builds a typology having three general categories: (1) polytheism, (2) monotheism, and (3) trinitarian monotheism. Tillich doesn't want his analysis to be unduly clear, so he frames the latter as a type of monotheism; but scrutiny reveals it to be the synthesis of a dialectic running from concreteness to ultimacy to concrete ultimacy. Polytheism, the first category, is subdivided into (a) universalistic, (b) mythological, and (c) dualistic types. Monotheism is also characterized by a three-way breakdown: (a) monarchic,

94. Alexander J. McKelway, *The Systematic Theology of Paul Tillich: A Review and Analysis* (Richmond: John Knox Press, 1964), p. 120.

(b) mystical, and (c) exclusive. Not to be confused with trinitarian Christianity, which falls under monarchic monotheism, trinitarian monotheism is the true religion and has no subdivisions.

The gist of Tillich's discussion of polytheism is that it is unbalanced in favor of concreteness. This emphasis on concreteness gives us a good look at what makes a god concrete. Universalistic polytheism offers the pervasive sacred power of *mana*, an impersonal spiritlike essence, embodied in quasi-personal divinities (spirits). Pantheism, with its universal essence permeating all elements of nature, is an offshoot. Tension radiates between the concrete and the ultimate because the universalistic divinities "are not sufficiently fixed and individualized" to be fully concrete. To paraphrase, real concreteness requires personality and individuality. In mythological polytheism, best represented by its Greek form, there are "individual deities of a relatively fixed character" representing various realms. Here concreteness is manifest in personality, which man creates because he "cannot be ultimately concerned about something which is less than he is, something impersonal." Tillich is indicating that a thing is concrete to the extent that it resembles a human being. Mythological polytheism is highly concrete but lacks ultimacy in the sense of a unifying element comparable to *mana*. The movement back toward ultimacy begins when the mythological gods are made subject to a transcending principle, such as fate. Dualistic polytheism is the next step toward ultimacy. The many special realms are reduced to two. Dualism, for example, Zoroasterism, projects a good god and a bad god, but the good god is superior and in the long run will win. This superiority is at once a further move toward ultimacy and a move toward monotheism.[95]

Treating polytheism as the thesis, concreteness, Tillich introduces monotheism as its negation, ultimacy. Monarchic monotheism carries the antithesis only tentatively, standing on the border between polytheism and monotheism. A god-monarch rules over angels and spirits and other inferior deities. Unlike polytheistic dualism, wherein the good god's unifying power is a matter of relative superiority vis-à-vis the bad god, monarchic monotheism gives the god hegemony with respect to all other divinity. Nevertheless, the many lesser divinities are evidence of strong residual

95. *ST–1*, pp. 222–23.

ties with polytheism. Mystical monotheism overcomes these: it radically negates the element of concreteness by completely dissolving the spirits and demigods. Anyway it tries to, although in popular Buddhism and other forms in which it is practiced mysticism allows the excluded gods to insinuate themselves back in. A degree of concreteness is restored. Exclusive monotheism (easily recognized as the Unitarian-liberal variety) tries to more adequately restore concreteness while retaining the element of ultimacy. The exclusive god is a personality. But instead of standing as the superior deity among inferior supernatural beings, the god stands alone. And he rules over all nations. Both by overcoming the fragmentation of polytheism and monarchic monotheism and by standing as a universal god, the god of exclusive monotheism qualifies as ultimate. At the same time, by embodying the element of personality, absent in mysticism, he restores a degree of concreteness. The trouble is, his personal traits tend to disappear as anthropomorphisms; ultimacy overshadows concreteness.

Trinitarian monotheism follows as the dialectical synthesis which absorbs the best elements of polytheism and monotheism. It is too early to go into the details of Tillich's trinitarian formula and, for that matter, he does not develop the subject in connection with his typology of religions. The important thing to note at this point is that trinitarian monotheism involves "the unity between ultimacy and concreteness in the living God."[96] It culminates the dialectic.

FOUR REQUIREMENTS. Two qualities associated with concreteness and two with ultimacy are visible in the typology. The first two—concreteness—represent the human side of the normative picture of the Christ. They convey the idea that God consists of separate, manlike individuals: concreteness includes, first, personality and, second, a multiplicity of embodiments of the divine. The next two qualities—ultimacy—are derived from the divine side of the Christ picture. They express the need for an impersonal abstraction which binds the individuals into a unified whole: ultimacy is impersonal and universal.

Personality—similarity to living persons—is a key characteristic of concreteness. The spirits of universalistic polytheism are only

96. *ST–1*, p. 228.

partially concrete because they lack personality. The mythological gods are exceedingly concrete, for they actually cavort among men. Dualistic gods are also concrete: heavily personified. A mystical "god" is wholly unconcrete, since it lacks any personality whatsoever. Other monotheistic gods are concrete to a degree—they are personalities—but the exclusive monotheistic (Unitarian) god loses concreteness to the extent that his anthropomorphisms are removed. In short, the more closely the divine resembles a human being the more concrete it is. Tillich claims that his god is *fully* concrete.

Universalistic and mythological polytheism each possess the second quality of concreteness, namely, numerous manifestations of the divine. Dualism moves away from the concrete and toward the ultimate: there are only two manifestations. Monarchic monotheism is accorded merely borderline status among Tillich's monotheistic religions because there remain numerous minor gods (angels, saints, etc.) manifesting divine qualities. In mysticism concreteness vanishes except where lesser divinities reappear in popular religion. Exclusive monotheism omits monarchic monotheism's subordinate gods and thereby suffers a lack of concreteness.

On the side of ultimacy, impersonality is the first quality. Universalistic polytheism is somewhat personal where the spirits are concerned but quite impersonal when it comes to *mana*. In contrast, what makes mythological polytheism so completely nonultimate is the absence of any such impersonal element. Dualism's gods may be less anthropomorphic, but they still reflect the image of man: dualism remains essentially concrete. The same manlike personality characterizes monarchic monotheism, which falls well short of full ultimacy. It is only with mystical monotheism, where the divine is completely impersonal, that genuine ultimacy finally materializes. Backsliding occurs with exclusive monotheism, for the divine again becomes anthropomorphic (or at least anthropopathic.)

Regarding universality, universalistic polytheism enjoys some ultimacy because *mana*, which pervades everything, binds the quasi-personal spirits. Except in the presence of a higher principle like fate, mythological polytheism's gods are markedly nonuniversal: each is limited to a special realm. Dualism moves toward ultimacy by combining the fragmented divine into just two powers, partially united through the good god's superiority (and expected victory) over the bad. Monarchic monotheism achieves even greater ultimacy by eliminating the second god; yet subordinate divinities with special powers remain, preventing full ultimacy. Mysticism swallows up the remaining fragments of divinity, thereby achieving full ultimacy. Exclusive monotheism is also fully universal: no lesser divinities compete with the one. Ultimacy, then, combines all divinity into a single universalized divinity.

To subtly emphasize the four requirements and the need for synthesis, Tillich has hidden two subordinate dialectics within the overall dialectic of polytheism, monotheism, and trinitarian monotheism. Each subordinate dialectic is a double one, presenting (a) a clash between personality and impersonality and (b) a clash between separateness and unity. Under polytheism the universalistic type is a *thesis* (less-than-personal spirits, the binding substance of *mana*), the mythological type is its *antithesis* (personal gods, many dominions), and dualism is a crude *synthesis* (more personal than spirits but less so than Greek gods, two realms as a compromise between one and many). Monotheism introduces the same concepts in reverse order. Monarchic monotheism is the *thesis* (personal god, some fragmentation of divinity), mysticism is its *antithesis* (impersonal god, all divinity consolidated), and exclusive monotheism is the *synthesis* (personal yet tending to lose anthropomorphisms, many realms—nations—under one ruler).

Taking the typology dialectic and its sub-dialectics together, here is the overall picture:

A. *Thesis*: Polytheism = concreteness (manifold divinity, personal)
   1. *Thesis*: Universalistic = relatively ultimate (one *mana*, impersonal)
   2. *Antithesis*: Mythological = relatively concrete (many *very* personal gods)
   3. *Synthesis*: Dualistic = compromise (two gods, moderately personal)
B. *Antithesis*: Monotheism = ultimacy (one divinity, impersonal)
   1. *Thesis*: Monarchic = relatively concrete (many demigods, personal)
   2. *Antithesis*: Mystical = relatively ultimate (one impersonal divinity)
   3. *Synthesis*: Exclusive = compromise (one divinity ruling over many nations, personal but tending to become impersonal)
C. *Synthesis*: Trinitarian Monotheism = concreteness *and* ultimacy

Although two of the dialectics reverse the usual one-many order for thesis and antithesis, this in no way belies the point that these are dialectics. The revised order is just a way of making the dialectical message hard to detect. It would look a little suspicious if an analysis purporting to deal with the "history of religion" had monotheism coming before polytheism.

THE LESSON APPLIED. Tillich's dialectical typology of religion constitutes a detailed set of specifications for the Tillichian God. Once the dialectical character of the typology is recognized, the message becomes abundantly clear. Everything is so plain that we would have no difficulty figuring out what Tillich means by "God" even if we had no advanced insight. Tillich advises that his God is both concrete and ultimate. Concreteness, he unmistakably indicates, requires (1) personality, that is, the form of a human being, and (2) manifoldness, or diversity. Ultimacy requires (3) impersonality, or abstraction, and (4) universality. What we are confronted with is a specific application of the classical Hegelian pattern. Tillich calls it the problem of the one and the many. We have already learned that the general solution always conforms to the "principle of identity": the one must be the general category comprising the many particulars. All we have to do to solve the immediate version of the problem, therefore, is determine what sort of particulars we are facing.

The six examples of what is or is not concrete, and in what degree, provide ample evidence that the particulars are human beings. The most concrete of all the gods of superstition are those of mythological polytheism. In Greek mythology, the gods were so nearly human that they mixed with humans, and many a child was said to have been sired by Zeus or one of his cohorts. A god is concrete, in Tillich's vernacular, insofar as it resembles a man (which is why the god of exclusive monotheism loses concreteness when he loses his anthropomorphisms). Perfect concreteness implies perfectly human character. Only man is perfectly human.

Everything now falls into place. Take the manifold aspect. Manifold means numerous and varied. In the religious context, it means numerous different embodiments of the divine. This is another reason why mythological polytheism ranks first in concreteness: it has many gods, individualized in personality. So it is with man. There are many men, each with his own personality. Or, from the "subjective reason" standpoint, there are (holds Tillich) many different preliminary concerns transparent to humanity.

Impersonality comes next. Individual human beings may be personal, but collectively they are impersonal. Humanity is not an individual or a personality; as Tillich says, it is not *a* being. Taken in its physical aspect, humanity is a conglomerate of human beings. Interpreted as an ultimate concern, it is a highly intangible abstraction. The paradox about God being personal and impersonal at the same time dissolves when we grasp that ultimacy and concreteness aren't two different things but two sides of the same thing.

Finally, humanity is universal. Universal, as illustrated by the typology, does not mean all-embracing in the pantheistic sense of excluding nothing. It means universal with respect to a relevant set of particulars. The god of exclusive monotheism has universality because he includes all *divinity*, not everything that is; he is not the universe or nature. By the same token, Tillich's God is universal because it includes all humanity. Humanity is the "unconditional"; Tillich refuses to accept any doctrine making man's divinity subject to the condition that certain groups or individuals are excepted.

THE LOGOS DOCTRINE. Confirmation of the foregoing interpretation of concreteness and ultimacy is found in what Tillich calls the Logos doctrine. "The Logos doctrine as the doctrine of the identity of the absolutely concrete with the absolutely universal is . . . the only possible foundation of a Christian theology which claims to be *the* theology." What is this doctrine and where is the identity between something concrete and something universal? Tillich declares that in the Christian doctrine that the Logos became flesh "Christian theology has received a foundation . . . which is absolutely concrete and absolutely universal at the same time." The concreteness, he continues, is not that of myth or mystical vision or divine law but "the concreteness of a personal life." Both the obvious allusion to Logos-God becoming a man and the direct reference to "a personal life" verify that concreteness refers to man. Looking now at universality, there is an analogy between philosophy's universal Logos, in which all human reason participated, and a God which is universal in the sense that all men participate in it. Therefore, "if Jesus is called the Christ he must represent everything particular and must be the point of identity between the absolutely concrete and the absolutely universal." Observe Tillich's repetition of the idea that the concrete must be *identical* with the universal. In the incarnation myth, the incarnate Logos is a man yet is identical with God. From this we must infer that the universal is God, that man and God are identical, and that—based on analogy to the universal Logos—God includes *all* men ("everything particular").[97]

The Logos doctrine has a correlate, the description of which provides still more evidence that the analysis is correct. In discussing the opposition between relativism and absolutism, after saying that something which is absolute and concrete at the same time can overcome the conflict, Tillich asserts, "The law of love . . . is absolute because it concerns everything concrete."[98] The "law of love," we can be reasonably certain, describes the commandment on which Tillich says his concept of ultimate concern is based: the commandment to love God with all one's heart, soul, mind, and strength. This commandment, together with the companion one to love one's neighbor (which means the same thing if God is man), is sometimes called "the law of love."[99] Tillich says it is absolute *because* it concerns *everything concrete.* Describing concreteness, he again identifies "a personal life" as "the most concrete of all possible forms of concreteness" we can encounter.[100] Absoluteness depends on concreteness ("because"), concreteness relates to man ("a personal life"), and no man is excepted ("everything concrete"); hence it is safe to conclude that the law of love commands, "You shall love all humanity as God." This sounds very much like the Logos doctrine. It too affirms the identity of the absolute and the concrete, and Tillich can describe it as "the principle of universality."[101] Stated as a principle, the Logos doctrine would go something like this: "God is identical with the entire universe of concrete human beings." This principle is, for Tillich, a law of sorts. And why shouldn't a Logos principle be regarded as a law in an analogical system? Tillich points out that, for Heraclitus, Logos meant "the universal law of reality."[102] In short, the Logos principle and the law of love are both laws expressing the idea that all

97. *ST–1*, pp. 16–17.   98. *ST–1*, p. 152.
99. See Charles Guignebert, *Jesus*, trans. S. H. Hooke (Hyde Park, N.Y.: University Books, 1956), p. 376.
100. *ST–1*, p. 150.   101. *ST–1*, p. 16.
102. *History*, p. 7.

humanity should be treated as God. Moreover, Tillich perceives that the early Christian apologists not only identified the Christ with the Logos but "equated . . . the divine commands with the rational law of nature,"[103] which means they equated the Great Commandment (among others) with the universal Logos. We have another pair of Tillichian correlates or, to be more exact, we have a variation of the earlier correlation between Logos and Word of God. For the law of love is a specific instance, and the most important at that, of a divine command. As such, it is a theological analogue of philosophy's rational law of the universe. Each law in its own way is absolute law. In their syntheses of universality (ultimacy) and concreteness, Tillich's versions of both laws direct man to love all mankind as God.

103. *Boundary*, p. 60.

CHAPTER 4

The Symbolic Christ

When a Christian liberal becomes disenchanted with the idea of a divine savior, something that happens rather frequently these days, the customary response is to remold Jesus into a moral leader and teacher. Tillich has conspicuously avoided this course of action, choosing to erect a Christology having "Jesus as the Christ" as its foundation. The Christ, not the historical Jesus, becomes the symbol for what Tillich calls "New Being." Jesus of Nazareth, as far as Tillich's doctrines are concerned, might never have lived. Not that Tillich has any real doubt about Jesus' historicity; he simply wishes to emphasize that it is the divine redeemer of traditional theology who is the symbol of New Being. Why is it the Christ that Tillich selects for his symbol? What is the New Being which is symbolized? What are the symbolic analogies between the Christ and New Being? These questions are the subject of the present chapter.

JESUS *VERSUS* CHRIST

To his larger audience Tillich presents several reasons for bypassing the historical Jesus. These reasons lack depth and are not hard to recognize as cover for more basic considerations which Tillich is unwilling to state candidly. A candid statement would unblock the ears of too many people who are not ready for anything stronger than a few bits and pieces of Tillich's No to supernaturalism. The basic reasons for which Tillich prefers the Christ as his symbol include ethical problems affecting the historical Jesus and unique values in the Christ picture.

147

Officially, there are three reasons why Tillich wishes to use "Jesus as the Christ" instead of Jesus as Nazareth as his central symbol. One is that he wants to maintain Christianity as a New Testament faith, not to revitalize the Old Testament religion. "The retreat in historical research to the 'teachings of Jesus' reduces Jesus to the level of the Old Testament and implicitly denies his claim to have overcome the Old Testament context."[1] The picture of Jesus as just another prophet, perhaps the greatest but still just a prophet, is not the "picture which created both the church and the Christian."[2] Note how adaptable this line of talk is to convincing listeners that he accepts the divinity of Jesus. But of course he doesn't, and for this very reason we cannot take seriously his pretense that the Christ concept is an essential element in any Christian formula. The fact is that scores of writers and theologians have managed to call themselves Christian while rejecting the traditional picture of Jesus. They have done so by the simple expedient of treating "Christ" as a surname and refurbishing the name through moral emphasis. If Tillich had seen Jesus in the same light as these liberals he could easily have done the same.

A second reason advanced by Tillich for using the Christ symbol is that the historical picture of Jesus cannot be made scientifically probable. The reports on which the gospels are based, he reasons, are too colored by the supernaturalistic orientation of the witnesses to be reliable. It would be pointless to argue that Tillich is wrong about how much can be known about Jesus, if Tillich really believes what he says. However, Tillich demonstrates in many ways his respect for historical research generally and biblical research in particular. The only thing he has strong doubts about is the possibility of writing an accurate biographical "life" of Jesus. When the historical requirement is reduced to knowledge of the teachings of Jesus, which is all the liberal approach requires, Tillich does not argue the impossibility of knowing what Jesus *said*. Instead he falls back on the first argument, namely, that a Christianity centered on the "words of Jesus" fails to overcome the Old Testament context.

The last of Tillich's superficial considerations concerns the possi-

1. *ST–2*, p. 106.   2. *ST–2*, p. 115.

bility that historical research might some day uncover evidence that Jesus never lived. In effect, Tillich says, "If we base theology on the supposition that Jesus was real and it turns out he wasn't, won't we be in a fix then?" This is the most obviously false of the three reasons. If historical truth were Tillich's criterion, Jesus as the Christ would be the first Jesus to be ruled out. Whereas Tillich definitely believes Jesus existed and does not seriously expect historical research ever to challenge the fact, he very emphatically does not believe that a supernatural Christ ever came to earth. Yet he doesn't hesitate to base his theology on a nonhistorical Christ. And if he is willing to base his doctrines on a nonhistorical Christ, he could just as well utilize a nonhistorical moralist; the real could be replaced by an ideal.

The Problem of Demonism

If the above considerations are superficial, what are Tillich's deeper reasons for turning his back on Jesus of Nazareth? The first of two explanations introduces the problem of demonism. Practically anyone familiar with Tillich will recognize demonism, also called idolatry, as one of his most pervasive concepts. Demonism relates to universality—the Logos principle—and is its opposite, for the concept of demonism embodies the thesis that all gods that represent less than the whole of humanity are demonic. A close look at this thesis provides a basis for understanding why Tillich lacks the liberals' enthusiasm for the historical Jesus. Significantly, it also reveals further evidence that the Tillichian God is mankind.

TRUE AND FALSE ULTIMACY. One can hardly fail to note that most of the ultimate concerns mentioned by Tillich in various places are unwholesome. Those which are something less than honorable Tillich calls demonic or, alternatively, idolatrous. A demon and an idol are the same thing—something worshiped, literally or figuratively, as ultimate when it is not truly ultimate. "The holy which is demonic, or ultimately destructive, is identical with the content of idolatrous faith."[3] Yet, by either label, the demon-idol remains an ultimate concern: "Idolatrous faith is still faith. The holy which is demonic is still holy."[4]

---

3. *Dynamics*, p. 16.   4. *Dynamics*, p. 16.

Describing demonism, Tillich draws a distinction between true and false ultimacy: "In true faith the ultimate concern is a concern about the truly ultimate; while in idolatrous faith preliminary, finite realities are elevated to the rank of ultimacy."[5] Here Tillich is employing the concept of a preliminary concern. Man, he explains, can react in one of three ways to a preliminary concern: (1) he can view it with indifference, (2) he can promote it to the rank of ultimate, or (3) he can treat it as a manifestation of the ultimate without actually making it ultimate. We need not discuss here the first and third alternatives. But what Tillich says about option number two provides basic insight into the nature of demonism. "Something essentially *conditioned* is taken as unconditional, something essentially *partial* is boosted into universality, and something essentially *finite* is given infinite significance (the best example is the contemporary idolatry of religious nationalism)." Any concern fitting this description signifies "idolatry."[6]

The idolatrous concern is "conditioned," "partial," and "finite"; and the example is religious nationalism. What does this mean? The quoted passage comes from volume 1 of *Systematic Theology*, the 1951 publication date of which strongly suggests that Zionism is the religious nationalism in question. In any event, an exclusive group is the heart of the matter. The religious state, viewed as a demonic concern, is subject to the *condition* that only certain people shall be treated with reverence; it includes only *part* of the human race; it is *finite* in the literal sense of being limited—limited to members of a particular country and creed. With most of mankind left out, the religious state, interpreted as a god, can hardly be labeled universal. From this description, demonism begins to jell as that which excludes certain elements of humanity from the area of concern.

Everything Tillich says about demonism is consistent with this interpretation. Thus he contends that there are "many degrees in the endless realm of false ultimacies."[7] For example: "The nation is nearer to true ultimacy than is success."[8] Why should the nation be closer to ultimacy than success? The nation represents millions of people. But success is among the most selfish of all gods: it rep-

5. *Dynamics*, p. 12.
7. *Dynamics*, p. 11.
6. *ST–1*, p. 13 (my italics).
8. *Dynamics*, p. 11.

resents just one individual. Following this example, we can postulate a rough hierarchy of gods ranging from success and allied selfish concerns (salvation, pleasure, money, etc.) at the bottom to humanity at the top. Within this hierarchy any ultimate concern not transparent to humanity as a whole is demonic in direct proportion to its exclusiveness. Family is less demonic than self, clan outranks family, party stands above clan, and nation is higher than party. The Church, embracing as it does more of humanity than a particular nation, lies still closer to true ultimacy; yet not until its "demonic exclusiveness" yields to a "holy community with universal inclusiveness" through humanistic reorientation will the Church cease being demonic.[9] Only humanity, at the apex of the hierarchy, has the universality necessary to support its claim to the title of God. This is what it means to say, "The claim of anything finite [limited] to be final in its own right is demonic."[10]

GODS OF SPACE. The above interpretation of demonism gets considerable support from Tillich's concept of the "spatial god." In Theology of Culture Tillich develops a concept of space which is not physical but something he calls "beside-each-otherness."[11] Space is less than infinite when it is restricted to a particular group. "Examples of spatial concepts are blood and race, clan, tribe, and family."[12] Tillich strongly disapproves of the spatial gods, gods "who give ultimate dignity and value to a special race and to a special community of blood."[13] He again brings out nationalism for special criticism: "The 'beside-each-otherness' necessarily becomes an 'against-each-otherness' in the moment in which a special space gets divine honor."[14] Definitely implied in the view that any ultimate concern which mirrors unconcern for persons outside one's own group is demonic.

Following through on the spatial concept, Tillich illustrates its positive aspect with the biblical story of Abraham. We need not be disturbed by his very obvious misinterpretation of the Bible: this is intentional and illustrates the use of "Jesus as the Christ" as the

9. ST-3, p. 262.
10. ST-1, p. 134. The same idea appears in Tillich's statement that demonism "is possible only in contradiction to the universal idea, that is, only in the particular." (Religion, p. 87.)
11. Culture, p. 32.   12. Culture, p. 32.
13. Culture, p. 32.   14. Culture, p. 33.

interpretive "norm" which demands that all biblical interpretations be consistent with the proposition that God is man. "The command to Abraham to leave his homeland and his father's house means the command to leave the gods of soil and blood, of family, tribe and nation; that is, the gods of space, the gods of paganism and polytheism, the gods who stand beside each other—even if one of them is the most powerful."[15] This same story is again used in *On the Boundary*, where Tillich describes Abraham's God as the one "who means to bless all the races" and "utterly demolishes all religious nationalism—the nationalism of the Jews, which he opposes constantly, and that of the pagans, which is repudiated in the command to Abraham."[16] In *Dynamics of Faith*, Tillich calls it the God "who, because he represents justice for everybody and every nation, is called the universal God, the God of the universe."[17]

The spatial dichotomy of nonuniversality and universality lays bare the structure of demonism. It explains why Tillich can say that it would have been demonic for theology's Christ to yield to Satan's temptations in the wilderness, making a god of himself and excluding all others from his concern.[18] It explains why polytheism's "demonic element" stands "rooted in the claim of each of the divine powers to be ultimate, although none of them possesses the universal basis for making such a claim."[19] And it explains why "a main characteristic of the demonic is the state of being split."[20] Anything is demonic to the extent that it is selfish or excludes other beings from the field of concern. Demonism is faith in a nonuniversal god; it is non-faith in humanity.

DEMONISM AND ESTRANGEMENT. For a final test of this interpretation of demonism, we can search for its correlate—an analogous philosophical concept. Where is it? If demonism is non-faith in humanity, it amounts to separation from God. That immediately suggests estrangement. But wasn't estrangement identified in Chapter 2 as the correlate of sin? The answer is that demonism *is* sin. In Christian tradition, sin is viewed as the work of the devil and his demons. Sin therefore constitutes allegiance to a god that is less than God—some instead of all.

15. *Culture*, p. 35.   16. *Boundary*, pp. 91–92.
17. *Dynamics*, p. 2.   18. *ST–2*, p. 126.
19. *ST–1*, p. 222.   20. *ST–3*, p. 103.

The correlative analogy between demonic sin and estrangement can be restated briefly. As mentioned above, both involve separation from God. Regarding sin: "The very heart of what classical Christianity has called 'sin' is the unreconciled duality of ultimate and preliminary concerns, of the finite and that which transcends finitude, of the secular and the holy. Sin is a state of things in which the holy and the secular [God and man] are *separated*, struggling with each other and trying to conquer each other."[21] This verifies what has been said about demonism: the ultimate and preliminary concerns are not reconciled; the finite concern is opaque to the infinite, humanity. As for estrangement, it describes the Hegelian notion of a self separated from its world through self's failure to recognize world as itself. Man split apart from himself is analogous.

Despite being correlates, demonism and estrangement have slightly different connotations. Both entail separation of man from man. But demonism emphasizes the moral aspect of the situation, whereas estrangement focuses on the psychological or tragic aspect. At the same time, demonism concerns man's attitude toward others; it "expresses what is not implied in the term 'estrangement,' namely, the personal act of turning away from that to which one belongs [the human race]."[22] Estrangement, as the quotation suggests, describes the condition of man which results from the demonism of his fellow man.

The Historical Jesus

Why is Tillich unwilling to defer to Jesus as a moral leader? We have just seen that Tillich holds as one of the basic tenets of his system that any concern is demonic to the extent that it is selfish or exclusive. The most demonic of all concerns are those which are purely selfish, for example, success. Other concerns are demonic in whatever degree they are restricted to a special group, excluding part of the human race from the area of concern. Tillich is contemptuous of demonism in any form. Yet the teachings of Jesus were—and no objective observer can fail to recognize this— demonic in many ways. Tillich therefore has no admiration for Jesus or for his teachings. Let us inquire about the specifics.

21. *ST–1*, p. 218 (my italics).   22. *ST–2*, p. 46.

PERSONAL SALVATION. The most crucial weakness in Jesus' ethic is that it is a selfish ethic; it is rooted in desire and fear. The moral precepts Jesus taught, both the good and the bad, were not offered for their intrinsic value but as the means of personal salvation. Jesus taught that we should be good—so we can enter the kingdom of God. He also taught us to avoid sin—so as thereby to avoid hell. In short, Jesus' ethic is one of hell's fire and brimstone.

The evidence on this point is written throughout the gospels. From the time Jesus began preaching, his constant message was, "Repent, for the kingdom of heaven is at hand."[23] The message announced the imminent destruction of the world, to be accompanied by the resurrection of the dead and the installation of God's earthly but supernatural kingdom. In Maurice Goguel's apt words, Jesus "believed that the present world, which was dominated by demons, was destined to disappear in the near future, and that it would be replaced by a new world-order in which God would be supreme."[24] There was no time to lose. Those who repented could enjoy salvation in the world to come; the rest were doomed to fiery agony. The message was sincere, but not wise or noble.

Scholars generally agree that Jesus did not deliver the Sermon on the Mount as an extended discourse on a single occasion. Nevertheless, we are indebted to Matthew for pulling together most of his principal sayings and presenting them in one place. As others have pointed out,[25] the Sermon continually alternates between threats and promises: "will never enter the kingdom of heaven," "your reward is great in heaven," "shall be liable to the hell of fire," "will reward you," "shall be liable to judgment," "have their reward," "your whole body [will] be thrown into hell," "will reward you," "will have no reward," "have their reward," "go into hell," "gifts," "destruction," "shall enter the kingdom of heaven," and "thrown into the fire."[26] Sometimes during the Sermon Jesus promises and threatens at the same time. Consider the original ending of the Lord's Prayer: "For if you forgive men their

23. Matt. 3:2.
24. Maurice Goguel, *Jesus and the Origins of Christianity*, trans. Olive Wyon (New York: Harper Torchbooks, 1960), II, 552.
25. For example, see Walter Kaufmann, *The Faith of a Heretic* (Garden City: Doubleday, 1961), p. 223.
26. Matt. 5–7, *passim*.

trespasses, your heavenly Father also will forgive you; but if you do not forgive men their trespasses, neither will your Father forgive your trespasses."[27]

The same mixture of cajolery and threats characterizes those pronouncements of Jesus recorded elsewhere in the gospels. He tells one man to sell his possessions and give to the poor, not for humanitarian reasons but to obtain "treasure" in the kingdom of God. Again, describing the kingdom, he says that "many will come from east and west and sit at the table with Abraham, Isaac, and Jacob in the kingdom of heaven, while the sons of the kingdom [of Satan] will be thrown into the outer darkness; there men will weep and gnash their teeth."[28]

Particularly striking evidence of the selfish basis of Jesus' ethic comes from words of praise for the disciples. Returning from a premature mission to announce doomsday throughout the land, the disciples were elated over some incidental success at faith healing: "Lord, even the demons are subject to us in your name!" Did Jesus find the healing of the sick good cause for such joy? No, it was not the healing of the sick but the promise of reward for which the disciples should be happy: "Nevertheless do not rejoice in this, that the spirits are subject to you; but rejoice that your names are written in heaven."[29]

The parables for which Jesus is so famous likewise present the picture of reward and punishment. With few exceptions, the parables carry no specific moral lessons. Rather, they are designed to point up the two alternatives: hell and the kingdom of God. In one the master beats a disobedient servant.[30] In another sinners are barred from a house wherein "all the prophets" dwell.[31] Still another compares the final judgment to the work of fishermen who, after drawing in their net, keep the good fish and throw away the bad.[32] Perhaps the most vivid of all the parables tells the story of the enemy (Satan) who sows weeds among the farmer's wheat. The farmer tells his servants to let the weeds grow with the wheat until the harvest, at which time they will be burned, while the wheat will be gathered into the barn. "Just as the weeds are

27. Matt. 6:14–15. 28. Matt. 8:11–12.
29. Luke 10:17–20. 30. Luke 12:47.
31. Luke 13:24–30. 32. Matt. 13:47–49.

gathered and burned with fire, so will it be at the close of the age. The Son of man will . . . gather . . . all evildoers, and throw them into the furnace of fire; there men will weep and gnash their teeth."[33]

Over and over as he roamed the countryside, Jesus preached his ethic of personal salvation. To him it was repent or perish. These are the very words Jesus used when he said (referring to some people who had been slain), "unless you repent you will all likewise perish."[34]

It all adds up to an ethic of fear—a fire and brimstone ethic. Its cardinal principle can be stated in two words: "Save yourself." If Jesus taught people to be good, he taught them to do so for selfish reasons, for the sake of heavenly reward. If he taught them not to sin, the teaching stressed the selfish consideration of eternal fire. In its emphasis on personal salvation, the ethic of Jesus is selfish from beginning to end. Even though no other faults could be found, this alone would qualify it as demonism in one of its worst forms.

SHEEP AND GOATS. The ethic of personal salvation is only the beginning of Jesus' flirtation with the demonic, however. Far worse than his advice to others is his own attitude toward humanity. Jesus was concerned about humanity but only a narrow segment of it. In his judgment most humans were fit to be burned alive and deserved what was in store for them. This outlook is brought out rather clearly in Jesus' description of the final judgment. He tells how the Son of man, attended by angels, will gather everyone before him to be judged. Next, "as a shepherd separates the sheep from the goats," the messiah will place the "sheep" on his right and the "goats" on his left. "Then the King will say to those at his right hand, 'Come, O blessed of my Father, inherit the kingdom prepared for you . . .' Then he will say to those at his left hand, 'Depart from me, you cursed, into the eternal fire prepared for the devil and his angels;' . . . And they will go away into eternal punishment, but the righteous into eternal life."[35]

The very idea of burning people alive in endless torture is in itself far removed from the humanistic point of view. But what

33. Matt. 13:24–30, 36–43. 34. Luke 13:3.
35. Matt. 25:31–46.

156

makes Jesus' attitude really appalling is that *Jesus himself planned to throw the "goats" into the fire.* For Jesus believed himself to be the messiah, or Son of man. Thus, at the synagogue in Nazareth, he publicly identified himself as the suffering servant of Isaiah,[36] whom he seems to have identified with the messiah. One man who wished to join his following was warned that, whereas foxes and birds have holes and nests, "the Son of man has nowhere to lay his head."[37] And when, at Caesaré a Philippi, Peter referred to him as the Christ, Jesus tacitly acknowledged the title by telling the disciples to keep it a secret.[38] Similarly, when the disciples asked at the Mount of Olives, "what will be the sign of *your* coming and of the close of the age?" Jesus answered, "many will come in *my* name, saying, 'I am the Christ,'" but he cautioned that the real end and his own appearance on a cloud from heaven would be preceded by earthquakes and other cataclysmic events.[39] Taken before the high priest and asked if he was the messiah, Jesus replied, "I am; and you will see the Son of man sitting at the right hand of Power, and coming with the clouds of heaven."[40] Nor can we overlook the fact that Jesus made a special effort to enter Jerusalem on an ass, thereby fulfilling a supposed prophecy from the Old Testament. What this messianic consciousness means is that Jesus not only approved of what the Son of man was going to do but actually expected to supervise personally the assignment of men and women to the holocaust: "And then will *I* declare to them, '*I* never knew you; depart from *me*, you evildoers.'"[41] (Those unwilling to accept the evidence that Jesus saw himself as the messiah should nevertheless ask themselves: is it possible to disagree that Jesus approved of what was going to happen?)

And this is not all. Those to be burned were not just a small minority of misfits. On the contrary, Jesus intended to relegate most of humanity to the eternal fire. He warned that "many" would enter the wide gate leading to destruction but that only a "few" would enter the narrow gate leading to eternal life.[42] Again: "For many are called, but few are chosen."[43] Remember, Jesus was planning to do the choosing.

36. Luke 4:16–21.
37. Luke 9:58.
38. Mark 8:27–30.
39. Matt. 24:3–33.
40. Mark 14:61–62.
41. Matt. 7:23.
42. Matt. 7:13–14; cf. Luke 13:23–24.
43. Matt. 22:14.

It seems that worthy individuals—persons who deserved his concern—were scarce. Jesus' standards of eligibility for salvation were set at levels close to perfection: "You, therefore, must be perfect, as your heavenly Father is perfect."[44] Accordingly, Jesus advised the rich man who had lived by the Ten Commandments that he still was not qualified for the kingdom. "Again I tell you, it is easier for a camel to go through the eye of a needle than for a rich man to enter the kingdom of God."[45] Jesus also advised that not just murder but the most picayune offenses would doom a man: "But I say to you that every one who is angry with his brother shall be liable to judgment; whoever insults his brother shall be liable to the council, and whoever says, 'You fool!' shall be liable to the hell of fire."[46] Mere lustful thoughts, whether or not they led to adultery, would also condemn a man. Small wonder a wide gate would be needed for the goats!

ETHNIC SHEEP. The moral exclusivism of Jesus easily qualifies as demonism, as Tillich uses the term. Yet this is still only part of the story, for Jesus' moral demonism is compounded by ethnic demonism of equally severe proportions. The sheep, it seems, were not to be found among all nationalities and creeds but only among the Jews: "I was sent only to the lost sheep of the house of Israel."[47]

This ethnic demonism, like the moral, is well documented. Fairly early in his ministry Jesus sent out his disciples to deliver what he then anticipated would be a final warning that the Day of the Lord was at hand. Instructing the disciples, he made it clear that the warning was intended only for the Jews. "Go nowhere among the Gentiles, and enter no town of the Samaritans, but go rather to the lost sheep of the house of Israel."[48]

On another occasion Jesus was confronted by a desperately worried woman. Mark identifies the woman as the Greek of Syrophoenician lineage; Matthew describes her as a Canaanite. She fell at Jesus' feet and begged him to cure her sick daughter. Jesus refused. "Let the children [of Israel] first be fed, for it is not right to take the children's bread and throw it to the dogs." ("Dogs" was a term of disparagement in the eastern world; it is paired with

44. Matt. 5:48. 45. Matt. 19:24.
46. Matt. 5:21–22. 47. Matt. 15:24.
48. Matt. 10:5–6.

"swine" in the Sermon on the Mount's admonition about casting pearls.) Only when the woman pleaded with him, comparing herself to the dog that eats the children's crumbs, did Jesus yield.[49]

Jesus' antipathy towards the Gentiles should come as no surprise. He was a Jew, and a devout one. His respect for the temple and for the Passover is well known. Once, after helping a leper, Jesus charged him to go at once to the Temple and offer the sacrifice which Moses commanded.[50] He defended the Jewish religious laws, about which he said "not an iota, not a dot" would pass away till heaven and earth did likewise.[51] As a Jew, he also accepted the messianic belief in an apocalyptic end of the world being followed by a paradisiacal kingdom of God on earth. God's kingdom was for Jews only; hence, as the messiah, he could promise his twelve disciples that in the kingdom they could sit beside him on twelve thrones, judging the twelve tribes of Israel.[52]

LOYAL SHEEP. If exclusiveness and selfishness are demonism, still more can be said about Jesus' demonic inclinations. A group restricted to Jews who can meet exceptionally high standards of morality may be exclusive indeed, but Jesus demanded that yet a third standard be met by the "sheep." This was the standard of personal allegiance to Jesus, a standard which is at once both exclusive and selfish. At least as far as those with whom he had personal contact were concerned, Jesus demanded that they abandon their families, even their children, and join his crusade for salvation.

Two striking examples of Jesus' attitude appear in Luke (with a parallel account in Matthew). In one case, a man who wished to follow Jesus requested, "Lord, let me first go and bury my father." Jesus rudely rejected the request: "Leave the dead [those to be denied entry to the kingdom] to bury their own dead; but as for you, go and proclaim the kingdom of God." Another man who was willing to leave house and loved ones to follow Jesus had this request: "I will follow you, Lord; but let me first say farewell to those at my home." Jesus' incredibly inconsiderate reply was, "No

49. Mark 7:25–29.
50. Mark 1:44.
51. Matt. 5:18.
52. Matt. 19:28.

159

one who puts his hand to the plow and looks back is fit for the kingdom of God."[53]

The latter incident illustrates Jesus' willingness to disrupt families in order to augment his personal following and advance the cause of salvation. Here is more of the same philosophy:

And every one who has left houses or brothers or sisters or father or mother or children or lands, for my name's sake, will receive a hundredfold, and inherit eternal life.[54]

Do not think that I have come to bring peace on earth; I have not come to bring peace, but a sword. For I have come to set a man against his father, and a daughter against her mother, and a daughter-in-law against her mother-in-law; and a man's foes will be those of his own household.[55]

The remark about the sword is sometimes misconstrued by those who would have us believe that Jesus advocated spreading Christianity (a faith he never anticipated) by the sword. It is evident, though, that Jesus was really referring to the sword which cleaves families, dividing them into those who follow Jesus and those who do not. To Jesus, salvation was far more important than family, especially in view of the fact that doomsday was just around the corner and the family was about to be extinguished anyway. Consequently, he was willing to have parents abandon their children and to pit son against father for the sake of saving additional individuals.

By example as well as by word Jesus upheld the principle of salvation-before-family. When he returned to Nazareth to preach, his mother and brothers came and stood outside the synagogue. Evidently worried about Jesus' messianic behavior, they "sent to him and called him." Those in the crowd sitting about Jesus told him, "Your mother and your brothers are outside, asking for you." Jesus answered "Who are my mother and my brothers?" Then, looking about him, he said: "Here are my mother and my brothers! Whoever does the will of God is my brother, and sister, and mother."[56] To Jesus, the family which counted most was his family of personal followers.

In Jesus we see the portrait of a man who, convinced not only

53. Luke 9:59–62.   54. Matt. 19:29.
55. Matt. 10:34–36.   56. Mark 3:31–35.

160

that he was the messiah but that God's kingdom was "at hand," took what must have seemed to him to be a logical step. He blinded himself to any concern for individuals who, by failing to heed the call of the messiah, branded themselves unworthy. In the process he turned his back on his own family and urged his followers to do likewise. "For whoever is ashamed of me and of my words in this adulterous and sinful generation, of him will the Son of man also be ashamed, when he comes in the glory of his Father with the holy angels."[57]

TILLICH AND SCHWEITZER. The foregoing analysis strongly suggests that Tillich is unwilling to make the historical Jesus his basic symbol because he finds Jesus to be the epitome of demonism. This assessment is certainly one which will be difficult for any committed Christian to accept, however. Three objections in particular are likely to be raised, and they might as well be dealt with in advance.

One likely objection stems from the tendency of some Christians, especially liberals seeking to remake Jesus in their own images, to write off as redactions any statements by Jesus which do not conform to their own twentieth-century morality. We cannot at this point enter into a long digression on biblical exegesis to disprove any such contentions. Suffice it instead to point out two things. First, there is fairly general agreement among biblical scholars about Jesus' messianic-eschatological orientation and about the derivative nature of his ethic. For example, David Bradley writes, "The parables of Jesus and his other ethical teachings appear basically to be adjunct to his proclamation of the imminence of God's judgment."[58] Second, and even more pertinent, there is no evidence that Tillich agrees with those who would salvage Jesus' liberal image by assuming he never said the things he said. On the contrary, Tillich insists that Jesus' words "are not the truth which makes us free" and "should not be used as such by our scholars and preachers and religious teachers."[59]

A second possible objection is that Tillich sometimes indicates

57. Mark 8:38.
58. David G. Bradley, *A Guide to the World's Religions* (Englewood Cliffs: Prentice-Hall, 1963), p. 50.
59. *New Being*, p. 70.

161

that Jesus was devoid of all traces of demonism and was wholly united with the ground of his being. This objection collapses under the weight of Tillich's christological "norm," to be discussed shortly. For the moment, we need merely understand that the "norm" demands that biblical interpretations be based not on the historical Jesus but on the mythological Christ, as adapted by Tillich. What Tillich says about Jesus as the Christ, and about Jesus' refusal to do business with the devil (does Tillich believe in the devil?), has no bearing on what he thinks of the real Jesus.

A third objection might be that I have borrowed Tillich's rude habit of reading one's own views into someone else's writing. There is certainly no denying that what has been said closely coincides with my own estimation of Jesus, though I find the term "demonic" a bit silly. Nevertheless, there is ample reason to believe that Tillich holds to the demonic interpretation. The concept of demonism is quite precise and unquestionably applies to exclusive interests such as those which have been attributed to Jesus, and nobody is better equipped to recognize a situation to which his own concept applies than Tillich. At the same time, Tillich has absolutely no commitment to supernaturalism or to Christian tradition, taken literally, such as would lead him to view Jesus through rose-colored glasses. Indeed, he pointedly asserts that we are "liberated from the authority of everything finite [limited] in him" and from the need to adopt "any legalistic understanding of his ethics."[60] Tillich specifically mentions Jesus' "special traditions" and "his rather conditioned world view" as aspects of his finitude.[61] Also: "Error is evident in his ancient conception of the universe, *his judgments about men,* his interpretation of the historical moment, his eschatological imagination."[62] Therefore: "When in our time Jesus . . . was portrayed as . . . a social benefactor, or as a moral example, or as a religious teacher, or as a mass leader—He ceased to be the one in whom we can believe, for He . . . was no longer the Jesus who is the Christ."[63]

Going beyond these specific remarks about Jesus, Tillich acknowledges the influence of two other enlightened observers, Schweitzer and Bultmann: "I owe my historical insights into the

60. *ST–1*, p. 134.   61. *ST–1*, p. 134.
62. *ST–2*, p. 131 (my italics).   63. *New Being*, p. 99.

New Testament principally to Schweitzer's *The Quest of the Historical Jesus* and Bultmann's *The Synoptic Tradition*."[64] These two scholars do not mince words about Jesus' eschatological orientation. Schweitzer in particular offers a damning appraisal of Jesus:

There is nothing more negative than the result of the critical study of the life of Jesus. . . . [Jesus'] image has not been destroyed from without, it has fallen to pieces, cleft and disintegrated by the concrete historical problems which came to the surface one after another, and . . . refused to be planed down to fit the design on which the Jesus of the theology of the last hundred and thirty years had been constructed . . . . [The Jesus of future theology] will not be a Jesus Christ to whom the religion of the present can ascribe, according to its long-cherished custom, its own thoughts and ideas, as it did with the Jesus of its own making. *Nor will He be a figure which can be made by a popular historical treatment so sympathetic and universally intelligible to the multitude.* . . . He passes by our time and returns to His own. What surprised and dismayed the theology of the last forty years was that, despite all forced and arbitrary interpretations, it could not keep Him in our time, but had to let Him go. . . . we must be prepared to find that the historical knowledge of the personality and life of Jesus will not be a help, but perhaps even an offence to religion.[65]

Tillich acknowledges that Schweitzer's constructive beginning has required corrections. Presumably he is alluding to such things as the supposed predestinationist element in Jesus' thought, Schweitzer's failure to place the blame for Jesus' execution on the Romans, and his unwillingness to use Luke as a source. But when Tillich credits much of his insight about Jesus to Schweitzer, can we fairly assume that he is in basic disagreement with the highly negative summation quoted above?

Jesus as the Christ

Tillich's aversion to demonism provides half the explanation for his refusal to adopt the historical Jesus as his central symbol. The other consideration involves the utility of the Christ concept, treated as a symbol. This brings us to what is, in terms of understanding Tillich, his most fundamental assertion. The assertion provides the rationale for his calling himself and his theology

64. *Boundary*, p. 49.
65. Albert Schweitzer, *The Quest of the Historical Jesus*, trans. W. Montgomery (New York: Macmillan, 1966), pp. 398–401.

Christian. At the same time, it is the essence of his Christology and perhaps the weightiest single piece of evidence that Tillich's God is man. The assertion: "The material norm of systematic theology . . . is the 'New Being in Jesus as the Christ.' "[66]

"AS THE CHRIST." The norm is offered as a criterion for interpreting the Bible and all other theological sources. As presented, however, it is far too vague for such use. Endless confusion has resulted among Tillich's colleagues. J. H. Thomas is typical. "What does it mean to say that 'the New Being in Jesus as the Christ' is the norm of our theology? We can understand that Christology is a central doctrine, a doctrine indeed to which all other elements of Christian doctrine must by definition be related. But even so this does not make it the norm."[67]

What Thomas should have said is that before it can be used as a norm, "Jesus as the Christ" must be interpreted. Fortunately, interpretation is not difficult once a person recognizes that Tillich not only rejects the supernatural but has no great enthusiasm for Jesus as an individual. "As the Christ" is the phrase on which to focus. We have seen that Tillich does not believe the doctrinal assertions that Jesus was the messiah, the Son of God, Savior, God incarnate, or otherwise divine. This could lead to the misunderstanding that some personal aspect of the historical Jesus, perhaps his ethic, is to be emphasized. Tillich warns us against this by stressing the Christ aspect of Jesus. He wants us to know that his norm is drawn not from the real Jesus but from the supernatural Jesus of theological fiction.

FULLY GOD AND FULLY MAN. What is there about theology's divine Christ that might become normative? Ever since the Council of Chalcedon (A.D. 431), Christian theology has held that Jesus was fully God and fully man—100 percent divine and 100 percent human. That makes him a 200 percent personality as it were. Tillich, of course, thinks this is absurd. His forte may or may not be arithmetic, but he no more believes that one plus one equals one than he believes the "logical nonsense" of the Trinity that three times one equals one.[68] Yet he intends to make the most of it. How

66. ST–1, p. 50.
67. J. Heywood Thomas, *Paul Tillich: An Appraisal* (Philadelphia: Westminster, 1963), p. 29.
68. ST–1, p. 56.

164

can he accept the proposition that the Christ was completely God yet completely human? *The Christ can be fully God yet fully man only if God is man!* For Tillich, God and man are the same. Their identity is symbolized by the theological Christ. The Christ can therefore serve as the norm by which the Bible, tradition, theologians, and other sources are to be interpreted (i.e., misinterpreted). Tillich is going to deliberately distort all source material into agreement with the proposition that God is man.

This interpretation of Jesus as the Christ is subtly propounded in Tillich's explorations of the work of the Councils of Nicaea (A.D. 325) and Chalcedon. Everything is carefully phrased so that the most naive readers will think Tillich literally accepts the decisions of the councils and therefore affirms the divinity of Jesus. But for those who can hear there is a hidden message. Arian teaching had made Jesus into what Tillich calls a "half-god" by contending that the Son had a beginning. The Niceans rejected the Arian position in favor of a declaration that in Jesus the eternal Logos, identified with God, became flesh. Tillich approves, averring that "the decision of Nicaea saved Christianity from a relapse to a cult of half-gods."[69] Some would take this to mean that Tillich accepts the Christ as a supernatural personage, the incarnation of God. What it really means, however, is that Tillich dislikes a doctrine saying one-half plus one-half equals one, because the arithmetically logical Arian formulation removes the necessity of equating God with man to purify the arithmetic.

Nicaea spurred the monophysitic controversy, monophysitism holding that Jesus had only one nature—divine—and not two. Chalcedon endorsed the contrary view that the Christ had two natures. Again, Tillich approves. "The church was right . . . in resisting the monophysitic distortion of the picture of Jesus as the Christ."[70] The Chalcedon decision "saved Christianity from a complete elimination of the picture of Jesus as the Christ," although it failed "to give a constructive interpretation" to the two nature formula.[71] Theology has never adequately solved the problem of "how to think the unity of a completely human with a completely divine nature."[72] The problem has been failure to distinguish between the

69. *ST–2*, p. 144. 70. *ST–2*, pp. 127–28.
71. *ST–2*, p. 141. 72. *ST–2*, p. 142.

concept of two natures and its substance. Theology "must be free from a confusion of its conceptual form with its substance, and it must be free to express this substance with every tool which proves to be more adequate than those given by the ecclesiastical tradition."[73] Interpreting, the form of the doctrine of the two natures must be kept but its substance must be changed: God must be changed from supernatural substance to human substance. Instead of two *separate* natures, the Christ must have two *identical* natures. Tillich's name for this transformation is "eternal God-man-unity."[74]

GOD INCARNATE. In addition to having been fully God and fully man the theological Christ is supposed to have been God (or the Logos) incarnate—God in the flesh. Tillich also regards this as nonsense: "the assertion that 'God has become man' is not a paradoxical but a nonsensical statement."[75] Once more, however, he is willing and even anxious to live with it, given the right to define God. He defines God as humanity and conceptualizes it as a concern. In parallel, he correlates the Logos with the "law of love": love God (and love your neighbor). Humanity, or the principle of love for humanity, can now be "incarnated" in any individual who becomes ultimately concerned about humanity. "The Incarnation of the Logos is not metamorphosis but his total manifestation in a personal life."[76] ("His" should be translated "its," and its antecedent, "the Logos," should be understood as referring to the law of love.) This solution to the incarnation retains the concept but, Tillich warns us, "removes the pagan connotations and rejects its supranaturalistic interpretation."[77]

Underscoring his desupernaturalization of the incarnation and the Christ, Tillich calls for a "low Christology." He defines a "high Christology" as one which emphasizes the divinity of the Christ and observes that "however high the divine predicates may be which are heaped on the Christ, the result is a Christology of low value, because it removes the paradox for the sake of a supranatural miracle." A Christ with cosmological or metaphysical over-

73. *ST–2*, p. 142.
75. *ST–2*, p. 94.
77. *ST–2*, p. 149.

74. *ST–2*, p. 148.
76. *ST–2*, p. 149.

tones is not for Tillich. To be acceptable, a Christology must stress the humanity of Jesus. It must find God in the Christ by finding man. It must interpret Jesus as the symbol for the unity within an individual of the universal and the concrete—for the incarnation of infinite humanity in finite man. This is what Tillich means in saying that a low Christology "actually is the truly high Christology."[78]

THE CHRIST AND METAPHYSICS. As this juncture it is appropriate to entertain a new argument giving further support to the conclusion that Tillich's God is not pantheistic, quasi-pantheistic, or otherwise metaphysical. This argument supplements the material in Chapter 1 but could not be presented there because crucial background points, now covered, were yet to be developed. These points deal with (1) ultimate concern, (2) demonism, and (3) Tillich's use of the Christ as his "norm" and as the basis for his analogical doctrine of incarnation. Taken together, the three concepts invalidate a certain metaphysical interpretation which seems to be ingratiating itself with Tillichian scholars.

Unlike some of the more careless interpretations of Tillich, the one in question shows an awareness of the fact that Tillich identifies God as one's ultimate concern. This view also recognizes and attempts to resolve the superficial inconsistency in Tillich's treatment of ultimate concern—his sometimes making ultimate concerns plural, allowing them to be practically anything (e.g., the nation or "the Christian message"), and other times speaking of God in the singular, implying that there is only one ultimate concern. Without actually being aware that Tillich is patterning ultimate concern after the two-sided Christ, analogically incarnating the "divine" (general) in the "human" (particular), the metaphysical interpreters manage to grasp the right type of solution: one general concern embodied in the many diverse concerns different people regard as ultimate. The assumption is that Tillich sees a metaphysical link between being-itself, conceived of as an ineffable supernatural essence, and the finite things men regard as their ultimate concerns. Because being-itself participates in (or is participated in by) everything that is real, any item of concern is *basically* being-itself.

78. ST–2, pp. 146–47.

This explanation would be logically adequate, though still in conflict with Tillich's many denials of supernaturalism and of any "second reality behind empirical reality," if it didn't gloss over a vital fact. That fact is that Tillich regards some ultimate concerns as demonic, or idolatrous. We have seen that Tillich makes a definite distinction between "true" and "false" ultimacy, between concerns "transparent" and those "opaque" to the divine. Now if every ultimate concern embodies the divine, which is what the metaphysical argument contends, how can there be such a thing as demonic concerns? How do we reconcile the idea that everything mirrors being-itself with the idea that idolatrous ultimate concerns don't? And, by the way, if everything is ultimately ultimate, what happens to Tillich's distinction between ultimate concerns—those generating "infinite passion"—and ordinary nonultimate ones? Clearly, the metaphysical argument proves too much: it proves Tillich has no doctrine of demonism, and maybe not even a doctrine of ultimate concern.

Once more we reach the conclusion that being-itself is not to be found lurking in the shadows of supernaturalism. It is to be found rather in a nonsupernatural ultimate, one reflected in some ultimate concerns but not others. This ultimate, moreover, must be one which justifies Tillich's insisting that the Chalcedon decision was correct in affirming that the Christ was fully God and fully man, even though Tillich knows this doctrine to be mythological in content. What is myth cannot be correct in any literal sense, so its "correctness" must be understood analogically or symbolically. Fully God and fully man is nonsensical unless interpreted as symbolizing the *full* (not partial) identity of God and man.

THE NEW BEING

Having covered the point that the mythological Jesus—Jesus as the Christ—is Tillich's christological symbol, we are ready to ask what the symbol represents. In Tillich's system, Jesus as the Christ symbolizes "the New Being." New Being relates to individuals and describes a state wherein a particular individual embraces the Tillichian God as his God. This state has close parallels in numerous Christian "symbols."

New Being and Humanism

Tillich's definition of New Being, like the rest of his definitions, is impossible to understand without knowledge of what he means by God. No matter how it is described, and Tillich offers many descriptions, it is recognizable as a state wherein the individual "gets religion." That is, a person becomes aware that he believes in and wants to serve the one true God. The only question is: who or what is that God? Since, for Tillich, the one true God is man, New Being can be defined as a state of humanism, that is, as holding an ultimate concern transparent to humanity. Were he willing to lay aside equivocation, Tillich could have no objection to this definition, for it corresponds almost exactly to his description of humanism. This description bears repeating: "For humanism the divine is manifest in the human; the ultimate concern of man is man."[79]

CHARACTERISTICS OF NEW BEING. Going beyond what I hope is a clear but simple definition of New Being, what are its detailed characteristics? The first thing that should be mentioned is where the term originates. It comes from 2 Corinthians 5:17. Tillich prefers his own translation: "If anyone is in union with Christ he is a new being; the old state of things has passed away; there is a new state of things."[80] From this translation we gather that New Being is a setting aside of old beliefs and attitudes and their replacement with something new. The new state of things involves "union" with the Christ. Since this union is obviously figurative, Tillich is implying that persons with New Being resemble the Christ in certain respects. These respects, and there are many, are analyzed in the following section of this chapter, dealing with the christological symbolism. By way of anticipation, however, it can be mentioned here that a very basic respect is the presence of God (appropriately defined) in a human being.

Aside from being a new state of things wherein humanity, as an ultimate concern, is embodied in man, the most significant characteristic of New Being is that it is dialectical. New Being is a dialectical synthesis, a double synthesis in fact. Two distinct dialectics culminate in New Being. One might be called the theological dia-

---

79. *Dynamics*, p. 63.   80. *New Being*, p. 15.

lectic, because it is based on religious doctrines concerning the Christ's separation from and return to God. The theological dialectic is a life, the dialectical life of Yes-No-Yes. This is an idealized human life which follows the Christ pattern of separation and reunion, that is, separation from and reunion with God. Life has three stages in relation to God: belief (union), unbelief (separation), and new belief (reunion). New belief is a blend of belief and unbelief, Yes and No; it is a synthesis. New Being is belief in a nonsupernatural God.

The second dialectic of which New Being is the synthesis can be termed philosophical: it features the Christ's philosophical correlates, essence and existence. As implied, the Christ has two correlates, and these represent two opposing tendencies united in the Christ's person. By analogy: "New Being is essential being under the conditions of existence, conquering the gap between essence and existence."[81] Essence, it will be recalled, describes both thesis and synthesis in the essence-existence-essence dialectic. It is union with God, either potential union, as embodied in the concept of humanity and symbolized by theism, or actual union—man united with mankind. Existence is the state of estrangement in which men, because others (and sometimes they themselves) reject mankind, must exist. Essence under the conditions of existence means that, with New Being, a person accepts mankind (essence) even though mankind does not reciprocate (existence). Two things are new about New Being in the philosophical sense: "it is new in contrast to the merely potential character of essential being; and it is new over against the estranged character of existential being."[82] Again note the distinction between potential essence and the realized essence of New Being.

The philosophical dialectic provides the basis for another characteristic of New Being. This one recalls Tillich's philosophizing about the fragmentary overcoming of estrangement. New Being is what fragmentarily overcomes estrangement, fragmentarily because only fragments of mankind—specific individuals—turn to mankind as their God. Estrangement can be fully overcome only if everyone accepts mankind as God, something Tillich does not expect to hap-

81. ST–2, pp. 118–19.   82. ST–2, p. 119.

pen. Perfect reunion must be a two-way street, but humanity in the aggregate does not return the love of individual men.

Two other facets of New Being can be noted briefly at this point. First, New Being is the state of self-transcendence discussed in Chapter 3 in connection with the concept of a self-transcending God. Man transcends his existential self when he accepts man as his God. And because man is God, God transcends "his" estranged self at the same time. Second, and here we anticipate Chapter 5, entry of the Spirit into the person who attains New Being is what brings New Being about. "Inasmuch as Jesus as the Christ is a creation of the divine Spirit, according to Synoptic theology, so is he who participates in the Christ [has New Being] made into a new creature by the Spirit."[83] The precise identity of the Spirit will be clarified shortly, but it obviously isn't a supernatural entity.

ANTI-HUMANISM: A SMOKESCREEN. There seems to be one flaw in the proposition that Jesus as the Christ symbolizes humanism: Tillich sometimes expresses hostility toward attitudes he identifies with humanism. Thus he asserts in one place that "a humanistic philosophy which tries to hide the ambiguities in the idea of humanism must be rejected."[84] In another passage he deplores the mistaking of cultural creativity for divine creativity, arguing that man "attributes infinite significance to his finite cultural creations, making idols of them, elevating them into matters of ultimate concern."[85] Similarly, he contends that "if we take socialism, humanism, and nationalism . . . as ultimate concerns . . . then we can only answer: If they are *really* ultimate, they become demonized; if, on the other hand, they are kept as manifestations of the ultimate and remain 'transparent,' then they are proper or acceptable, ethically speaking."[86]

Remarks like these may seem to express a lack of enthusiasm for humanism, but they actually constitute a smokescreen, laid down by Tillich to hide his own humanism from the larger audience. As Tillich's reference to "the ambiguities in the idea of humanism" indicates, humanism can be used in more than one sense. (Is humanism in art the same as ethical humanism?) Only in some meanings does Tillich find humanistic attitudes deficient. The first two

83. *ST–2*, p. 119. 84. *ST–3*, p. 85.
85. *ST–2*, p. 51. 86. *Dialogue*, p. 29.

criticisms above, the second of which helps explain the first, involve what might be termed cultural humanism. The philosophy being attacked is one that confuses man's artistic, literary, and other cultural creations with man himself. The third criticism is directed toward the elevation of ethical humanism to the status of an ideology. When humanism *as an ideology* is one's ultimate concern, it goes between socialism and nationalism in the demonic sandwich. When an ideology is worshiped, it becomes an idol and is idolatrous; but when it is a transparent window through which a deeper concern for man can be seen, then it is man who is revered and the ultimate concern becomes "proper."

The distinction between perverted humanism and genuine humanism is brought out rather clearly in *Dynamics of Faith*. There Tillich classifies different types of faith. He identifies three types of "ontological faith" and three types of "moral faith." One form of ontological faith is "romantic-conservative" humanism, which romantically sees the ultimate in existing nations, cultures, social systems, and the like. Tillich opposes this and other types of ontological faith because they accept things as they are rather than looking toward what ought to be. Under moral faith, a particular variety is identified as "progressive-utopian" humanism. It characterizes, among other people, the Enlightenment leaders, who "fought for freedom from sacramentally consecrated bondage and for justice for every human being."[87] In short, humanism can be good or bad. The only variety which Tillich espouses is the kind wherein "the ultimate concern of man is man."

This brings us back to Tillich's Christ symbolism. In one of his mock attacks (such as it is) on humanism, Tillich appears actually to contrast his Christ symbol with a humanistic symbol, damning the latter with faint praise. Declares Tillich, "I myself believe that the humanistic ideal is inferior to the Christ concept, but their concern is genuine."[88] It sounds as though Tillich prefers his own concept of Christianity to humanism, implying that they are different. But closer inspection of his words shows he is merely indicating a preference for one *symbol* over another. Jesus as the Christ is preferred to man ("the humanistic ideal") as a symbol of concern for

87. *Dynamics*, p. 69.   88. *Dialogue*, p. 22.

humanity. As an avowed apologist for Christianity, Tillich must say that the "Christ concept" is better, but he does this with the secret reservation that humanism is what the Christ symbolizes.

Parallel Symbolism

New Being is a general heading under which can be subsumed many other symbols, referring now to symbols in the narrow sense of expurgated concepts and doctrines. There are a dozen such symbols, not counting some relatively obscure ones such as regeneration and ecstasy. The first six—revelation, salvation, resurrection, grace, atonement, and last judgment—all mean about the same thing. They relate to the onset of New Being and emphasize slightly different facets of this event. The other six describe the state of New Being, either in its personal or its collective aspect. These are the symbols of incarnation, providence, faith, religion, the cross, and the Church. In line with the point that analogy is what defines a Tillichian symbol, note that each of the new meanings is analogous to the old. And, regarding the further point that theological symbols are paired with philosophical correlates in Tillich's thought, note also that each symbol has its correlate.

REVELATION. We have already observed that revelation is the process of becoming aware, or making a value judgment, that God is man. Tillich refers to it as the manifestation of our ultimate concern (humanity) and as the event wherein the mind is grasped by the ground of being. Just as in traditional revelation God takes possession of the human mind, so in Tillichian revelation does humanity "possess" the mind as a concern. God is revealed to a person. This event correlates philosophically with the participation of the human *logos* in the universal Logos, that is, with the manifestation of reason (the Logos) in the human mind. By either analogy, the union of the ultimate with the human marks the onset of New Being.

SALVATION. "The identity of revelation and salvation"[89] is freely acknowledged by Tillich, but he nevertheless wishes to give salvation its own emphasis. In a way salvation is the product of revelation, although the two occur simultaneously. In traditional the-

---

89. *ST–1*, p. 146.

ology salvation means being saved from sin and damnation, from the enslaving power of the devil and his demons. At the same time, according to Tillich, salvation means healing. By combining the idea of being saved with the idea of being healed, Tillich is able to treat salvation as both the saving of enslaved minds (enslaved by demonism) and the healing of estrangement. "Salvation happens whenever the enslaving power is conquered, whenever the wall is broken through, whenever the sickness is healed."[90] Only God can do this, through "revelation." When it happens, New Being materializes.

RESURRECTION. The resurrection of Jesus, in Christian theology, refers to Jesus rising from death into new life. Tillich sees existence and estrangement as the analogues of death. New Being is the analogue of new life. Resurrection, then, is the process of rising from existential estrangement into New Being. Tillich even goes a half step beyond analogy by interpreting Jesus' life and his death on the cross as subjection to "existential estrangement." His resurrection was thus victory over estrangement. Hence, by analogy, any person who enters New Being is resurrected from existence and enters a new life of essential unity with mankind.

GRACE. Traditionally, grace means God's mercy and forgiveness; it is a forgiving act of God by which a person is saved. Just as resurrection overcomes death, grace overcomes sin. Now in Tillich's thought, sin is the theological correlate of estrangement: it is demonism, or the state of being split apart from one's fellow man. Grace is what overcomes demonic sinfulness and brings harmony with mankind. "Grace is the *re*union of life with life, the *re*conciliation of the self with itself. Grace is the acceptance of that which is rejected."[91] This means that in grace love unites one human life with all others; man is reconciled with man. Grace is accepting God after God has been rejected—accepting humanity after the supernatural God has been rejected. It is the beginning of New Being.

ATONEMENT. Jesus atoned for the sins of man, or the sin of Adam if one prefers, by dying on the cross. It makes little difference whether atonement is viewed as substitution, sacrifice, ransom, or quasi-military conquest of the devil and his legions. Whatever the

<hr>

90. *Eternal Now*, p. 115.　　　　91. *Foundations*, p. 156.

mechanism, man is removed from the grip of sin. In Tillich's analogy, sin is estrangement. What overcomes sin, freeing man from the grip of estrangement, is the act of entering into New Being. "The doctrine of atonement is the description of the effect of the New Being in Jesus as the Christ on those who are grasped by it in their state of estrangement."[92] The analogy is carried a little farther by the fact that New Being remains subject to the conditions of existence, just as in his atoning act the Christ subjected himself to the conditions of existence.

LAST JUDGMENT. The last judgment, in Christian theology, is an event associated with the second coming of Christ and the general resurrection of the dead. The Christ arrives on a cloud from heaven and separates the sheep from the goats. Sometimes it is God who will do the judging; but this makes little difference, since God is in Christ. Separation of what is good from what is bad is the distinctive characteristic. The Tillichian last judgment is similar. God, as an ultimate concern for humanity, is incarnated in him who judges. The false concerns and the demonic are put aside, and man's true concern—humanity—is accepted. "This is what 'last judgment' means—to separate in us, as in everything, what has true and final being from what is merely transitory and empty of true being."[93] When this happens and what has true being is judged to be God, the individual who judges moves from existence to essence.

INCARNATION. Christianity has long taught that, in Jesus, God became flesh. In early Logos Christology it was the Logos that was embodied in Jesus. Either way, the doctrine has been called the "incarnation." Tillich purges it by eliminating the notion of metamorphosis, which he calls an "absurdity" (that word again). Metamorphosis is replaced with an inverted adoptionist view wherein man adopts a preliminary concern transparent to God and the Logos. Transparency is the incarnation side of things. Naturally, the God and Logos thus incarnated are also redefined: God is humanity, as an ultimate concern, and Logos can be interpreted either as reason (a "rational" concern) or as the "law of love" for humanity. Otherwise, incarnation remains God's—or the Logos's—"manifestation in a personal life."[94] Concern or love for humanity

92. *ST–2*, p. 170.   93. *Eternal Now*, p. 35.
94. *ST–2*, p. 149.

175

is, indirectly, embodied in a personal life. Incarnation, thus defined, is identical with New Being.

PROVIDENCE. The conventional meaning of "providence" is God's loving care and intervention in human affairs; its philosophical counterpart is courage. Loosely speaking, providence is that which enables us to face life and even death courageously. In Tillich's thought as in real Christianity, God gives us this ability. Tillich just happens to be speaking of a different God when he says of providence: "It means the courage to accept life in the power of that which is more than life. Paul calls it the love of God."[95] He who has New Being has the courage of providence.

FAITH. We have already talked about faith. In Tillich's vocabulary it means a state of being ultimately concerned. Alternatively, it means being grasped by an ultimate concern, by a power which is greater than we are, by the power of being, or by God. In what Tillich calls true faith (contrasted with demonic faith) the ultimate concern is humanity. The analogy to traditional faith is apparent. Strictly speaking faith means believing what you are supposed to believe about religious matters, but in effect it means being concerned about, or resting in the grip of, God. As for the correlate, being grasped by God is analogous to the appearance of the universal Logos in the human *logos*.

RELIGION. Like incarnation, providence, and faith, Tillich's version of religion is identical with New Being. Since religion and faith are employed interchangeably in normal usage ("the Christian religion," "the Christian faith"), Tillich makes religion a precise synonym for faith. He says that "religion is being ultimately concerned about that which is and should be our ultimate concern."[96] Similarly, "religion is ultimate concern; it is the state of being grasped by something unconditional, holy, absolute."[97] Philosophically speaking, it is courage, essence, and self-realization.

THE CROSS. One can ordinarily interpret the symbol of the cross in several ways. It can symbolize the Christian Church, Jesus, or the atonement. But for Tillich it stresses the idea that Jesus' unity with God (incarnation) was so perfect that he endured the worst of fates without separating from God. The cross means that "he who

95. *New Being*, pp. 57–58. 96. *Culture*, p. 40.
97. *Protestant*, p. 59.

is the Christ subjects himself to the ultimate negativities of existence and that they are not able to separate him from his unity with God."[98] In terms of symbolism, therefore, the cross supports the idea that when a person experiences New Being his attachment to humanity is so firm that it is maintained despite his continued subjection to the divisive influences which characterize the estranged conditions of human existence. As the interpretation suggests, estrangement and existence are the philosophical correlates of the cross.

THE CHURCH. Having redefined faith, religion, and the cross in his own peculiar manner, Tillich is not going to retain the orthodox meaning of "the Church." Therefore, whereas the Church normally refers to the community of individuals who are faithful to the Christian God, Tillich converts it into a symbol for "the Community of the New Being."[99] It is not organized religion but "a group of people who express a new reality by which they have been grasped."[100] As one of this group, Tillich can maintain that "a church which raises itself in its message and its devotion to the God above the God of theism" is what he believes in.[101] Regarding correlation, a lucid explanation is difficult prior to our considering, in Chapter 5, Tillich's philosophy of history. Briefly, however, as the dominant group in Christian history the Church correlates with the Germanic people and the working class, the "meaning bearing" groups in the dialectical histories of Hegel and Marx.

CHRISTOLOGICAL DIALECTICS

Since Jesus as the Christ is a symbol for New Being, there must be an analogy between the two. Actually there are many. To find them we must explore in somewhat greater detail the two dialectics outlined in connection with New Being. This will entail previewing certain material developed in the next chapter for, as Tillich has explained, the different parts of his system are intricately related. Reviewing, the two dialectics are (1) the theological dialectic (belief-unbelief-new belief) and (2) the philosophical dialectic (essence-existence-essence). The thesis, the antithesis, and the syn-

98. ST–2, p. 158.
100. Culture, p. 212.
99. Culture, p. 212.
101. Courage, p. 188.

thesis of each dialectic all relate to different characteristics of the Christ.

The Theological Dialectic

Broadly speaking, the belief-unbelief-new belief (or Yes-No-Yes) sequence mirrors the Johannine story of the Logos-Son's movement from heaven to earth and back to heaven: the Son is initially united with God, later separated for a sojourn on earth, and finally reunited with God. But in a narrower sense, which Tillich finds more amenable to symbolism, life's three stages correspond to three milestones in the Christ's life on earth: incarnation (God united with man), crucifixion (God separated from man), and resurrection (God and man reunited). These milestones symbolize the three stages of the dialectical life of which New Being is the climactic third stage.

INCARNATION. Life's first stage, which is also one element of the eventual synthesis, witnesses man in union with God. Specifically, this is union with the God of theism, but abstractly it represents union with whatever is absolute. Tillich repeatedly indicates that Jesus as the Christ is the ideal symbol for New Being because the Christ was in perfect union with God. "The New Being is manifest in the Christ because in Him the separation never overcame the unity between Him and God, between Him and mankind, and between Him and Himself. . . . In Him we look at a human life that maintained the union in spite of everything that drove Him into separation."[102]

Observe in the above quotation how carefully Tillich's ideas are phrased for the benefit of the larger audience. The reference to "a human life" (the Christ was "fully man") makes it sound very much as if Tillich is talking about the historical Jesus. He seems to be saying that Jesus of Nazareth, who incidentally happened to be the Christ, is a perfect example of dedication to God coupled with selfless concern for mankind. No interpretation could be more erroneous. Tillich is talking about the theological Christ, not the historical Jesus. Jesus as the Christ was in perfect union with God because he *was* God. The Christ of theology was God incarnate

102. *New Being*, p. 22.

178

("fully God"). Furthermore, Tillich is interpreting the gospels in accordance with "the norm." The norm assumes that Jesus was fully God and fully man because God and man are the same. This makes it a matter of dogma that the Christ was in perfect union with mankind, hence the reference to unity "between Him and mankind." By exploiting ambiguity in the word "unity," Tillich equivocally suggests emotional unity between the Christ and mankind when the unity is really biological. The unity is that described by a normative picture, a mythological picture as it happens, and has nothing to do with the psychology of the historical Jesus.

The symbol, Jesus as the Christ, is a picture, a work of the imagination. For Tillich it has no more reality than Santa Claus, who could have served an equivalent purpose had Tillich elected to use pagan symbols for his "theology" of humanism. The element of unity, man with man, in the picture of what commends it to Tillich as an appropriate analogical symbol for the situation of any human being ultimately concerned about humanity.

Only by keeping the norm constantly in mind can we avoid the many traps Tillich has set for the unsuspecting members of his larger audience. When describing Jesus he conveys two false impressions which cloud his hidden message. The more superficial of the two is that he accepts Jesus as the Christ. Most people are not going to be misled on this score, so Tillich also tries to make it sound as though he admires Jesus as a moral leader passionately devoted to both God and man. But the careful reader will notice where Tillich hedges. For example:

In all its concrete details the biblical *picture* of Jesus *as the Christ* confirms his character as the bearer of the New Being or as the one in whom the conflict between the essential unity of God and man and man's existential estrangement is overcome. Point by point, not only in the Gospel records but also in the Epistles, this *picture* of Jesus *as the Christ* contradicts the marks of estrangement which we have elaborated in the analysis of man's existential predicament.[103]

How easy it is to interpret this as referring to a historical Jesus who, "point by point," proved his unfaltering devotion to God and man. Tillich has warned us, however, that each piece of biblical

103. *ST–2*, pp. 125–26 (my italics).

evidence must be interpreted "under the norm." In addition, twice in the quoted material he mentions that "the biblical picture"—which we know he regards as myth—is his point of reference. He also adds the qualifying phrase "as the Christ" in two places, which should certainly be enough to alert anyone who can recognize that Tillich is not a religious conservative.

It boils down to this: Jesus as the Christ symbolizes New Being's Yes to God because the mythological Christ was "one man in whom God was present without limit"[104]—physically present, that is. Perfect physical union of God and man becomes the analogue of perfect mental unity. The "without limit" part of the analogy compares the "fully God" aspect of the Christ with New Being's unlimited commitment to humanity. "The message of Jesus as the Christ is universal in embracing all mankind, all classes, groups, and social stratifications of mankind."[105]

CRUCIFIXION. Incarnation is the thesis in the Christ's life of separation and return; crucifixion is the antithesis. Correspondingly, whereas incarnation symbolizes the Yes to God which defines stage one of the ideal life, crucifixion symbolizes the No of stage two. Theology's Christ was a supernatural being—messiah, Son of God, God incarnate, savior—and as such a proxy for all religious supernaturalism. On the cross, man rejected and killed the supernatural. Something comparable happens whenever man says No to God: he rejects the supernatural, killing it among his thoughts and beliefs. And, because New Being, the synthesis, takes the No into itself, the crucifixion's symbolism extends to New Being. The symbolic analogy: man's physical crucifixion of the supernatural represents man's mental crucifixion of the supernatural.

Tillich has coined the phrase "accepting acceptance" to describe the process. The best known expression of the idea comes from *The Courage to Be*, where "acceptance" is used to describe "absolute faith" (New Being). "It is the accepting of the acceptance without somebody or something that accepts."[106] This declaration is preceded by an attack on the God of theism, a supernatural being who stands as an "invincible tyrant" who destroys man's individuality with his all-knowing mind and arbitrary law. Man

104. *New Being*, pp. 178–79.   105. *History*, p. 29.
106. *Courage*, p. 185.

rebels, rejecting the divine tyrant. That is, man *accepts* the fact that there is no supernatural God or realm. Does the God of theism retaliate, perchance by smiting man with a plague or withholding providential favors? No, God *accepts* man's acceptance that there is no God. "He" cannot do otherwise, for in reality there is no supernatural "somebody or something that accepts."

Tillich's meaning comes through more clearly in *The Shaking of the Foundations*. There he tells how men symbolically reject the supernatural when they reject the divine messiah. "Yet when the Divine is rejected, It takes the rejection upon itself. It *accepts* our crucifixion, our pushing away, the defence of ourselves against It. It accepts our refusal to accept, and thus conquers us."[107] These remarks are in the context of an assault on divine rule and divine law, reviewed in Chapter 1. Tillich is arguing that man loses his freedom, dignity, and humanity by submitting to supernatural authority. "*Whenever the Divine appears, It is a radical attack on everything that is good in man, and therefore men must repel It, must push It away, must crucify It.*"[108] Man must crucify the Christ to enter New Being. "To the Crucified alone we can say: 'Thou art the Christ.'"[109]

In various other books, Tillich reiterates the acceptance theme. One version is that man must have "the courage to accept the unacceptable"[110] in order to enjoy New Being. What is "unacceptable"—if only to a devout believer—is the premise that there is no Supreme Being, no divine providence, no supernatural salvation. In another instance Tillich, using his norm, interprets Jesus' acceptance of the "Christ" title offered by Peter as a stratagem for destroying Christly supernaturalism. "He accepts it under the one condition that he has to go to Jerusalem to suffer and to die," because he wants to slay the idea that there can be another God besides man.[111] In a similar vein, Tillich interprets that the temple tore its curtain when Jesus was crucified, to signify the destruction of religion. "When the curtain of the temple was torn in two, God judged religion and rejected temples."[112] That is, man, represented by those who rejected the divine messiah, judged religious super-

---

107. *Foundations*, p. 147 (my italics). 108. *Foundations*, p. 147 (my italics).
109. *Foundations*, p. 148. 110. *Morality*, p. 63.
111. *Culture*, p. 67. 112. *New Being*, pp. 177–78.

naturalism and rejected it. Tillich counsels: "Our final wisdom is to accept our foolishness and to look at the place in history in which wisdom itself appeared in the garb of utter foolishness, the Cross of the Christ."[113] By this he means that men who have believed in the supernatural should accept as foolish their old beliefs and view the crucifixion as a putting aside of supernaturalism, represented by the Christ. He is saying that Jesus as the Christ is a symbol for the negative element of New Being, rejection of the supernatural.

The same point is delivered, now more cautiously, in *Systematic Theology*. There Jesus as the Christ is termed the "final revelation." This means, explains Tillich, that it is the "criterion" for all revelation: it determines which value judgments as to what is god are true and which are demonic. Tillich insists that revelation can be final only "if it has the power of negating itself without losing itself."[114] Jesus as the Christ negates Jesus Christ. Yet the Christ is not lost; he is retained as a symbol for that which accepts the crucifixion of the supernatural—New Being.

Driving home his point, Tillich accents the Christ's "sacrifice of everything he could have gained for himself" from his unity with God.[115] As God incarnate, the Christ could literally have played God. He could have yielded to the "temptation to exploit his unity with God as a means of advantage for himself."[116] In this regard, the disciples "tried to induce him . . . to avoid the cross" and "tried to make him an object of idolatry."[117] Instead, the Christ surrendered himself and his divinity to the cross. "Only in view of the crucifixion can the Fourth Gospel have him say that 'he who believes in me does not believe in *me*' (John 12:44)."[118] Although members of the larger audience have occasionally gulped the bait by interpreting these words as endorsing some form of the doctrine of atonement, their actual meaning is that only that which symbolizes man's crucifixion of theism can symbolize New Being.

RESURRECTION. In the third stage of the life of Yes-No-Yes, man returns to God—a new God, humanity. Belief and unbelief are replaced by their synthesis, new belief (New Being). Stage three is symbolized by the resurrection. After the crucifixion, an act which

---

113. *Eternal Now*, p. 172.
114. *ST–1*, p. 133.
115. *ST–1*, p. 135. ·
116. *ST–1*, p. 136.
117. *ST–1*, p. 133.
118. *ST–1*, p. 136.

separated man from God, the Christ was raised from death. In the living Christ, God and man were again united; the movement of separation and return was complete. (If one prefers, the resurrection can be interpreted in terms of what happened shortly afterward: the Christ ascended on a cloud to heaven, there to rejoin God, at whose right hand he thereafter sat—and sits.) Two symbolic analogies stand out: (1) the analogy between the christological reunion and man's return to God and (2) the analogy between new life and new belief.

Unwilling to settle for just two resurrection analogies, Tillich has invented a third. This one relates a hypothetical spiritual reawakening in the disciples following the crucifixion to the spiritual reawakening experienced by individuals through New Being. The analogy comes from Tillich's interpretation of the resurrection. This interpretation, it must be stressed, is symbolic; it is not an attempt to describe what actually happened, as McKelway, Tavard, and Armbruster wrongly suggest.[119] As Tillich tells the story, the disciples accepted Jesus as the messiah, "him whose being was the New Being." Then he was crucified, and the disciples were filled with negativity and doubt: the messiah was not supposed to die. Perhaps Jesus was not really the messiah. Soon, however, in an "ecstatic" experience, the disciples became convinced that Jesus "is present wherever the New Being is present." (The amusing implication that the disciples might have read Tillich is one giveaway to the symbolism.) In other words, they reinterpreted their original belief symbolically. The thesis that Jesus was literally the messiah was followed by the antithesis that he wasn't which in turn gave way to the synthesis that he was but he wasn't, that is, that he was figuratively the messiah—Yes, No, Yes. In this interpretation, the Christ represents God and supernaturalism. Belief gives way to unbelief; unbelief leads to new belief; new belief combines belief and unbelief. Dialectically symbolized are the elements that must be combined to produce personal maturity.[120]

119. See Alexander J. McKelway, *The Systematic Theology of Paul Tillich: A Review and Analysis* (Richmond: John Knox Press, 1964), pp. 169–70; George H. Tavard, *Paul Tillich and the Christian Message* (New York: Scribner's, 1962), pp. 136–37; and Carl J. Armbruster, *The Vision of Paul Tillich* (New York: Sheed and Ward, 1967), pp. 199–200.

120. *ST–2*, pp. 156–57.

The Philosophical Dialectic

Moving on to the second of the two dialectics which culminate in New Being, we have the one built of essence and existence. These philosophical concepts are analogous to union and separation in relation to God. The dialectic moves from essence to existence to their synthesis, essence under the conditions of existence. There is a separation from and return to essence. Because Jesus as the Christ correlates with essence under the conditions of existence, which in turn describes New Being, the philosophical dialectic provides additional symbolic analogies relating the Christ to New Being.

ESSENCE. Essence, the philosophical thesis, is very similar in substance to the theological idea of perfect union with God. But, at least in Tillich's writing, essence accentuates the negative. Tillich speaks of it as resistance to estrangement. Essence is a state wherein the individual is not estranged from the divine. In Hegelian terms, it is where the divine, instead of being divided against itself, is in its essential state of self-integration. For Tillich the divine is man; so if the Christ can be shown to be free of attitudes tending to separate him from man, essence is indicated.

Estrangement and demonism, we have seen, are the respective philosophical and theological terms for an attitude of unconcern toward elements of the human race. They indicate a lack of universality in man's attitude toward himself. The ailments are severe when one's concern turns inward in a quest for power, wealth, or recognition; they are relatively mild when only a few people are treated as strangers; but severe or mild, they are incompatible with New Being. Jesus as the Christ symbolizes the complete absence of unconcern for even the lowest elements of humanity. Perfect unity with God, in short, is recast as non-unity with any god which is less than "fully God."

Tillich likes to use the temptation stories to illustrate the Christ's unwavering resistance to demonic estrangement. In the first of these Satan tempts Jesus in the wilderness. Jesus refuses to exploit his station for personal gain. In the second, when Peter challenges Jesus' decision to go to Jerusalem, Jesus rebukes him: "Get behind me, Satan!" He says this because Peter is unwittingly acting as the devil's intermediary in tempting Jesus to base his actions on personal considerations, thereby avoiding the threat that awaits him. (A reminder: unless Tillich believes in the devil, and he doesn't, he cannot be referring to the historical Jesus in discussing Jesus' resistance to demonism.) Just as the Christ refused to bend to selfishness, those who enter into New Being resist the temptation to put themselves ahead of others. The synthesis, New Being, includes the thesis.

Jesus as the Christ, interpreted under the norm, remains open to even the most rejected members of society. He mingles freely with sinners and prostitutes. And, on the cross, he "humiliates himself as a slave and experiences the death of a slave."[121] (In case one wonders how Tillich can use such an example when Jesus not once spoke out against the worst institution of his day, slavery, and even used slaves in parable with matter-of-fact acceptance, the answer again is that Tillich is talking about the normative Christ and not the historical Jesus.) By the same token, no element of society is regarded as alien when one is in essential union with mankind.

EXISTENCE. Estrangement, which Tillich presents as the basic condition of human existence, is the antithesis of essence. The term implies separation. The separation that concerns Tillich is the separation of man from man. This separation, because it is unavoidable, is an aspect of New Being. Even in his essential state, individual man remains estranged from humanity because of the exclusiveness, or demonism, of others. How does the Christ symbolize the estrangement in New Being? In two ways: abstractly in his separation from God and concretely in his separation from man.

From the abstract viewpoint, God separated from himself and, as the Christ, went out from himself in heaven to earth. During the process of going out from and later returning to himself—to his essentially divine self—God passed through a state of estrangement from himself. The manifestation of this self-estrangement was God's simultaneous presence in heaven and on earth. Thus God, as the Christ, was able to pray to himself: "Our Father, who is in heaven, . . ." The Christ's physical estrangement from God (or

121. *Dialogue*, p. 156.

himself) symbolizes the mental estrangement of man from man which defines the existential environment of New Being. (This separation also supplements the more narrowly defined separation of the crucifixion in symbolizing the No—man separated from belief in God—but the No type of estrangement should not be confused with the estrangement of man from man.)

From a concrete standpoint, referring to the human as opposed to the divine, the Christ again symbolizes the estrangement of man from man. The Christ, who had no place to rest his head, was forced to flee from one place to another. He was betrayed and mocked by men, stoned, spat upon, and made to wear a crown of thorns. Then he was nailed to a cross. His rejection and ultimate crucifixion by man point to the separation of man from man. They symbolize the existential suffering to which one remains subject even in the state of New Being.

EXISTENTIAL ESSENCE. In the Christ essence and existence become a synthesis, essence under the conditions of existence. The synthesis analogically symbolizes New Being, wherein individuals imitate the normative Christ (if not the historical Jesus) in accepting *all* men despite being rejected by many of them. By accepting his fellow man, unconditionally, the initiate into New Being overcomes the torment of the estrangement to which he remains subject. The overcoming of estrangement is the basis of a final set of analogies relating the Christ to New Being. This might sound like too many analogies, but Tillich is quite specific that there are many angles to consider. Thus at one point, after enumerating three specific aspects of the christological symbolism, he says: "So I could go on. . . . We must see all the different relations."[122]

Four analogies remain. First, New Being buries the old life of despair, which we recall as the concomitant of estrangement. The Christ was also buried, and with him his existential despair. Second, New Being brings salvation. According to Tillich, salvation means healing, the healing of estranged relations. The Christ is called "savior." Third, New Being cleanses man of sin, or demonism, which correlates with estrangement. In his atoning death on the cross, the Christ did the same thing. Finally, what enables New

122. *Dialogue*, p. 156.

Being to conquer estrangement is the presence of love for humanity. New Being is the Logos, or "law of love," manifest in a person. In the Christ the Logos became flesh.

A "HOME STRETCH" RECAPITULATION

Before entering the home stretch in this analysis of Tillich's thought, it might be a good idea to pause and survey the ground that has been covered. This should help us to see in perspective the various portions of the system as we follow Tillich's thoughts down the tortuous path leading through the concepts of divine Spirit, Trinity, and "life" to Tillich's philosophy of history and its goal of the Kingdom of God. We began with the finding that Tillich is a complete atheist who lost his belief while completing his higher education. Intellectually, he despises Christianity, and few Christian doctrines have escaped his hard-worked slur "absurd." Still, being the son of a clergyman and having a fondness for religious life and traditions, Tillich's feeling toward the Church is ambivalent. Tillich has met this ambivalence by deciding to have his cake and eat it too. He is going to remain with the Church for the purpose of undermining Christianity from within, a procedure which incidentally allows him to develop on the side his Grand Synthesis of theology and philosophy.

The Grand Synthesis is a superficially vague "philosophical theology," that is, a theology based on rational interpretation of traditional doctrine. It is designed to lead each listener to whatever level of religious sophistication he is ready to accept. The most naive and unquestioning will find a simple affirmation of Christian faith, including faith in the divinity of Jesus; incipient doubters will be encouraged to honor their most pressing doubts; liberal and agnostic Christians will be drawn toward a metaphysics which, whether they recognize this or not, entails rejection of the most fundamental of all Christian beliefs, the belief in a personal God; and a few may even be converted to humanism. Tillich has guardedly stated his purpose by declaring his words to be "particularly directed" toward "the few" who recognize "the shaking of the foundations." In an unusually bold sermon, he has actually acknowledged his intent to emulate Paul and become "all things to all men." The theologian (himself) must behave "as though weak" in order to reach the weak (Christians). He must go about his mission by working "not from the outside, but from the inside" in disseminating his message.

His message is a message of humanism, a dialectical humanism cast in the Hegelian mold. It is based on a popular German philosophical notion with roots reaching back to Kant's concept of *homo noumenon*. This is the notion that God is man, best expressed in the thought of Feuerbach and Marx but probably mediated to Tillich more by Schelling than anyone else. Tillich's humanistic message uses the mythological Christ—"Jesus as the Christ"—as its "norm," meaning that Tillich's God is to be an imitation of the Christ, fully God and fully man. Within the framework of a rational ("philosophical") theology, the only way to have a God that is *"fully* God and *fully* man" rather than half God and half man is to define God to mean humanity. Tillich does this. Carrying out the divine-human theme, he conceptualizes humanity as the general concern (divine) embodied in those "preliminary" concerns (human) that are "true," rather than "demonic." Humanity also becomes the analogue of Hegel's universal-particular Spirit; philosophy participates equally with theology in shaping the Tillichian God. The Hegelian analogy treats the ultimate concern as equivalent to the Spirit's universal side and preliminary concerns as counterparts of the manifold embodiments of Spirit in nature and history. Alternatively, the general (one) and particular (many) can be viewed as humanity and individual men.

Tillich's theology, then, is really a pseudo-theology. Its author calls it an "apologetic" theology. An apologetic theology, as far as he is concerned, is one which tries to achieve a *synthesis* of two opposing points of view, that of the apologist and that of his opponents. For Tillich, "the great synthesis between Christianity and humanism" is the goal and has been acknowledged as such in several places. With explicit reference to the conflict between religion and humanism, Tillich has identified reconciliation through synthesis as "my own way"; and again explicitly he has said that this synthesis "has found its final form" in his *Systematic Theology.* Elsewhere, Tillich has defined apologetics by example as telling one's opponents that their God is the apologist's under another name (synthesis). The example is the Logos, which early

Christian apologists equated with God in speaking to hellenistic audiences. So, apologetics is achieving a synthesis of two conflicting positions by equating one God with another, and the two positions that concern Tillich are Christianity (God is the absolute) and humanism (man is the absolute). Hence, to "those who have ears," Tillich has spoken his apologetic message: God is man. The "hard of hearing" are in trouble, however, for a complex and hitherto misinterpreted "system" muffles the hidden message. The system amounts to a code of sorts, the purpose of which is to protect Tillich's standing in the Church. It utilizes three building blocks: symbolism, correlation, and dialectics.

Symbolism and correlation relate closely: both are based on analogy. A Tillichian symbol is linked by analogy to its object. Accordingly, being-itself can symbolize humanity: being-itself is the absolute of philosophy while humanity is the absolute of humanism. Similarly, "dynamics" and "form" can symbolize man and God, because dynamic means changing and change implies "many"—many men—whereas form implies singularity, or the oneness of God. Correlation, meanwhile, does not mean what Tillich's deliberately misleading explanation seems to indicate, namely, a correlation of questions and answers. It refers instead to the correlation of analogous theological and philosophical concepts. The analogous concepts jointly symbolize a Tillichian concept, creating a triangular analogy. As an example, God and being-itself ("God is being-itself"), the respective theological and philosophical absolutes, are correlates, and both symbolize humanity. Sin, or separation from God, correlates with estrangement, the separation of a metaphysical self from itself. Both symbolize Tillichian estrangement, which is simultaneously the separation of man from God and the separation of man from himself, because God and man's self are identical.

Dialectics is the workhorse of the system. This means the Hegel-Marx dialectics of thesis-antithesis-synthesis, not Barth's nonsequential and unresolved oppositions. Cleverly disguised dialectical formulations permeate every corner of the system. Estrangement is thus identifiable as the antithesis of an ontological dialectic moving from (a) the thesis of *potential* human unity, or essence, to (b) the *actual* separation of man from man, or existence, toward (c) *actual-*

ized potentiality, where man realizes himself as God, and where essence = existence. Again, in the symbolic conglomeration that passes for an analysis of "reason and revelation," everything revolves around the dialectic of union, separation, and reunion. "Subjective reason" (individuals) and "objective reason" (humanity) start out essentially united as "ontological reason" (thesis), then are existentially separated in three "conflicts in reason" (antithesis), and finally are brought back together through the "revelation" that the "depth" of both forms of reason is God (synthesis). The many and the one are merely two sides—human and divine— of the Tillichian God.

"Being and God" continues the dialectical theme. Tillich's abstruse philosophizing about "being" and about being's dichotomy of "self and world" is almost pure Hegel; only the God has been changed. "Self" (men) and "world" (humanity) are potentially united as "being" (God), but existentially they are estranged through self's failure to recognize world as itself. The many selves comprising humanity can become the one "world" which is God by recognizing that humanity is God. After exhausting this dialectic, Tillich creates what purports to be a semi-historical typology of religions. However, it is really another dialectic in disguise. And, as usual, it carries the hidden message that God is man.

In his christological symbolism, Tillich uses "Jesus as the Christ" to symbolize New Being. More dialectics. New Being is humanism, the synthesis of a dialectic advancing from (*a*) life's initial Yes to God to (*b*) its subsequent No to supernaturalism to (*c*) the union of Yes and No which affirms the nonsupernatural God, humanity. Here the stages of belief, unbelief, and new belief are symbolized respectively by incarnation, crucifixion, and resurrection. Incarnation describes a union of man and God, representing the original Yes; the crucifixion depicts the No, or the death of the supernatural; and the resurrection symbolizes the "new life" of New Being. Subsumed under resurrection is a sub-dialectic—not a "theory"—dealing with the disciples' imaginary shift from "Jesus *is* the messiah" (Yes) to "Jesus is *not* the messiah" (No) to "Jesus is a *symbolic* messiah" (Yes + No).

Theology's Christ concept correlates with two philosophical concepts, essence and existence. Each instance of New Being is a fragmentary instance of the self-realization of humanity as God. Therefore, New Being is a synthesis in the additional sense (in addition to Yes + No) of "essence under the conditions of existence." And "Jesus as the Christ" further symbolizes humanity's—each man is a particle of humanity—dialectical movement from essence to existence to existential essence. The Christ's resistance to demonic temptation now represents essence, his existential persecution and suffering signify existence, and the synthesis of both characteristics in one individual—the Christ's accepting man despite being rejected by him—provides the symbolic analogy for existential essence.

This brings us to the end of the territory covered by volumes 1 and 2 of *Systematic Theology*. The next chapter proceeds through the conceptual realm of volume 3 to the end of the system. There we shall find, to adapt one of Tillich's punlike aphorisms, that the end of systematic theology is the end of theology.

CHAPTER 5

Dialectical Humanism

When Tillich claims that estrangement can be overcome only fragmentarily, he is not just being a realist or perhaps a pessimist; he is being a dialectician. The reunion of man with man *must* be limited by the forces of estrangement, and essential being *must* remain subject to the conditions of existence, because New Being—the goal of life and of history—*must* as a matter of philosophical structure be a dialectical synthesis. And synthesis cannot, according to the rules of dialectics, overpower and destroy thesis and antithesis but must take them into itself. Tillich's passion for dialectics is overwhelming; thesis, antithesis, and synthesis permeate his thought. We saw in Chapter 2, where dialectics was introduced, that Tillich himself has suggested that his thought be called "dialectical." Since he is constrained not to openly acknowledge the humanistic character of his God, it has been necessary to help him in completing the label. As we pull together the pieces of Tillich's philosophies of God, life, and history, it should become evident why the overall picture can most accurately be described as dialectical humanism.

SYNTHESIS AND THE SPIRIT

It might seem a bit odd, after devoting separate chapters to God and the Christ, to confine the Spirit to the introductory section of another chapter. After all, the Holy Spirit is a full-fledged member —well, anyway a member—of the Christian Trinity. Moreover, in *Systematic Theology* Tillich devotes as many pages to the Spirit

(Part IV) as to God and the Christ combined (Parts II and III). Nevertheless, there are valid reasons for treating the divine Spirit, which is what Tillich calls it, in this manner. From a substantive viewpoint, the Spirit is of minor import in Tillich's thought; like incarnation and faith, it amounts to a kind of second-line symbol for New Being. The fact that Tillich belabors the Spirit for almost three hundred pages in *Systematic Theology* (while scarcely mentioning it in his other books) does not alter this evaluation.[1] But from the viewpoint of structure, the Spirit is the basic ingredient in Tillich's philosophy of humanism. In this sense, the entire present chapter is about Tillich's divine Spirit.

The Traditional Holy Spirit

In discussing symbolic analogies between God and Christ, on the one hand, and humanistic concepts on the other, one can take it pretty much for granted that the traditional terms are well enough understood. With the Holy Spirit, though, the situation is different. The traditional concept is so remote from modern modes of thought that many Christians can only think of it vaguely as the third member of the Trinity, something to be referred to in liturgy but otherwise ignored. It may also be dimly conceived of as God's omnipresence, Christian motivation in man, or simply an aspect of God's personality. I have known theology students who thought they knew what the Holy Spirit was but simply could not articulate their ideas. A background discussion therefore appears to be in order.

Among primitive people, ideas about soul, spirit, and breath are bound together in a mélange of related images. Man is thought to have an invisible, immaterial inner self which is the seat of life and intelligence. After death this inner self—the soul or spirit—is what becomes immortal or is reincarnated. When Jesus said on the cross, "Father, into your hands I commit my spirit!" he was referring to his soul. Some primitives have equated the soul with breath, because breath is what disappears when a man dies; the word "spirit"

---

1. The great length of Part IV is contrary to Tillich's original plan. In the Preface to the second volume, containing Part III (the Christ), Tillich said that part would be "the largest of the five parts of the system" (p. vii). He failed to reckon that Part IV would overinflate: compared to the Christ's 162 pages, the Spirit boasts 289.

is actually derived from the Latin *spiritus*, breath. Gods as well as men are credited with having soul, spirit, or breath. Thus in some primitive religions animal gods have been ceremonially butchered for the dual purpose of allowing the devotees to consume the gods' flesh and blood (to absorb desired traits from the divinity) and releasing the gods' spirits for reincarnation in younger, healthier animals.

Although it may incorporate reflections of Zoroasterism's Holy Spirit, which was a separate entity apart from *Ahura Mazdah*, Christianity's Holy Spirit is basically another deity's inner self: it is God's soul, spirit, or breath. In Greek, the language of the New Testament, the word for Holy Spirit is *pneuma* (as in pneumatic). It literally means breath and designates the spirit or soul. Again, in the Old Testament, *ruah* is the breath of Yahweh which inspired the early prophets to speak. The same general idea of God having a soul is carried over into the Elizabethan translation, "Holy Ghost," for a ghost is a disembodied soul or spirit. Now the notion that God could have a spirit may sound strange in an age when most people look at God himself as a spirit. But during the formative years of Christianity and long afterwards, God was a highly anthropomorphic being who sat on a throne with Jesus at his right hand and ruled over a kingdom having streets of gold.

As God's inner self or soul, the Holy Spirit was an agent sent out on special errands while God remained behind in heaven. The ancients were firm believers in spirit possession, as illustrated by belief of Jesus and his contemporaries that human ailments were indicative of possession by demons, or evil spirits. Early Christians (like some of today's) therefore had no difficulty believing that the Holy Spirit could enter a person to effect a wide variety of results. The Holy Spirit impregnated the Virgin Mary,[2] led Jesus into his ministry,[3] gave the disciples the power to work miracles,[4] caused converts to speak in tongues,[5] and enabled men to prophesy.[6] Mythologically speaking, God was present in men through the Holy Spirit in all such events. The Holy Spirit was uniting God and man.

2. Matt. 1:18, 20. 3. Matt. 3:16, 17; 4:1.
4. Acts 1:8; 5:12–16. 5. Acts 2:4; 10:44–46.
6. Acts 19:6.

The Spirit as New Being

Since a symbol, as Tillich uses the term, is analogous to that which it symbolizes, we should expect "divine Spirit" to have a humanistic meaning analogous to the religious one. If the Holy Spirit of Christian tradition is the soul or spirit of God which goes out from the deity to possess man, what might the Spirit represent in a humanistic pseudo-theology where God is man? What we are seeking is some essential aspect of humanity—God—which becomes spiritually manifest in the individual. Ultimate concern immediately comes to mind. A reasonable hypothesis is that Spirit possession in the Tillichian system refers to a person being united with man through ultimate concern for man. If this is the case, divine Spirit and Spiritual Presence, two terms used interchangeably by Tillich, are additional symbols for New Being.

With this hypothesis in mind, we can turn to Tillich's definition. "The Spirit of God is the presence of the Divine Life within creaturely life. The Divine Spirit is 'God present.' "[7] In a similar vein: "God Himself in us: that is what Spirit means."[8] These words aren't hard to recognize as a description of New Being. In New Being man is ultimately concerned about man; humanity, as a concern rather than in its physical aspect, is present in man. God is present. God is in us. Very clearly, divine Spirit and Spiritual Presence are indeed additional symbols for New Being. They describe a state of humanism.

The symbolic relationship of the Spirit to New Being is verified in some of Tillich's remarks about revelation, faith, and New Being itself. Revelation, we recall, is an event marking the onset of New Being: God, as an ultimate concern, manifests itself in an individual in a manner analogous to the spirit possession of religious revelation. Tillich asserts that "the presence of the divine Spirit" is a definitive aspect of revelation.[9] Hence, considering that revelation precipitates New Being, Spiritual Presence is also a definitive aspect of New Being. We have seen that faith is usually defined as a state of being grasped by an ultimate concern or by the ground of being (God). So when Tillich declares that faith can also be defined as

---

7. *ST–3*, p. 107.   8. *New Being*, p. 137.
9. *ST–1*, p. 112.

"the state of being grasped by the Spiritual Presence"[10] we know that Spiritual Presence is interchangeable with faith as a secondary symbol for New Being. There are, in addition, statements in which Tillich directly links the Spirit with New Being. One of these was noted when we examined New Being: Tillich says that, just as the Christ was created when the Spirit descended upon him, so is a person "made into a new creature by the Spirit."[11] Also, Tillich indicates that since mankind "is continuously under the impact of the Spiritual Presence, there is always New Being in history."[12]

Correlating the Spirit

Though well enough documented, the above interpretation of the divine Spirit somehow appears lacking. For one thing, the heavy emphasis given the Spirit in Tillich's discussion of Trinitarianism leaves the impression that some important feature of the Spirit remains to be explored. Furthermore, it is not yet evident what the philosophical correlate of the Spirit is. We know that in Tillich's system each theological concept is supposed to have a philosophical correlate to which it relates by analogy and which helps clarify what is symbolized. Revelation has been correlated with reason, God with being, salvation and resurrection with the overcoming of existential estrangement, and the Christ with reunion (or essence) under the conditions of estrangement (or existence). But where is the philosophical correlate of the Spirit, and what insight does it offer into the symbol's meaning?

A clue to the Spirit's correlate comes from Tillich's discussion of "the trinitarian principles." Here we must preview some of the material bearing on Tillich's Trinity, for it is not possible to satisfactorily cover either subject—Spirit or Trinity—without some reference to the other. After mentioning "power" in connection with the first of three principles and "meaning" in connection with the second, Tillich declares that the Spirit, as the third principle, unites power and meaning. Synthesis! The Spirit correlates with dialectical philosophy's triadic third stage. The Holy Spirit unites God and man; synthesis merges thesis with antithesis; and, by

10. *ST–3*, p. 131.   11. *ST–2*, p. 119.
12. *ST–3*, p. 140.

dual analogy, the Tillichian divine Spirit combines religion with atheism in humanistic synthesis.

In correlating the divine Spirit with dialectical synthesis, we reach a novelty in the system. Why do you suppose Tillich bothers to rename the Holy Spirit, calling it the divine Spirit? Could it be his way of planting another clue? And could that clue have something to do with the initials for divine Spirit—the initials DS? DS also stands for Dialectical Synthesis, and this strikes me as too much of a coincidence to be accidental. Why else rename the Holy Spirit? I won't push this point too hard, because there is the barest possibility of a coincidence and, in any case, we have other ways of identifying the Spirit. Still, I am substantially convinced that the common initials DS are of deliberate design. In typically oblique fashion, Tillich is making the point that the Spirit signifies a dialectical synthesis of Yes and No, revelation and reason.

This understanding of what Spirit means to Tillich is supported by an unusually explicit remark: "In the concept of the Spirit the highest *synthesis* is given between the Word of God which comes from the outside and the experience which occurs inside."[13] This is Tillich's way of saying that Spiritual Presence is the third stage of a dialectical movement running from revelation (thesis) to reason (antithesis) to Spirit (synthesis). Revelation and reason can be thought of as two opposing modes of life. Early life is the life of revelation, a term for which "Word of God" is substituted in the quotation. This life is that of traditional religion. Divine inspiration —God's will, as mediated through the Bible, religious hierarchies, ministers, and even personal experience—provides guidance. Man accepts the outside authority which says there is a God that commands allegiance. But eventually man rebels against religious supernaturalism and turns to the life of reason. This happens because within the minds of rational men no God is experienced: the inner voice of reason ("the experience which occurs inside") says No to God. Neither revelation nor reason, standing alone, is adequate in Tillich's eyes. Revelation is based on the false premise that there exists a divine being who reveals to man his wishes and

13. *Perspectives*, p. 21 (my italics); cf. *Religion*, where Tillich writes that in the Spirit "the ideal synthesis of revelation is clearly expressed" (p. 107).

commands. Reason is closer to what is needed but fails to provide the necessary goal in life; life becomes "ambiguous." The conflict between the external authority of biblical tradition and the internal authority of reason is resolved through synthesis. Spiritual Presence merges God with no-God. Revelation and reason embrace, with revelation providing the goal which reason requires for proper functioning. This is not the revelation of old, of course, but Tillich-style revelation. A nonsupernatural Spirit possesses man and reveals to him that humanity is the God toward which reason should direct life.

It isn't hard to recognize that this dialectical movement from revelation to reason to Spirit (or rationalized revelation) is substantively identical to the theological dialectic outlined in the last chapter. That dialectic portrays New Being as the synthesis of a movement from belief to unbelief to new belief. Both dialectics, then, are ways of describing a life which separates from and returns to belief in a god. Both tell of the Yes which changes to No, then becomes a new Yes without ceasing to be No. What this means is that Spirit is more than a symbol for the presence in an individual of ultimate concern for humanity; it is more than just Yes. Spiritual Presence means that whoever is "possessed" unites dialectically in his person two elements: unconditional affirmation of humanity and unconditional denial of the supernatural.

The Spirit and the Christ

At this point you may wonder what the difference is between the two symbols, "the Spirit" and "Jesus as the Christ." We have just seen that the Spirit, alias Spiritual Presence, symbolizes a dialectical synthesis of Yes to God and No to God: God is simultaneously affirmed and denied. We have also seen that the Spirit is a secondary symbol for New Being. But in Chapter 4 almost the same thing was said about Jesus as the Christ, except that the Christ was spared the "secondary" label. Jesus as the Christ was said to symbolize New Being, and the principal analogies between the Christ and New Being were identified with the thesis Yes and the antithesis No. The first analogy stresses the Christ's perfect unity with God, which compares with not only the original Yes of theistic belief but the regenerated Yes which is the hallmark of

New Being. The second analogy spotlights man's crucifixion of the supernatural—his saying No to God. The two analogies are blended in New Being, with man saying No to the God of supernaturalism by saying Yes to the God of humanism. Where then is there any difference between the two symbols?

There really isn't any. Nor should there be under Tillich's reasonably orthodox explanation of biblical theology. The Holy Spirit, according to the Bible, descended on Jesus when he was baptized and led him away into the wilderness. It remained with him thereafter on earth. Jesus as the Christ in essence *was* the Spirit of God (in addition to being God himself and the Son of God). The two symbols are essentially the same thing; hence, they might as well symbolize essentially the same thing. There are nuances of emphasis: Jesus as the Christ highlights the completeness of man's union with God and the firmness of his rejection of the supernatural; the Spirit plays up the actual synthesis, or combining of the opposing elements. But in substance both symbols represent the third stage of a dialectic, which third stage synthetically unites the first two.

A DIALECTICAL TRINITY

A curious feature of previous discussions of Tillich's Trinity is their failure to give more than nominal recognition, if any, to its dialectical nature. One gets the impression that many theological writers are unfamiliar with Hegelian dialectics and its distinctive characteristics of sequence and synthesis; they think Tillich is speaking of the nonsequential and unresolved oppositions (e.g., heaven and earth) which characterize the theological "dialectics" of Barth and others. J. H. Thomas, for example, seems to associate Tillich's dialectics with "Barthian ideas."[14] David Kelsey sees nothing describable as dialectical in Tillich's Trinity: he thinks it is God, Christ, and the Spirit symbolizing three aspects of the saving event of revelation.[15] What has been overlooked is that Tillich plainly states and additionally implies that his Trinity is dialectical and symbolizes a three-stage life. It has no "members" in the

---

14. J. Heywood Thomas, *Paul Tillich: An Appraisal* (Philadelphia: Westminster, 1963), p. 18.
15. David H. Kelsey, *The Fabric of Paul Tillich's Theology* (New Haven: Yale University Press, 1967), pp. 167–70.

orthodox sense, only attitudes or states of mind identified by symbols. It is the life of thesis, antithesis, and synthesis manifesting itself in numerous ways but always in relation to belief in God and the supernatural.

The Symbol of the Trinity

In many different places Tillich indicates that his Trinity is a dialectic rather than a numbers game. "The doctrine of the Trinity —this is our main contention—is neither irrational nor paradoxical but, rather, dialectical."[16] According to Tillich, the notion that three can be one and one can be three is "the worst distortion of the mystery of Trinity."[17] Luther, he feels, was right in rejecting "a theology which makes the Trinitarian dialectic into a play with meaningless number combinations."[18] It is not the number three which is decisive but "the unity in a manifoldness of divine self-manifestations."[19] What Tillich means by this is that there is not just one manifestation of his God, comparable to the Christ manifestation, but millions—one for every personalized ultimate concern transparent to the unifying God—and he is therefore unwilling to define trinities in the usual manner. (If you wonder how he gets away with this when there was only one Christ in the prototype theology, Tillich is apparently willing to view incarnation more broadly to include the many instances of possession by the Holy Spirit, the Christ being merely the normative case.) Three, he argues, relates to "the intrinsic dialectics of experienced life" and describes life "going out from itself and returning to itself."[20] Certain tongue-in-cheek evidence "that the trinitarian symbolism is dialectical" is presented and, while not meant to be taken seriously as evidence, serves to further emphasize the point.[21]

Note that Tillich starts to get specific when he mentions life going out from and returning to itself. The idea is repeated frequently. "The doctrine of the Trinity . . . describes in dialectical terms the inner movement of the divine life as an eternal separa-

16. ST–3, p. 284.
18. ST–2, p. 144.
20. ST–3, p. 293.

17. ST–3, p. 284.
19. ST–3, p. 293.
21. ST–3, p. 293.

tion from itself and return to itself."[22] Similarly: "But the trinitarian symbols are dialectical; they reflect the dialectics of life, namely the movement of separation and reunion."[23] And, regarding the "trinitarian principles" which we shall inspect in a moment, they "are moments within the process of the divine life."[24] These remarks leave hardly any room for doubt that the Trinity relates to the three-stage (trinitarian) life of belief-unbelief-new belief, or revelation-reason-Spirit, described in connection with the two symbols, Christ and Spirit.

Any lingering uncertainty on this point melts when Tillich explores his religious and philosophical typologies. After covering polytheism, representing concreteness, and monotheism, which stresses ultimacy, Tillich comes to his own "trinitarian monotheism." This is not Christian trinitarianism, which he has already described under the rubric "monarchic monotheism," but something Tillich calls a "description of life-processes."[25] He defines the "trinitarian problem" as that of "the unity between ultimacy and concreteness in the living God."[26] Tillich is alluding to the three-stage life. Ultimacy (ultimate concern) relates to God and the life of revelation; concreteness concerns the concrete world of human reason, a personal life being the chief mark of concreteness. The point is further clarified when Tillich describes "dialectical realism, the philosophical analogue of trinitarian monotheism."[27] He refers to this as "thinking" which "moves through 'yes' and 'no' and 'yes' again."[28] The conceptualization, he indicates, presupposes that life itself moves to "self-affirmation" through a dialectical process. Here Tillich has inconspicuously identified the dialectical three-step as the correlate ("philosophical analogue") of the Trinity. He has thereby identified the Trinity itself as "thinking" which moves dialectically to thoughts wherein man affirms himself as God ("self-affirmation"). With these points resolved, it is a simple matter to deduce that the Trinity symbolizes the three-stage life moving from theism to atheism to humanism, or from union (Yes) to separation (No) to reunion (Yes). "In his Son, God separates Himself

22. *ST–1*, p. 56.
24. *ST–1*, p. 250.
26. *ST–1*, p. 228.
28. *ST–1*, p. 234.

23. *ST–3*, p. 284.
25. *ST–1*, p. 228.
27. *ST–1*, p. 234.

from Himself, and in the Spirit He reunites Himself with Himself."[29]

The analogy connecting the symbol of the Trinity to the three-stage life adds a small detail to the earlier analogy between the Christ's separation and return and New Being's return to God. That detail grows out of the subsequent analogy between the Spirit (unites God and man) and New Being (unites mankind and man). *God* (stage one) goes out from himself as his *Son* (stage two) and then returns to himself, leaving behind the *Holy Spirit* (stage three) to maintain the revelatory union between God and man. Here is Tillich's official reading of orthodox theology: "After the return of the Logos-Incarnate to the Father, the Spirit will take his place and reveal the implication of his appearance. In the divine economy, the Spirit follows the Son, but in essence, the Son *is* the Spirit."[30] The crucial point: Spirit follows Son. The trinitarian analogy, then, compares three stages in human "thinking" to the three physical states exhibited by God in the supernatural Trinity.

The Trinitarian Elements

A tentative introduction to the trinitarian symbols and what they represent is provided in the analysis of "the trinitarian principles." Found in volume 1 of *Systematic Theology*, this little gem of obfuscation is so esoteric as to be quite useless to anyone not already privy to Tillich's Trinity. The first of three principles is not really spelled out but only described—vaguely. It is what "makes God God." Under Tillich's definition, God is an ultimate concern, and what makes God God is the ultimacy of the concern. This element Tillich further identifies with "the ground of being," the "power of being," and the "abyss" of the divine. All of these are used by Tillich in various places as alternative labels for God, and this confirms that the first element of the Trinity relates to God. The second principle is identified as *logos*. It involves "meaning and structure." The lower case spelling of *logos* is a clue: we know that *logos* stands for human reason, as opposed to the divine reason of the Logos. As for "meaning and structure," they refer to the "shaping" function of "subjective reason" (the *logos*), which

29. *Love*, p. 107.   30. *ST–3*, p. 148.

function cannot operate properly without the guidance of "objective reason" (the Logos). Reason, then, is the second element of the Trinity; and by implication it is reason without aim or guidance. Tillich states that the third principle is the Spirit. As already mentioned, it unites power (God, the power of being) and meaning (reason). To repeat what we have already discovered, the Spirit as the third trinitarian principle is a dialectical synthesis of God and reason. God, of course, signifies the life of revelation, and reason is the life of reason.[31]

In these "principles" we don't have the actual trinitarian symbols, except for the Spirit, but we do have clues as to their content. The full development of the principles into meaningful symbols occurs in volume 3. There Tillich specifically identifies the "symbolic names" he is going to work with as "Father, Son, and Spirit"; and he associates these with "the threefold manifestation of God as creative power, as saving love, and as ecstatic transformation."[32] Power and God go well enough together (thesis), and so do ecstatic transformation and the Spirit (synthesis). But doesn't love conflict with reason as the second principle and the second stage of the three-stage life? Not really. Theologically speaking, God's saving love manifests itself in the Logos' becoming flesh, and—here Tillich exploits the ambiguity of Logos—Logos means reason. Also, the "Logos principle" correlates with the "law of love." This takes care of the link between love and reason but raises a second conflict. Isn't it the Son rather than the Logos which is to be the middle symbol? Tillich's answer is that both symbols are to be used for the same purpose. A moment ago we saw that Tillich interprets orthodox theology as equating the "Logos-Incarnate" with the Son who goes out from and returns to the Father. That Tillich accepts this identity for symbolic purposes is verified by a reference to "God and his Logos (also called Son)."[33] In the same paragraph, Tillich also identifies "God and his Logos" with "the Father and the Son"[34] and mentions the "Logos-Son" of ancient theology.[35]

Three final points clarifying the trinitarian symbols and what they symbolize appear in some remarks about "Reopening the

31. *ST–1*, pp. 249–52.
33. *ST–3*, p. 288.
35. *ST–3*, p. 289.

32. *ST–3*, p. 283.
34. *ST–3*, p. 289.

Trinitarian Problem" which conclude Part Four of *Systematic Theology*. Superficially Tillich is directing some mild jibes at the sexuality of Christianity's divine images, but at a deeper level he is explaining his own symbols. Noting that Protestantism has discarded the Virgin Mary, Tillich complains about the male-dominant aspect of its "symbols." He would like to think that "ground of being," as a kind of alter ego for the Father, can symbolize "the mother-quality of giving birth, carrying, and . . . calling back" the created. Tillich is hinting at his first trinitarian symbol's function: God, as the object of superstitious belief in life's first stage, figuratively gives birth to stage two and calls man back at stage three for the purpose of bestowing the name "God" on a new god. Tillich next takes up the sexuality of the Logos, as embodied in the Christ, and finds it to be "the negation" of sexuality. Affirmation, negation, and negation of the negation is the alternative formulation of thesis, antithesis, and synthesis; "the negation" is a final reminder that the Logos-Son symbolizes the antithesis in the dialectical life of man. Moving along to the divine Spirit, Tillich observes that it "transcends" the male-female symbolism of the Father, Son, and Holy Virgin. As another final reminder, Tillich is saying that the Spirit, symbolizing a dialectical synthesis of God and reason, transcends both.[36]

One other point should be clearly understood regarding the three trinitarian symbols. They do not add up to God; they are not "God in three persons." When Tillich denies that his God is a numerical paradox, he means it. Man, the God of Paul Tillich, is trinitarian, and there is a Trinity; but the Trinity is not God.

The Divine Life

The preceding description of the trinitarian "divine life" of separation and return may have left the impression that it refers to the lives of individual men: the divine life has been pictured as a personal life which moves from theism to atheism to humanism. Perhaps it also sounds like a description of reality. Actually, things are a bit more complicated. Tillich's divine life does relate to individuals in some contexts, but in others it concerns mankind. Either

36. *ST–3*, pp. 293–94.

way there are elements of reality, but the action is basically symbolic. The symbolism conforms to the same general pattern for
both applications. This pattern involves four levels of correlation:
(1) At the highest level of generalization Hegelian dialectics is correlated with the Trinity. (2) The dialectical movement from thesis
to antithesis to synthesis—from Yes to No to Yes—is correlated
with the Son's going out from and returning to the Father, the
movement from God to man to God. (3) The dialectical stages of
thesis, antithesis, and synthesis are correlated with Father, Son,
and Spirit, the last being what unites God and man upon the Son's
return. (4) As a specific application of the elements, there is a correlation of union, estrangement, and reunion (or essence, existence,
essence) with innocence, sin, and salvation.

NEO-HEGELIANISM. The distinction between the Trinity's application to individual man and its application to mankind is based on a
parallel distinction between the early and the mature thought of
Hegel, summarized in Chapter 2. To restate a few essentials, Hegel
was an atheist as most men understand the term. He interpreted
the myth of the fall figuratively. Man's fall was a falling away
from belief in God. Harmony with God could be restored through
self-recognition: man needed to seek infinity in himself. In effect,
Hegel described a movement from thesis to antithesis to synthesis,
with the synthesis standing as a metaphysical variety of humanism.

Imitating Hegel, Tillich devises for man a similar three-stage life
with a somewhat different synthesis. Stage one gets many labels,
one of which derives from Hegel's interpretation of the fall. Before
the fall, Adam was innocent; hence Tillich can use the term
"dreaming innocence" in disparaging reference to the childlike
beliefs associated with life's first stage, theism.[37] Man starts out in
a dream world. Because it is belief in *a* god, however, dreaming
innocence can be subsumed under the general principle of belief. It
therefore embodies potentiality—potentiality for belief in *the* God
—and represents essence. Essence becomes the philosophical correlate of innocence. When man awakens to reality, rejecting supernaturalism, he separates—"falls"—from God. Inasmuch as traditional theology describes Adam's separation from God as sin, stage

37. *Culture*, p. 156.

two of life metaphorically becomes sin. Sin is estrangement, the basic condition of human existence, so estrangement and existence are other names for stage two. Actually man has been estranged from the true God, humanity, all along, but at the moment we are referring to estrangement from the God of theism. (This is not the usual meaning of estrangement or of sin in Tillich's thought.) In time, man returns to God; he experiences salvation. Correlatively speaking, man returns to essence. But this is not the essence of old, not potential essence; it is the realized essence of belief in humanity. As in Hegel's early dialectic, man finds the infinite in himself. God and no-God reach a synthesis.

In his mature thought Hegel shifted his perspective from man to the divine. The divine was the metaphysical World Spirit, the world as a supernatural self emerging into self-consciousness. In its essential state, the primordial state of nature, the world was in union—thesis. But man, the metaphysical organism's seat of consciousness, divided the Spirit against itself. Man, though essentially part of the world, regarded nature as alien; subject saw itself as a separate and hostile object. Hence, through man, the Spirit became alienated (estranged) from itself. Thesis gave way to antithesis. Finally, in Hegel's philosophic mind, the Spirit developed self-awareness. The essential unity of man and the rest of the world was recognized, and with the reunion of the estranged, a dialectical synthesis took place. It was a return to essence. Tillich summarizes Hegel's story this way: "The world is the process of the divine self-realization."[38] God and man are "reconciled by the reconciliation in the philosopher's head."[39]

Following through on the contrasting perspectives—man and Spirit—of Hegel's early and later thought, Tillich gives the "divine life" a second meaning. As opposed to three stages in the development of an individual, the second meaning concerns three stages in the development of humanity. We are still dealing with the symbolic "life" of the divine, but attention shifts from God's human side to "his" divine side. Self-transcending man becomes self-transcending God. To effect the change, Tillich takes Hegel's dialectic of union, estrangement, and reunion and substitutes his God

38. ST–2, p. 24.   39. Perspectives, p. 163.

206

for Hegel's—humanity for the metaphysical world. Humanity's latent unity becomes a new form of "dreaming innocence," also called essence. As already explained, this essence is not a stage in history; it is potentiality. When the human race appeared on earth there simultaneously appeared the capacity for unity which the term "humanity" implies. But, as "dreaming" suggests, the essential stage of union among men was never realized. Instead, the actual existence which stands in tension with the potential is a state of estrangement (sin). Man is and always has been alienated from man; the self is divided against itself. This existential separation is manifested in selfishness, predatoriness, exclusivism, hatred, and strife. In the context of the divine life of separation and return, therefore, man is said to be in the antithetical state of separation. Nevertheless, a dialectic always moves toward synthesis. Tillich's synthesis materializes fragmentarily whenever self-recognition takes place, whenever individual men recognize that humanity is God. Because this fragmentary "reunion" occurs in the face of continued estrangement within humanity as a whole, the synthesis can be described as combining thesis and antithesis, essence and existence.

SOME MISCONCEPTIONS. Against this analytical background, a few words must be said about Guyton Hammond's erroneous interpretation of the divine life and about related tendencies to take Tillich literally. Hammond takes cognizance of Tillich's statements that (a) life goes out from and returns to itself and (b) God, as the power of being, is that which overcomes nonbeing. Substantially ignoring all warnings about symbolism, he jumps to the literal conclusion that Tillich's God is Life, conceived of as a metaphysical entity. This entity is constantly threatened by nonbeing, or death. It therefore seeks to "affirm itself"[40] through "a metaphysical 'movement' "[41] in which it separates from itself, goes out to man for some dimly conceived enrichment, and then returns to itself. Affirmation takes place with man's self-awareness, by which Hammond means man's becoming conscious of himself as an indi-

40. Guyton B. Hammond, *The Power of Self-Transcendence: An Introduction to the Philosophical Theology of Paul Tillich* (St. Louis: Bethany Press, 1966), p. 38.
41. *Ibid.*, p. 42.

vidual apart from others. Self-awareness in the mundane sense of self-consciousness is supposedly what Tillich means by self-transcendence. It results in estrangement, because in becoming aware of his existential identity as a person man overlooks his essential identity with Life.

One place Hammond goes astray is in failing to see the analogy between the "divine life" of separation and return and the Christ's life of separation from and return to God. Had he seen this he might have realized that he was dealing with symbolism and not a literal description of reality. (Hammond does acknowledge symbolism in the divine life, but his idea of symbolism is God symbolizing Life.) Hammond compounds his difficulty by supposing that death or non-life is the nonbeing which Tillich says is overcome by being. Actually, in the context of the divine life, Tillich is talking about the nonbeing of God and some supernatural companions, a subject to be considered shortly. Hammond, although familiar with Hegelian dialectics, further errs in concluding that Tillich patterns his dialectics mainly after Plato's dialogues (question and answer). He therefore sees nothing dialectical about the divine life and does not seek an antithesis. Were he looking for one he could hardly ignore the fact that estrangement is the negative element, or antithesis, in the divine life and materializes before, rather than after, self-awareness. The upshot of Hammond's analysis is that, whereas Tillich is merely trying to state symbolically that man should reject the supernatural (including metaphysics) and treat humanity as God, Hammond has turned him into a hopelessly ludicrous metaphysician.

This brings us back to symbolism. The fact of the matter is that the divine life is essentially symbolic, a parable of sorts. It provides an idealized description of human moral achievement. Consistent with the parable technique, it has something of a true-to-life quality: man *is* estranged, in Tillich's sense of the word, and some individuals *do* start out as theists, become atheists, and then revert to "religion" by espousing humanism. Also, Tillich's Yes is especially directed at those who are entering the No stage of life and, in his judgment, need a substitute God. However, Tillich obviously is not saying that beginning life as a theist is preferable to a humanistic upbringing. Neither is it reasonable to suppose that he sees some particular advantage in an ex-believer's going through a totally nonreligious antithetical phase before turning to humanism. A parable, moreover, is not an allegory; it offers a central point rather than a continuous symbolic description. The point Tillich wants to put across is that a mature attitude towards life unites two principles: unconditional rejection of the supernatural and unconditional acceptance of humanity. Tillich's Trinity symbolically describes this unity.

Variations on a Theme

The divine life, states Tillich, has "three elements which appear in different ways in all sections of systematic theology and which are the basis for the trinitarian interpretation of the final revelation."[42] The "different ways" are the many terminological disguises in which Tillich outfits life's three stages. To read Tillich, one must learn to recognize alternative labels for the same concept. We have already looked at such alternatives as (1) belief-unbelief-new belief, (2) revelation-reason-Spirit, (3) innocence-sin-salvation, (4) essence-existence-essence, and (5) union-estrangement-reunion. Six other instructive variations on the trinitarian theme are summarized below. In the next section of this chapter still another—being, non-being, and the courage to be—will be explored in much greater depth.

YES-NO-YES. The most rudimentary expression of the dialectical life is that outlined by Tillich in raising the counterpart philosophy of "dialectical realism," which he pairs with "trinitarian monotheism." Dialectical realism is thinking that moves from Yes to No, then back to Yes. The initial Yes affirms the reality of the supernatural. Man starts out living the life of religion; he believes in God, salvation, divine law, the revelatory wisdom of the Bible, and other supernaturalistic paraphernalia. The No marks a retreat—a permanent one—from supernaturalism. Man goes out from God, denying the validity of religion, God, and revelation. But the life of No (as Tillich sees it) leaves man with a feeling of emptiness and purposelessness: "The undialectical No is as primitive and unproductive as the undialectical Yes."[43] Searching for meaning, man

42. ST–1, p. 156.   43. Absolutes, p. 41.

returns to "God." The terminal Yes affirms that indeed there is a God—humanity—but, taking the No into itself (synthesis), continues to deny the supernatural.

HETERONOMY-AUTONOMY-THEONOMY. Closely related to the earlier dialectic of revelation, reason, and Spiritual Presence is that of heteronomy, autonomy, and theonomy. These terms, like "dreaming innocence," can be used in either a socio-historical or a personal context. Heteronomy is life under the rule of a stranger (*heteros*, strange; *nomos*, law); Tillich uses the term to describe submission to external authority. The authority can be a religious or a political ideology, but Tillich is naturally thinking mainly in terms of religious authority—the Bible for Protestants, the hierarchy for Catholics. Heteronomous rule characterizes the initial phase of life. When man rebels against religion, he provides his own law; he turns to the life of reason. This is autonomy (*autos*, self). The trouble with autonomy is that it is *logos* without the Logos: it is human reason unsupported by the divine reason which is the law of love. A synthesis is needed, and this is theonomy. Theonomy (*theos*, God) is reason united with external authority. Love for mankind supplies the orientation which autonomous reason needs to function properly.

CATHOLIC-PROTESTANT-HUMANISTIC. Tillich has on occasion spoken favorably about the Catholic Church, finding in it a substance that is genuine though hidden beneath a hard crust. Perhaps for this reason, many Catholic writers have been attracted to him. Catholic and Protestant writers alike, moreover, have discerned ecumenical possibilities in Tillich's thought, possibilities looking toward a synthesis of Catholicism and Protestantism. What these writers don't realize is that, whereas the synthesis is there, it is strictly symbolic. Catholicism, Protestantism, and humanism are heteronomy, autonomy, and theonomy all over again. The Catholic Church, with its unified structure and papal authority, is analogous to God (one, authority), and God is the focus of the life of theism. The more highly developed ritual and dogma of Catholicism further contribute to its suitability as a symbol for stage one of life. Protestantism contrasts sharply. It is fragmented and lacking in authority; each denomination and sect goes off in its own direction, answering to itself. Protestantism can therefore symbolize life's antithesis, the stage where man substitutes personal autonomy for religious authority. Protestantism also signifies protest, and protest means No. This makes the symbol doubly suitable. Humanism combines Protestantism and Catholicism, one and many, authority and autonomy, Yes and No.

UNAMBIGUOUS-AMBIGUOUS-UNAMBIGUOUS. The divine life can also be interpreted as a quest for the unambiguous life. To keep our list from growing too long, this dialectic can be treated in combination with the quest for a centered life. At the outset, man's life has meaning: man exists to serve God. Life is centered on God. Then meaning dissolves, and the center disappears. Life becomes ambiguous. Reason—technical reason—can tell man how to get somewhere but cannot tell him where to go. Man therefore goes off in all directions; his life is ambiguous. From the narrower standpoint of morality, each act becomes ambiguous, for there is no longer a divine code saying what is right and what is wrong. Ambiguous life is uncentered life. As Tillich explains it, a center is a point and a point can't be divided. Mankind cannot be split into demonic groups and still constitute a unified center giving direction to life. Finally man is grasped by the Spirit, and life is again meaningful. Its aim, service to mankind, is unambiguous. Once again, life is centered on God. (It is fair to ask whether this dialectic has not gone astray by letting the synthesis destroy rather than include the antithesis. Tillich seems willing to let proxies like reason and estrangement represent ambiguity in the synthesis: "Life always includes essential and existential elements; this is the root of its ambiguity."[44])

ULTIMATE-CONCRETE-CONCRETE ULTIMACY. Tillich identifies one of several "factors which have led to trinitarian thinking" as "the tension between the absolute and the concrete element" in God.[45] The typological dialectic explored in Chapter 3 traced the course of religious history from polytheism (concreteness) through monotheism (ultimacy) to trinitarian monotheism (concrete ultimacy). Tillich is probably just a little unhappy that the historical sequence must be rearranged to put thesis and antithesis in standard order;

44. *ST–3*, p. 107. 45. *ST–3*, p. 283.

but this can't be helped, and the synthesis is unchanged. Ultimacy describes life's first stage: there is one God who overrides all other concerns. Concreteness then appears as the negation of ultimacy. Many "gods," all of them on the human plane, beckon to man when he tries to live by reason alone—just as many quasi-human gods beckon in polytheistic religion. Trinitarian monotheism, as the negation of the negation, stands in tension between the opposing pulls of ultimacy and concreteness. Man exhibits many diverse preliminary concerns, each of them embodied in a personal life—concreteness. Yet man's subjective reason has "shaped" each of these from man's deeper concern for humanity, which concern is at once unifying and universal—ultimacy.

THEOLOGY-PHILOSOPHY-HUMANISM. In several places Tillich describes his thought as standing on the boundary between theology and philosophy. These two opposing modes of thought symbolize the two opposing approaches to life which the humanistic synthesis brings into unity. The early years of the divine life are lived under the influence of theological and religious doctrines. These doctrines affirm the existence of God and the reality of a supernatural world. Life's adolescence corresponds to a philosophical approach to life. Man seeks the guidance of his own reason. (Admittedly, it is a serious distortion of the nature of philosophy to treat it as the antithesis of supernaturalistic thought, since metaphysical concepts and related ideas about God ruled philosophy for many centuries; but philosophy at least views itself as rational.) The mature years of New Being are represented by humanism which, as developed by Tillich, is a synthesis of theology and philosophy, revelation and reason.

A PHILOSOPHY OF LIFE

Tillich develops his ideas about trinitarianism into what he seems to regard as a "philosophy of life."[46] (This somewhat misleading phrase serves to differentiate between dialectical thought which relates to man and that which relates to history.) Each of the trinitarian formulations just reviewed expresses this philosophy concisely but perhaps too symbolically to allow full appreciation of

46. See ST–3, pp. 11 ff.

Tillich's ideas. For savoring the real flavor of his thoughts on the inner life of man, there is no better place to turn than to *The Courage to Be*. Chapters 2 and 6 of this small book present in narrow compass Tillich's basic ideas about religion, doubt, and the God who gives courage to live in the face of doubt. Indeed, these chapters can be recommended as the best place to start reading Tillich regardless of one's focus. By taking some liberties with Tillich's arrangement of material, we can extract a detailed picture of the self-realization of man.

Religion and the Courage of Supernaturalism

The thesis of the life dialectic is religion, or being (saying Yes to the being of God or some other religious absolute). As Tillich sees it, man is threatened by three forms of anxiety: (1) about death, (2) about a meaning of life, and (3) about right and wrong. Religion attempts to overcome this three-fold anxiety by turning to the supernatural for support. The religious approach can lead in several directions. Two extremes are "participation" and "individualization," represented by mysticism and theism. In mysticism man tries to participate in—become a part of—the higher reality. Theism treats man and the deity as separate individuals and seeks to establish a person to person relationship. In all religions one tendency or the other is "dominant";[47] Tillich is not suggesting that mysticism is devoid of individualization or that theism totally excludes participation. (Mystics may personify the supernatural power with which they seek union, and Christian theists may seek to participate in God by eating the flesh and drinking the blood of his son.)

The two approaches to overcoming anxiety operate in different ways. In mysticism man strives to participate in the divine power by actually identifying himself with that power. The identifying experience convinces man that the world of time and space and material reality is ultimately unreal; hence, he sees death only as the negation of the negative. In similar fashion, by denying the significance of ordinary life, the mystic dissolves the very question of its meaning. Moral guilt over failure to meet the demands of successively deeper levels of mystical experience may occasionally

47. *Courage*, p. 156.

be felt, but the certainty of fulfillment prevents any sense of condemnation. Theism, typified by Christianity, provides different solutions. Man treats the ground of his being as a person who, in the divine-human encounter, removes the causes of anxiety. God promises security against the threat of death for those who observe the requirements of prayer, service, and devotion. He provides life with a divine purpose. And, through his law, he provides the answers to what is right and what is wrong.

Both avenues of religion are lacking in Tillich's judgment. Mysticism tries to assume away anxiety and meaninglessness rather than solve the problem. "It plunges directly into the ground of being and meaning, and leaves the concrete, the world of finite values and meanings, behind."[48] Mystical courage, moreover, is a transitory phenomenon lasting only for the duration of the encounter with the divine. Theism, for its part, is wrong because it makes God "a being beside others and as such a part of the whole of reality."[49] (Tillich plainly doesn't think that reality includes a supernatural being.) Worse yet, the God of theism is an all-knowing all-powerful tyrant who dictates man's actions and pries into his personal life. "This is the God Nietzsche said had to be killed because nobody can tolerate being made into a mere object of absolute knowledge and absolute control."[50] Herein lie the roots of atheism, "an atheism which is justified as the reaction against theological theism and its disturbing implications."[51]

Despite these drawbacks, Tillich is prepared to acknowledge elements of virtue—symbolic virtue, that is—in mysticism and theism. In doing so, he is again employing the polarity of individualization and participation, terms we first encountered as "ontological elements." By relating these polar concepts to mysticism and theism, he is also re-employing a polarity he first discussed in his 1912 dissertation, *Mysticism and Guilt-Consciousness in Schelling's Philosophical Development.*[52] This polarity, as outlined by Tillich in other works, uses mysticism to symbolize the principle of identity and guilt-consciousness to represent the principle of contrast.

48. *Courage,* p. 186.   49. *Courage,* p. 184.
50. *Courage,* p. 185.   51. *Courage,* p. 185.
52. For a summary of this treatise see David Hopper, *Tillich: A Theological Portrait* (Philadelphia: Lippincott, 1968), pp. 101–26.

The latter principle appears in theism's picture of estranged relations between man and God—sinful man cowering before God.[53] With these opposing concepts Tillich moves toward the conclusion that true faith is where both extremes, participation and individualization, "are accepted and transcended"[54] by man. To know the power of being (God), man must participate in it. Mysticism provides the "courage to be as a part."[55] At the same time, man must receive "the courage to be as oneself"[56] (a separate individual) if he is to accept himself despite the conditions that produce existential despair—which brings us to the second phase of the dialectic.

Doubt and the Threat of Nonbeing

When man awakens from the dreaming innocence of religion, be it the mystical or the theistic variety, he is faced with the threat of nonbeing. Introducing this concept, Tillich formulates still another variation on the trinitarian theme: "being and the negation of being and their unity."[57] The initial "being" is God or, more loosely, the life of religion. It is being in the senses that (a) the being or existence of God is affirmed, (b) God is a supernatural being, and (c) being is the philosophical correlate of God. Nonbeing is "the negation of every concept"[58] (including God). For meaning it "is dependent on the being it negates."[59] Tillich identifies three forms of being so negated, and by implication a fourth. Together, the several forms of nonbeing spell despair.

The three forms of being which nonbeing specifically negates are religion's answers to the three types of anxiety defined previously. To anxiety about death, religion answers that there is a life beyond the grave. The religious man dreams of eternal salvation, but the man who knows doubt is aware of "the nonbeing which remains nonbeing even if it is filled with images of our present experience."[60] At first man tries to argue away the finality of death, but his attempts are futile. "Even if the so-called arguments for the 'immortality of the soul' had argumentative power (which they do

53. *Perspectives*, p. 171.
54. *Courage*, pp. 156–57.
55. *Courage*, p. 163.
56. *Courage*, p. 163.
57. *Courage*, p. 32.
58. *Courage*, p. 34.
59. *Courage*, p. 40.
60. *Courage*, p. 38.

not have) they would not convince existentially."[61] So omnipresent is the threat of death that anxiety arises and persists even in the absence of immediate threats to man's life.

To man's anxiety about the meaning of life, religion replies that man exists to serve God. But as religion fades into doubt, feelings of "emptiness" and "meaninglessness" begin to attack man's spirit. Meaninglessness refers to the feeling that existence has no meaning, a feeling which Tillich believes accompanies the rejection of God. "The anxiety of meaninglessness is anxiety about the loss of an ultimate concern, of a meaning which gives meaning to all meanings."[62] Emptiness is associated with being cut off from the inspiration provided by the cultural and ceremonial aspects of religion. "A belief breaks down through external events or inner processes: one is cut off from creative participation in a sphere of culture, one feels frustrated about something which one had passionately affirmed, one is driven from devotion to one object to devotion to another and again on to another, because the meaning of each of them vanishes and the creative eros is transformed into indifference or aversion."[63]

To anxiety about right and wrong, religion says there is a divine moral code which will tell man what to do and what not to do. God stands above man as a judge. Under the condition of nonbeing, however, supernatural morality is reduced to another superstition. The divine judge disappears, and man is forced to judge himself. Man doesn't know what to do and experiences a deep sense of guilt. "A profound ambiguity between good and evil permeates everything he does, because it permeates his personal being as such. . . . The awareness of this ambiguity is the feeling of guilt."[64] In extreme situations, man is driven toward utter self-rejection.

The deeper implications of Tillich's analysis are difficult to escape. If there is no afterlife, no divine purpose, no judge but ourselves, then by implication there is no God. When Tillich says the three types of anxiety "are immanent in each other"[65] he is indicating that they arise simultaneously when God disappears. This is what Tillich means when, anticipating his development of the syn-

61. *Courage*, p. 42.
62. *Courage*, p. 47.
63. *Courage*, pp. 47–48.
64. *Courage*, p. 52.
65. *Courage*, p. 42.

thesis, he says that "facing the God who is really God means facing also the absolute threat of nonbeing."[66] The word "absolute" is his way of saying that the No to the supernatural is unconditional —not relative only to certain facets of supernaturalism and not subject to the condition that God is excepted.

Tillich goes on to talk about the despair which arises from man's anxiety. There is no salve for death, no meaning of life, no way of telling right from wrong—this is the gist of Tillich's appraisal. What frustrates man and leads him to regard life as futile is not the presence of the unknown so much as the existence of "the unknown which by its very nature cannot be known, because it is nonbeing."[67] Tillich wrings this point for all (and considerably more than) it is worth, but we need not spend much time on it. It was mentioned earlier, when we investigated Tillich's concept of estrangement, that this pessimism is more than a little artificial. Despair, Tillich admits in other places, is an abstraction from life and is not a description of life itself.

The Courage to Be

Tillich, having pushed man into a desperately uncomfortable position, poses a question: Does there exist a courage which overcomes doubt and meaninglessness, a courage which can "resist the power of nonbeing in its most radical form?"[68] (It should not be necessary to clarify what he means by the most radical form of nonbeing!) There is such a courage, the courage to be. Unsurprisingly, it is produced by a dialectical synthesis of being and nonbeing. In Tillich's words, "the self-affirmation of being is an affirmation that overcomes negation."[69] Continuing: "We could not even think 'being' without a double negation: being must be thought as the negation of the negation of being."[70] In the dialectical synthesis, "being 'embraces' itself and nonbeing,"[71] that is, being in both the sense of reality and in the sense of the true God includes the nonbeing of the supernatural God, supernatural salvation, supernatural meaning, and supernatural law. In the moment of self-realization man discovers this: he discovers that God is

66. *Courage*, p. 39. 67. *Courage*, p. 37.
68. *Courage*, p. 174. 69. *Courage*, p. 179.
70. *Courage*, p. 179. 71. *Courage*, p. 34.

man, hence that there is an essential unity between being (God) and nonbeing (the unreality of a *supernatural* God). "Being has nonbeing 'within' itself as that which is eternally present and eternally overcome in the process of the divine life."[72]

One way of discovering that man's self-recognition as God is what enthrones this negation of the negation is to observe what happens to mysticism (participation in God) and theism (individual relations with God), the two elements of the dialectic's thesis. Though separate and competitive in conventional religion, that is, at stage one of the dialectic, these elements merge at stage three: there is a synthesis within the synthesis. This inner synthesis appears as part of a description of what Tillich calls Protestantism. "The courage of the Reformation transcends [is a synthesis of] both the courage to be as a part and the courage to be as oneself."[73] What he is calling Protestantism, of course, is really Tillichian Protestantism—literally a protest against what has gone before. How does this unique brand of Protestantism unite participation in God with having a person to person relationship with God? Individual men are parts of humanity, hence they participate in humanity. Individual men also have person-to-person dealings with each other; hence they stand as individuals in relation to the rest of humanity. The seemingly paradoxical requirement of simultaneously being a part of and separate from God is easily met when God is defined as humanity.

Tillich defines the courage to be as "the courage to accept oneself as accepted in spite of being unacceptable."[74] We encountered a slightly different version of this expression in discussing the symbol, Jesus as the Christ. At that point a negative meaning having to do with God's acceptance (nonretribution) of man's acceptance that there is no God was stressed. Now there is a positive angle to consider. The divisive forces of estrangement and of demonism make us unacceptable to humanity as a whole. Our love is unrequited because we belong to the wrong race, class, or nation, and especially because we have excluded ourselves from membership in the religious community. Yet, despite being unacceptable to humanity, we accept it as our God. When we do this, humanity

72. *Courage*, p. 34. 73. *Courage*, p. 163.
74. *Courage*, p. 164.

218

"accepts" us by giving us "the power of being." "Power is the possibility a being has to actualize itself against the resistance of other beings. If we speak of the power of being-itself we indicate that being affirms itself against nonbeing."[75] Translation: Other men rebuff our efforts to live by the law of love, but love for humanity gives us courage and motivation despite the nonbeing of (a) reciprocal love and (b) supernatural answers to the questions producing anxiety.

A minor alteration in the definition makes courage "the accepting of the acceptance without somebody or something that accepts."[76] Look closely at the words "accepting of the acceptance." They are a semantic transformation of "negation of the negation." Tillich is indicating, now a little more subtly, that the courage to be is a dialectical synthesis. It is the negation of the negation of God. Tillich identifies three elements of "absolute faith," which faith grows out of the chain of acceptances. Each element is a part of the dialectic, and therefore part of its synthesis too. The first element is "the experience of the power of being" and refers to the thesis, which is belief in God, the power of being. The second element involves "the experience of nonbeing" and, Tillich reminds us, is dependent on the first. Unbelief is born of belief in God. The third element is "the acceptance of being accepted." Man accepts the power of being—that which overcomes nonbeing—and this power constitutes humanity's indirect acceptance of man.[77]

The power of being, incidentally, has more connotations than the above discussion indicates. The general meaning of power of being is the power to overcome nonbeing. As part of his policy of confusing people—of giving words many connotations centered around a controlling meaning—Tillich gives nonbeing many meanings. Sometimes it means the hypothetical nonexistence of humanity or, occasionally, of life. With respect to individuals it can mean the relative absence of a will to live (despair) or, less ominously, an antithetical state wherein the individual has rejected the God of theism and not yet found the true God. Nonbeing is also a synonym for estrangement, referring here to the nonbeing of mutual love among men. Lastly, nonbeing can signify the unreality of the

75. *Courage*, p. 179. 76. *Courage*, p. 185.
77. *Courage*, p. 177.

supernatural God and all he stands for—immortality, a "meaning of life," divine law, and such things. Humanity, as the power of being, overcomes all of these forms of nonbeing in various ways which are self-evident.

When man accepts the power of being, he accepts "the God above God."[78] Here is a crucial statement about this higher God: "Only if the God of theism is transcended can the anxiety of doubt and meaninglessness be taken into the courage to be."[79] There is a double meaning to this statement, with both meanings conveying the same point. First, the God of theism—and this means the rational, self-aware (if spiritlike) personality of Christian faith—must be transcended in the sense of being removed. Second, both the word "transcend" and the words "taken into" refer to a dialectical synthesis, which by definition transcends thesis and antithesis by taking them into itself. Doubt and meaninglessness can be brought into the synthesis, instead of simply being replaced, only if the object of doubt and the source of meaning—God—continues to be rejected. Tillich is saying we cannot just return to the thesis but must bring only that part of it which is vital into the synthesis. What is vital, as far as Tillich is concerned, is the word "God" and the concept of an absolute which stands at the center of one's life. For Tillich this absolute, the God above God, is humanity. *"The courage to be is rooted in the God who appears when God has disappeared in the anxiety of doubt."*[80]

An Ontological Footnote

By focusing on "individualization and participation" and on "despair," prominent terms in the foregoing analysis, we can perceive additional parallels between Tillich and Hegel. The first goes back to the structure of dialectics. In its simplest form, a dialectic has three parts: thesis, antithesis, and synthesis. Tillich emphasizes this simple structure in dialectical formulations concerning the idealized human life. But a more complex structure, based on that used by Hegel in his ontology, is employed for "ontological analysis" describing the "world," that is, humanity. This more elaborate

78. *Courage*, p. 186.   79. *Courage*, p. 186.
80. *Courage*, p. 190.

structure employs Hegel's two elements, the universal and the particular, as subdivisions of each part. The thesis is the elements' potential unity (essence), the antithesis their existential separation (existence), and the synthesis their ultimate "reunion" (essence = existence). Here one must be careful, for ambiguous terminology makes it easy to mistake the two elements for thesis and antithesis. In the simple dialectic of God, man, God = man, the thesis and antithesis are God and man, representing belief and unbelief. In the ontological dialectic, however, God and man become the elements, representing universality and particularity. Now the dialectic is God and man united, God and man separated, and God and man reunited. The basic idea is the same, but some terms have been redefined.

In *The Courage to Be* the simple dialectic, and the one on which we have concentrated our attention, is the one describing the life of a "self" or person; it is the movement from being to nonbeing to the courage to be. Again, this is just a variation of revelation, reason, revelation = reason and of God, man, God = man. Underlying this simple dialectic is the more complex one of individualization and participation: potentially united, existentially separated, then essentially reunited. Fundamentally, this is an ontological dialectic describing humanity. In a sense, however, it also symbolizes a personal life. Theism (individualization, particularity) and mysticism (participation, universality) are the ontological elements. And, if we think in terms of a personal life, the courage to be is their synthesis. As for thesis and antithesis, the simple and complex dialectics correspond conceptually but not temporally. Just as theism and mysticism stand in potential unity as a thesis, belief in a supernatural god (whether theistic or mystical) can be treated under "being" as potential unity with the true God: each thesis embodies the concept of potentiality. But temporally, both being *and* nonbeing correspond to existential separation of the elements, for in neither of these stages does man recognize that he is at once the universe (God) and an individual interacting with it.

Moving along to "despair," as the most general characteristic of nonbeing, there is a definite similarity between it and Hegel's unhappy consciousness. It would be hard to state with confidence that the former copies the latter—they have a common foundation

—but some resemblances are noteworthy. Unhappy consciousness describes the antithesis in an ontological dialectic employing the two elements, universality and particularity (or one and many). Hegel introduces the elements in this context as master and servant: one and many. The master expresses universality and is loosely equivalent to God lording over man; he is the infinite which projects itself into the finite particulars (servants) through fear, obedience, and the like. Potentially, the master and the servant are the same (Spirit); existentially, each regards the other as "object." This existential separation is carried by Hegel through several stages of antithesis, each slightly closer than the last to the goal of identifying the self with the universal without abandoning self's particularity. These stages include Stoicism, which is part universal and part particular but ultimately favors particularity, and Skepticism, which alternates between poles but spends most of its time being universal. Things approach a climax when the unhappy consciousness emerges. It is a human consciousness with the world view of medieval Christianity, a consciousness which sees itself as the "changeable" at the mercy of the "unchangeable" yet which identifies with the latter in certain ways (man as God's image, God's incarnation in man, participation through communion). The unchangeable is misconstrued as another being; this is the why and wherefore of estrangement and the meaning of "unhappy."

Compare all this with Tillichian nonbeing and its "despair." Nonbeing is also an antithesis, two in fact. In the simple dialectic of being, nonbeing, and the courage to be, it is the middle term. And in the ontological dialectic it shares with being the condition of separation between theistic particularity and mystical universality. In his antithetical plight man is unhappy; he knows despair. (This conceptual similarity is another reason for regarding "despair" as an abstraction and not taking it too literally.) One might even want to associate theist and mystic with stoic and skeptic: the mystic's denial of this world, for example, resembles the skeptic's annihilation of the objective world of manifold particularity. However, Hegel's half-and-half characterizations really don't provide a close fit, and if Tillich was copying he made a lot of alterations in the process.

Dialectical Humanism

A PHILOSOPHY OF HISTORY

Tillich feels constrained by theological and philosophical precedent to expand his thought to include a philosophy of history. He proceeds by discussing where history is headed, by what processes it moves, and whether it can reach a climax. History's aim is the Kingdom of God; it moves dialectically; and it foretells an endless series of ever higher climaxes.

The Kingdom of God

The central concept in Tillich's philosophy of history is the Kingdom of God. It is the humanistic counterpart of Christianity's Kingdom of God and of such philosophical utopias as Hegel's Germanic monarchy and the world communism of Karl Marx. To understand what Tillich has in mind, therefore, we must first relate his Kingdom of God to its theological and philosophical analogues.

RELIGION AND PHILOSOPHY. The Kingdom of God was borrowed by Christianity from Judaism, which in turn borrowed it from Zoroasterism. Zoroasterism, the ancient Persian religion, saw history as a twelve-thousand year struggle between good and evil, light and darkness. Its climax would begin with the arrival of a *saoshyant*, or prophet, the last of several miraculously born sons of the founding prophet Zoroaster. The dead would be resurrected and passed through a stream of molten metal. To the good it would feel like warm milk, but the evil would be scalded and purified. (The latter would previously have endured the torments of hell's fire, which is a pre-Kingdom purgatory in Zoroasterism.) This event would mark the final defeat of the Evil Spirit, the end of the age, and a new beginning—the Kingdom of *Ahura Mazdah*, the Wise Lord.

Judaism came in contact with Zoroasterism following the close of the Babylonian exile (538 B.C.). The Jewish people, immersed in poverty and robbed of the legendary glory of the earlier kingdom of David, found many answers to their needs in Zoroastrian ideas. Among the borrowings were the hell of fire, the messiah (*saoshyant*), the resurrection of the dead, and God's post-historical kingdom. In Daniel 7:10, the "stream of fire" issuing from before the Lord at the end of the world is patterned after the Zoroastrian molten metal. Unlike the Zoroastrian Kingdom, Judaism's was to be preceded by a final judgment and would exist side by side with hell. Some Jews visualized the Kingdom of God not as the supernatural realm of apocalyptic Judaism but as a political restoration of the kingdom of David, with the messiah, a descendant of David, ruling on behalf of God.

The more supernatural version, depicted by Jesus as the alternative to a fiery hell, was adopted by Christianity. Jesus, as the Son of Man (messiah), would arrive on a cloud from heaven—amid earthquakes, bloodshed, famine, eclipses, and other horror—for the Last Judgment. The dead would be called from their graves and a new world launched. Only the good were to be admitted to the Kingdom of God; the bad would receive eternal fire. At least this was the original idea. As Christianity became increasingly hellenized, the Zoroastrian-Hebrew notion of resurrection was gradually replaced by the Greek idea of an immortal soul. Correspondingly, the Second Coming, Last Judgment, and earthly paradise faded almost out of sight as a celestial heaven took over. But this celestial kingdom, which parallels history rather than being a part of history, is not the basis of Tillich's analogy.

The Kingdom of God has its correlates in numerous utopias and near-utopias advanced by philosophy. Tillich compares the thought of the Enlightenment, which looked to an "age of reason," to Christianity's final stage. For Auguste Comte, a period of positive sciences, flowing from earlier eras of religion and metaphysics, was man's earthly salvation. Hegel saw the emergence of the Germanic nations, attendant with the self-realization of the world-self, as the climax of history. A classless society following the overthrow of capitalism was Utopia for Marx. Other ideas, developed in varying degrees, exhibit similar characteristics.

TILLICH. What treatment does Tillich accord the Kingdom of God? Since he is not given to defining his terms, we must go by inference and test our inferences against the meager descriptions provided. There can be no doubt that we are dealing with something within the historical frame, for the analogous kingdom of early Christianity was a phase of history (actually post-history) and not something beside history. Another Christian feature to be mimicked is that of having every participant in the kingdom ruled by God. This is really the key feature. God is humanity, as an object of ultimate concern. Logically, then, the Kingdom of God should be a situation wherein everyone is ruled by concern for humanity—all humanity, not just demonic groups. As a hypothesis, then, let us say that the Kingdom of God is where everyone experiences Spiritual Presence, that is, where God is humanity in its entirety to every human being.

Does this hypothesis square with Tillich's description? "The real fulfillment of the Kingdom of God is when God 'is all to all,' as Paul says."[81] Also: "According to the visionary who has written the last book of the Bible, there will be no temple in the heavenly Jerusalem, for God will be all in all."[82] If it is accepted that Tillich's God is humanity, one can hardly question the meaning of "all to all." It means God is all humanity to all human beings. The same idea is carried in this passage: "But the Kingdom of God is also the place where there is complete transparency of everything for the divine to shine through it. In his fulfilled kingdom, God is everything for everything."[83] The word "transparency" indicates that Tillich is now talking about ultimate concerns, for they are what he commonly describes as being either transparent to (true concerns) or opaque to (idolatrous concerns) the divine. In the Kingdom of God everything—every concern—is transparent to humanity: everyone treats humanity as his God. In the Kingdom of God the entire universe of individuals must experience the fulfilment of New Being. "Fulfilment within the unity of universal fulfilment. The religious symbol for this is the kingdom of God."[84]

At one point Tillich lists four characteristics of the Kingdom of God. These agree with the interpretation suggested. First, the Kingdom of God is political, and its "political quality" is "power." This simply means that, in a figurative sense, God rules, and in a related sense, men have the power of being. Second, the Kingdom is social, and the social characteristic embodies the ideas of peace and justice. Man, in the social context, is peaceful and just toward man. Third, the Kingdom is personalistic in the sense of involving "the fulfilment of humanity in every human individual." This is about as plain a statement as Tillich will make about any symbol and requires no explanation. Fourth, the Kingdom has universality.

81. *Dialogue*, p. 123.
83. *ST–1*, p. 147.
82. *Culture*, p. 8.
84. *Love*, p. 65.

Tillich again refers to Paul's expression about "God being all in all" in the Kingdom.[85]

History as Dialectical

History, as described by Tillich, is a quest of sorts for the Kingdom of God—the utopian state of universal humanism. But Tillich's Kingdom is not the final stage of history; it is something which is always present, albeit fragmentarily. The purpose of history is constantly to enlarge the Kingdom, while rolling back periodic incursions of demonism. Progress is dialectical, if only in a heavily qualified sense.

TWO PROBLEMS. There is no question that Tillich wants to follow Hegel and Marx in presenting a dialectical philosophy of history, but it is apparent that he has had to struggle to remain in contact with reality. He acknowledges two problems with dialectical and other mechanistic histories. One is that it is hopelessly unrealistic, almost predestinarian, to treat history as a straightforward dialectical process. Tillich concedes that deterministic forces may be powerful in a given situation. "Nevertheless," he says, "the existence of chances, balancing the determining power of trends, is the decisive argument against all forms of historical determinism—naturalistic, dialectical, or predestinarian."[86] There is "no logical, physical, or economic necessity in the historical process,"[87] and dialectical activity must therefore be interpreted as largely incidental to the course of history.

The second problem is that the dialectical histories of Hegel and Marx brought historical dynamics to a rather abrupt termination. History became a static condition following the final synthesis. Regarding Hegel, Tillich inquires why the principle of negation should suddenly become impotent with the emergence of the German nations. Regarding Marx, he wonders why the classless society should not generate its own antithesis. "An absolute stage as the end of the dialectical process is a contradiction of the dialectical principle."[88] (Interestingly, Tillich is quite willing to settle for one antithesis and one final synthesis when it comes to "the divine life.")

85. *ST–3*, pp. 358–59.　　　　86. *ST–3*, p. 327.
87. *Protestant*, p. 48.　　　　88. *Protestant*, p. 42.

226

In order to overcome these two problems Tillich proposes an interpretation of history in which dialectics is not only restricted to ethical activity but is (a) nondeterministic and (b) unending. Tillich's history undulates from crest to crest: "History has its ups and downs, its periods of speed and of slowness, of extreme creativity and of conservative bondage to tradition."[89] Although it is not made explicit, one senses that each crest is a little higher than the previous one: "History . . . drives toward the creation of a new, unambiguous state of things."[90] In this drive, dialectical forces operate in two directions. First, ethical history and world history move on parallel courses, interacting in what can be loosely conceptualized as a dialectical manner: a development on one side (thesis) will influence events on the other (antithetical reaction) and lead to further developments on the first side (synthesis). There exists between world history and "church history"—the "church" is the humanistic community—"a highly dialectical relationship, including several mutual affirmations and negations."[91] Second, within ethical history one can always break time into arbitrary periods which a competent dialectician, if nobody else, can interpret as thesis, antithesis, and synthesis. These dialectical forces, both lateral and forward-moving, are nondeterministic because ethical progress merely influences, and is influenced by, history but cannot overcome the many chance factors at work. There is no end, no final synthesis, because the Kingdom of God can be approached but never fully realized.

History's unendingness requires elaboration. Tillich is quite emphatic about the fragmentary nature of the Kingdom's successively closer approximations. Man, he believes, cannot achieve the ultimate, but "fragmentary anticipations are possible."[92] Dreams of utopia ignore man's imperfectible nature: "The Kingdom of God can never be fulfilled in time and space. . . . Improvements in education and environment may serve to raise the general ethical level of a people and to polish its original crudeness, but such improvements do not affect the freedom to do good and evil as long as man is man. Mankind does not become better; good and evil are

89. *ST–3*, p. 371.
90. *ST–3*, p. 332.
91. *ST–3*, p. 382.
92. *Love*, p. 124.

merely raised to a higher plane."[93] Perhaps this sounds like common-sense realism, but Tillich is actually negative about the very concept of a realized Kingdom. He speaks as though an undivided world would be devoid of fun, excitement, and anticipation and contends that "a world without the dynamics of power and the tragedy of life and history is not the Kingdom of God, is not the fulfilment of man and his world."[94] Why be so negative? Because the real substance of these assertions is not realism but dialectics. In the introduction to this chapter it was pointed out that New Being *must* remain subject to the conditions of existence in order to dialectically include the antithesis—existential estrangement—in the synthesis. By the same token, each realization of the Kingdom *must* be partial so that the antithetical forces of demonism can be taken into the synthesis. If demonism were simply extirpated, the Kingdom of God would not be a synthesis. That would spoil the dialectic and corrupt Tillich's system.

KAIROS AND THEONOMY. The Greek word "kairos," taken from the New Testament, is used by Tillich to designate the beginning of an ascent to a new historical peak. In the New Testament it signifies such events as God's sending his Son to earth, the time of Jesus' death, and the Kingdom's being "at hand." Tillich finds analogies in historical moments pregnant with humanism. "In each kairos the 'Kingdom of God is at hand,' "[95] and each "is a turning-point in history."[96] The criterion for identifying a kairos, in the general sense, is the unique event of the "great *kairos*," the appearance of Jesus as the Christ as the center of history.[97] Don't be fooled by the way Tillich speaks of the Christ's appearance on earth as the central event of history. He is talking about theology's mythological history: Eden, the fall, sin, the incarnation, the Church, the second coming, and the Kingdom of God. The central mythological event is real history to millions of Christians but not to Tillich. He uses it only to symbolize actual historical events wherein man rejects the supernatural and becomes united with "God."

"The philosophy of the kairos is closely related to the dialectical interpretations of history."[98] For history "comes from and moves

93. *Boundary*, p. 77.
95. *Protestant*, p. 47.
97. *ST–3*, p. 370.

94. *Love*, p. 124.
96. *Protestant*, p. 45.
98. *Protestant*, p. 48.

toward periods of theonomy," and with each kairos "a new theonomy" begins.[99] Theonomy, it will be recalled, is the synthesis of
heteronomy (rule of authority) and autonomy (rule of reason); it
is reason guided by the "authority" of love for humanity. Heteronomy, autonomy, and theonomy now become a cultural dialectic
analogous to the personal one described earlier. Each cultural theonomy leads to (but does not deterministically generate) an antithesis which might be either heteronomous or autonomous. If
heteronomy follows, there is a new era of ecclesiastical rule or
political dictatorship. But if the reaction is autonomous, it is "not
necessarily a turning-away from the unconditional."[100] Autonomy
is nonhumanistic rather than antihumanistic; reason, science, and
empiricism for their own sakes bring progress outside the ethical
sphere and prepare the way for a new kairos.

The reader who attempts to understand Tillich's highly abstract
description of ethical progress in terms of actual history is wasting
his time. Like Hegel, Tillich is ready to read thesis, antithesis, and
synthesis into almost anything; like Marx, he has little inclination to
be specific. His only reasonably decent effort to apply heteronomy,
autonomy, and theonomy to world history is found among his 1963
Santa Barbara lectures. There he labels six historical periods:
(1) *heteronomy*—the early Greek period of ritual and liturgy,
(2) *autonomy*—the era of Greek philosophy, ethics, and religious
criticism which reached its apex around 100 B.C., (3) *theonomy*—
the first thousand years or so of Christianity, (4) *heteronomy*—the
period of the medieval church and the Inquisition, (5) *autonomy*—
the Renaissance, Reformation, and Enlightenment—roughly the
sixteenth, seventeenth, and eighteenth centuries, and (6) *heteronomy*—the secularization of the Kingdom of God idea into Nazi-
ism, communism, and other "quasi-religions."[101] The difficulties
arising from such arbitrary classifications as these are apparent.
Why ignore the growth of Yahwism, the mystery cults, and other
religious movements during the Greek philosophical period? What
on earth was basically humanistic about the period we call the
Dark Ages? (Here the answer is that Tillich is catering to the larger
audience: having called the incarnation the center of history and

99. *Protestant*, p. 47.   100. *Protestant*, p. 45.
101. *Dialogue*, pp. 32–33.

the "great kairos," he would be giving away his mythological referents if he failed to acknowledge theonomy in early Christianity.) Regarding the postmedieval period, why ignore the Thirty Years' War, the atmosphere which brought Galileo to his knees before the Pope, the witch trials, the rise of monarchic dictatorships, and the Napoleonic wars? By what standard is there less humanism today than in A.D. 500? Why is communism more heteronomous than the czarism of an earlier period? Why focus on particular continents and countries? If there has been only one theonomy, where are all the kairoi and the peaks among the ups and downs Tillich repeatedly mentions? These questions are raised not as criticism, though that they certainly are, but to underscore the futility of trying to reduce Tillich's abstractions to a coherent description of actual history.

THEORY VS. MESSAGE. The truth is that Tillich has no theory or interpretation of history, and neither has he deluded himself into believing he has. He is simply going through the motions of rounding out his analogical system by developing a highly abstract symbolic history based on analogies to Christian, Hegelian, and Marxian histories. This portrait of history is kept on its high level of abstraction to conceal the fact that, despite a plenitude of random comments about people and periods, Tillich really has nothing cohesively theoretical to say about history. His historical analysis, such as it is, is merely another exercise in encoding the hidden message of dialectical humanism. As such it belongs in the same category as Tillich's mislabeled "theories" of religious symbols, estrangement, the self-world relationship, religious typologies, and the resurrection. All purport to be profound descriptions of little understood aspects of reality. But the only genuine reality is the fact that none is really intended as a theory of reality or as anything else but a combination of No and Yes—No to Christian doctrine and Yes to humanity.

The Church in History

Tillich again tries to mislead the larger audience by speaking of Christianity as the key to the Kingdom of God. History, he says, is the story of groups. But we must be careful not to take what he says at face value. In bringing up the subject of groups, Tillich is back to his favorite activity: analogy building. Both theology and philosophy offer theories about groups assuming central roles in the fulfilment of history. For theology, the group known as the Christian Church carries the burden of taking history to its dramatic triumph, the Kingdom of God. For philosophy, two accounts of the group in history stand out: the dialectical accounts of Hegel and Marx. Hegel believed that history was the history of groups and that these groups were nations in whose national mentality (culture, "spirit") the consciousness of the Spirit progressively unfolded. The Germanic people, whom Hegel saw as embodying history's highest cultural values and among whom the Spirit (through Hegel, a German) achieved full self-realization, stood as the principal history-bearing group. As for Marx, we know that he regarded the proletariat as the group in whose hands the climax of history—communism—rested. Once more, then, we are dealing with theological and philosophical correlates. Correlates are symbols, so we must look for a symbolic meaning. The group Tillich is going to talk about will be not the one he seems to be discussing but an analogous one. It will be the group which relates to the Tillichian versions of the Kingdom of God, Germanic monarchy, and Marxian communism.

One particular group, asserts Tillich, holds the key to the meaning of history. Specifically, "it is Christianity in which key and answer are found."[102] One might suppose from this that the Kingdom of God means universal Christianity—everyone converted. The supposition is tenable, however, only if one knows what Tillich means by "Christianity." He uses the word interchangeably with "the Church" which, we noted earlier, is defined as "the Community of the New Being." Sometimes he clarifies his position by referring to the "latent church," as opposed to people who call themselves Christian: "Therefore, if we say that the churches are the leading forces in the drive toward the fulfilment of history, we must include the latent church (not churches) in this judgment."[103] The institutional churches are also involved, but only insofar as Tillichian reform movements make them vehicles for fighting supernaturalism. Fights "against the demonic and the profane in

102. ST–3, p. 349.   103. ST–3, p. 376.

the church . . . can lead to reformation movements, and it is the fact of such movements that gives the churches the right to consider themselves the vehicles of the Kingdom of God, struggling in history, including the history of the churches."[104] For the Kingdom of God to be realized, church-sponsored supernaturalism would have to be eradicated, because "the end [goal] of history is the end [destruction] of religion."[105]

James Luther Adams is quite wrong (for certainly he is not equivocating) when he writes that Tillich's key to history "is participation in . . . that group—the Christian church—for which the center is Jesus as the Christ, the power of the New Being."[106] Adams has stumbled on two of Tillich's many ambiguities. Tillich's Christian Church includes everyone who, consciously or otherwise, rejects the supernatural and makes concern for his fellow man the ultimate criterion of personal conduct; and Jesus as the Christ is a purely imaginary being symbolizing man incarnated as God in man —fully God and fully man. It is true that Tillich has said, with reference to the institution, that only the Christian Church can express "its devotion to the God above the God of theism without sacrificing its concrete symbols" in the process.[107] If we grant Tillich's faulty premises that (a) a church might want to switch to man as its God and (b) a switch requires the use of symbols derived from Christian belief, then what he says is obviously true. What other church already uses Tillich's "symbols"? But notice that Tillich does not say that other churches could not reform by sacrificing their symbols, and much less does he say that churches are necessary. On the contrary: "In Eternal Life there is no religion."[108]

DIALECTICS IN REVIEW

In examining his widely misunderstood method of correlation, we saw that Tillich is attempting a Grand Synthesis of theology and philosophy. There are four levels of synthesis: (1) the disciplinary level, correlating theology and philosophy, (2) the ontological

104. *ST–3*, p. 377.   105. *ST–3*, p. 403.
106. James Luther Adams, "Tillich's Interpretation of History," *The Theology of Paul Tillich*, ed. Charles W. Kegley and Robert W. Bretall (New York: Macmillan, 1952), pp. 295–96.
107. *Courage*, p. 188.   108. *ST–3*, p. 403.

level, correlating the two absolutes, God and being, (3) the historical level, correlating Christian history with Hegelian-Marxian dialectical history, and (4) the level of a personal life, correlating the
Christ's going out from and returning to God with the abstract
movement from thesis to antithesis to synthesis, and more loosely
with "life" and "process" philosophies. The synthesis is always
humanistic: humanism, the God of humanism (humanity), a humanistic conception of history, and a humanistic parable of life. In
creating his syntheses, Tillich unfolds an impressive number of dialectical formulations which in one way or another symbolically
state the hidden message that God is man. These bring theology
and philosophy into correlation while simultaneously declaring the
divinity of mankind.

The most important, though not all, of the dialectical triads will
be reviewed here so as to tie together the more crucial elements of
Tillich's system. A series of tables will be helpful toward this end.
Each table has three horizontal divisions, representing theology, philosophy, and Tillichian humanism. In reading these tables, observe
that the dialectics—each line is a dialectic—always conform to at
least one of four patterns:

	Thesis	*Antithesis*	*Synthesis*
(1)	Yes	No	Yes + No
(2)	God	Man	God = Man
(3)	One	Many	One = Many
(4)	Union	Separation	Reunion

The last three patterns relate closely. There are many men but
only one God. Many is loosely implied in separation, and union
describes the singular. Also note that, in the first pattern, union
and reunion are implied in the separation from and return to Yes.

The Disciplinary Synthesis

Tillich's correlative synthesis of the two disciplines, theology and
philosophy, is unique among those to be summarized in that thesis,
antithesis, and synthesis lie in different divisions. Table 1 summarizes the picture. It shows three sets of correlates. Theology correlates with philosophy to produce humanism. Revelation and reason,
the opposing sources of theological and philosophical knowledge,

combine to yield rationalized revelation, that is, "revealed" doctrines made rational through nonsupernatural interpretation. The Word of God, another term for revelation, joins the Logos, which connotes both law and reason, to symbolize the "law of love": You shall love humanity with all your heart, soul, mind, and strength. Theology-philosophy-humanism could also be presented left to right as dialectic, but revelation and reason are so closely identified with their respective disciplines that an extra triad would be redundant.

TABLE 1
DIALECTICS BASED ON CORRELATION OF DISCIPLINES

	THESIS	ANTITHESIS	SYNTHESIS
Theology	Revelation (Word of God, or Divine *Law*)		
Philosophy		Reason (Logos, or Rational *Law* of the Universe)	
Humanism			Rationalized Revelation (*Law* of Love for Mankind)

The Ontological Synthesis

The second level of correlation presents a merger of the theological and philosophical absolutes, God and being (or being-itself). These jointly symbolize humanity, the absolute of humanism. Table 2 summarizes the most significant dialectics in the area of ontology. Starting at the top, Tillich has devised a typology of religions which employs monotheism, belief in *one* God, to symbolize humanity and polytheism, belief in *many* gods, to symbolize individual men. By calling for a synthesis of the two, Tillich endorses one God consisting of many individuals. A second religious dialectic, based on the divine-human encounter, is a favorite of Tillich's. As presented in *The Courage to Be*, mysticism now represents the one (or union) and theism the many (or separation). Since the theism described here is monotheism, there might seem to be a contradiction between the use of monotheism to represent one in the typology of religions but many in the divine-human encounter. However, the second dialectic covers not just divinity but divinity *and* humanity: theism represents plurality, or the separateness of

234

man and God, whereas in mysticism the divine "swallows" man. (But when Tillich uses mysticism and "monarchic monotheism" as elements of a sub-dialectic in his typology, theism's plurality derives from angels and other demigods subordinate to the monarch.)

TABLE 2
DIALECTICS BASED ON CORRELATION OF ABSOLUTES

	THESIS	ANTITHESIS	SYNTHESIS
God:			
Typology of Religions	Monotheism (one)	Polytheism (many)	Trinitarian Monotheism (one comprised of many)
Divine Encounter	Mysticism (union)	Theism (separation)	Mysticism + Theism (union and separation)
Being:			
Structure of Reason	Ontological Reason (potential unity)	Subjective-Objective (actual separation)	Depth of Reason (actual unity)
Ontology	Being	Nonbeing	Being + Nonbeing
Humanity:			
Physical	Humanity (one)	Individual Men (many)	Humanity = Individuals (one comprised of many)
Mental	Ultimate Concern	Preliminary Concerns	Ultimate Reflected in Preliminary

In the philosophy division of the table ("Being") Tillich's two broadest ontological formulations are summarized. The dialectic labeled "Structure of Reason" constitutes the basic framework of Part I of *Systematic Theology*. Ontological reason is the thesis, the potential unity of mankind. This unity is shown by ontological reason's use as a general heading which subdivides. The two subdivisions, equivalent to what are elsewhere called the ontological elements, are objective (humanity) and subjective (individuals) reason. In the antithesis, these two elements are in conflict, symbolizing the divine divided against itself. Revelation conquers the antithesis, rendering both subjective and objective reason transparent to their depth and thereby establishing their synthesis as "the

235

depth of reason." In Part II Tillich dusts off being and nonbeing and uses them as thesis and antithesis in his "ontology." The thesis is the being of the *one*, humanity, or rather its potential being as God. Nonbeing has several connotations relating it to individual men or the *many* (e.g., men are not immortal), but the one to be emphasized is the nonbeing of mutual love among men. When being—realized being this time—reappears as the synthesis, the identity of the one and the many is symbolized. In another sense, the synthesis also combines the being of *a* God with the nonbeing of the supernatural God.

Under humanity there are again two dialectics. In a physical sense humanity is a universe, analogous to matter, but it also consists of concrete individuals; it is one (thesis) and many (antithesis). The potential unity of the many as the one is realized in the synthesis, where humanity becomes God. From a mental standpoint humanity is an ultimate concern, analogous to mind, and it is also the manifold preliminary concerns ("ultimate concerns" in a looser sense) which embody the ultimate. Either way, Tillich's God is a synthesis. The general (divine) is "incarnated" in the particular (human) in accordance with "the norm," Jesus as the Christ.

The Historical Synthesis

Things get a bit more complicated when it comes to interpretations of history. The historical dialectics are shown in Table 3. This table, more than any of the others, illustrates what Tillich regards as the basic pattern of dialectics. "The movement of life from self-identity to self-alteration and back to self-identity is the basic scheme of dialectics," he explains.[109] The modified column headings used in Table 3 emphasize this particular pattern; each dialectic follows it. The dialectics come in pairs. Under each side category one dialectic is labeled (*a*) states and the other (*b*) periods. "States" refers to the state of divine-human relations, which oscillate from union to separation (estrangement) to reunion. The divine, meanwhile, varies from God to Hegel's metaphysical world (Spirit) to humanity, depending on which system one is examining. The "periods" dialectics each divide history into three periods.

109. *ST–3*, p. 329.

These imitate the abstract pattern of separation and return characterizing the divine-human relationship. Authority, except in the case of Marx, is that from which man separates and to which he returns; in Marx, man separates from and returns to communal property, that is, his labor.

TABLE 3
DIALECTICS BASED ON CORRELATION OF HISTORIES

	UNION (ONE)	SEPARATION (MANY)	REUNION (MANY = ONE)
Christian:			
(a) States	Innocence: man and God united	Sin: man vs. God	Salvation: man and God reunited
(b) Periods	Pre-history: Eden (authority)	History (autonomy)	Kingdom of God (authority)
Dialectical:	Potential Essence	Actual Existence (estrangement)	Actualized Essence
Hegel:			
(a) States	Metaphysical World	Man vs. World	Man = World
(b) Periods	Oriental Despotism (authority)	Ancient Democracy (freedom, autonomy)	Germanic Monarchy (authority + freedom)
Marx:			
(a) States	Economic Man	Worker vs. Capitalist	Worker = Capitalist
(b) Periods	Primitive Communism	Slavery, Feudalism, and Capitalism	Final Communism
Tillichian:			
(a) States	Humanity (potential unity)	Man vs. Humanity (estrangement)	Man = Humanity (actual unity)
(b) Periods	Heteronomy (authority)	Autonomy (reason)	Theonomy (authority + reason)

To start with theology, Christianity interprets man's relations with the divine as a three-stage process wherein man separates from and then returns to God. This is paralleled by prehistory (Eden), where man submits to God's authority; history, where man rebels; and the Kingdom of God, where God rules once more. Philosophy's answer to Christian history is found in the dialectical histories of Hegel and Marx. These histories can be described in the language of philosophy as movements from essence to existence and back to essence. Hegel's three states in the divine-human relationship witness man separating from, then reuniting with, metaphysical world. The world-self (Spirit) moves from its potential unity as all reality to actual separation within itself—man views the objective world as a hostile entity—to realized potentiality wherein Spirit, through man, discovers itself in all "objects." The three periods in Hegelian history, in turn, mimic (but do not temporally correspond to) the divine-human situation generally and Christianity's separation and return to authority in particular. The difference is that Hegel's authority is not God but an earthly ruler. In Marx's dialectical materialism, God is proletarian man. Man is torn apart from and reunited with his labor (himself), or the fruits thereof (represented by the capitalist, etc.). Marxian history's broadest periods progress from communism to exploitative (private property) systems back to communism. Hegel and Marx each culminate their histories with utopias—Germanic monarchy and world communism—corresponding to the Kingdom of God.

Now for Tillich. He uses all that has gone before to symbolize his own dialectical history. The divine becomes humanity, and the "states" dialectic moves from potential human unity to the actual estrangement of man from humanity ("God") to actual human unity under conditions of estrangement. As for historical periods, Tillich has his own version of the now familiar movement from authority to autonomous freedom back to authority. However, in Tillich's case, this movement is a never-ending cyclical process: the Kingdom of God can be approached but never fully realized.

Tillich's two historical dialectics bring out some further correlations. Innocence and essence correlate to symbolize the potential unity of mankind; sin and estrangement correlate to symbolize the actual separation of man from man; salvation correlates with actualized essence (reunion) to symbolize self-transcending man; and the Kingdom of God correlates with Germanic monarchy and world communism to symbolize theonomous approximations to the Tillichian Kingdom, namely, universal humanism.

The Personal Life Synthesis

The fourth and last level of correlative synthesis is that of personal history—a personal life. Table 4 shows the principal dialectics involved. Three theological (Christian), three philosophical

238

(dialectical), and three Tillichian triads are included; although the last set could be greatly enlarged. Again, modified column headings are used in place of "thesis," "antithesis," and "synthesis," for the movement of separation and return is once more present. An idealized personal life separates from and returns to God.

TABLE 4
DIALECTICS BASED ON CORRELATION OF "LIFE"

	UNION	SEPARATION	REUNION
Christian:			
Trinity	Father	Son (separates)	Holy Spirit (unites)
Christ	Incarnation	Crucifixion	Resurrection
Disciples	Jesus is Christ	Jesus not Christ	Jesus a Symbolic Christ
Dialectical:			
The Triad	Thesis (Yes)	Antithesis (No)	Synthesis (Yes + No)
Alternate 1	Affirmation	Negation	Negation of Negation
Alternate 2	Essence	Existence	Essence = Existence
Tillich's "Divine Life":			
Version 1	God	No God	Nonsupernatural God
Version 2	Revelation	Reason	Humanism
Version 3	God	Man	God = Man

This table is easier to explain starting from the bottom. Tillich's "divine life" is a parable depicting the evolution of personal wisdom as a three-stage process. The idealized human life moves from theism to atheism to humanism, that is, from God to no God to a nonsupernatural God. The third stage is, in dialectical language, a synthesis of Yes to God and No to the supernatural. The progression can alternatively be described as a movement from revelation to reason to humanism, with humanism regarded as a synthesis. By associating revelation with God and reason with man, we can also identify a movement from God to man to God = man. The three versions are, one can see, substantially identical.

Moving up in the table, the "Christian" and "Dialectical" divisions hold a new group of correlates: Tillich mates the three members of the Trinity with the three stages of the dialectical triad.

The three resulting pairs of symbols respectively point to the three stages of the divine life. Beyond the Trinity, Tillich finds in Christianity two more ways to symbolize the divine life. The "Christ" triad—incarnation, crucifixion, and resurrection—represents Tillich's basic christological symbolism. Incarnation describes perfect union of man and God, symbolizing the divine life's thesis; the crucifixion, where man slays the supernatural, symbolizes stage two; and the resurrection, which reunites Jesus (man) and God, symbolizes stage three. The "Disciples" dialectic comes from Tillich's pseudo-theory of the resurrection. Note its point for point correspondence with the christological symbolism. The disciples at first view Jesus as the Messiah (Yes); then he is crucified and belief turns to doubt (No); and finally there is a spiritual resurrection through which the disciples visualize Jesus as a symbolic rather than a supernatural Christ (Yes + No)—the Christ who symbolizes New Being. Under the "Dialectical" heading there are two triads besides the basic one mentioned above. These are alternative ways of labeling the elements of a dialectic, hence of employing philosophical terminology to symbolize the divine life.

The Essential Tillich

The foregoing review makes it amply clear that Tillich's thought is long on mechanics, short on substance. Stripped of its dialectical cover, the philosophy that some commentators have hailed as profound is seen to hold little beyond the proposition that humanity is God. "God is man" is the essence of Tillich; all other doctrines are corollaries or close to it. The corollaries can be reduced to the ten listed below. A more extensive list could be offered but would entail excessive overlap and repetition. The ten corollaries:

1. God includes *all* mankind.
2. Any "god" (paramount concern or interest) reflecting concern for something less than or other than all humanity, for example, a special group, is demonic.
3. Any doctrine directly or indirectly affirming a supernatural god or metaphysical essence is demonic.
4. There is no supernatural God, no supernatural anything.

5. Rules of conduct governing human relations can be formulated only by man himself.
6. Human progress is measurable by the degree to which human beings accept humanity as God and comport themselves accordingly.
7. The goal of history—the main social objective toward which men should strive—is the recognition of all humanity as God by all human beings ("all in all").
8. Recognition of humanity as God brings personal satisfaction.
9. Not all men recognize humanity as God; hence man is estranged from himself.
10. Man will always be estranged, because some men will always prefer demonic gods to humanity. Personal essence will therefore always be limited by existence—synthesis will always include antithesis.

Nowhere is this philosophy better epitomized than in *On the Boundary*, the autobiographical sketch which Tillich has adorned with some of his choicest passages. "Today the idea of 'mankind' is more than an empty notion. . . . The increasing realization of a united mankind represents and anticipates, so to speak, the truth implicit in a belief in the Kingdom of God to which all nations and all races belong. Denying the unity of mankind . . . includes, therefore, denying the Christian doctrine that the Kingdom of God is 'at hand.' " Tillich illustrates his idea of a united mankind with the example of America, where "all nations and races" blend together. America "is a kind of symbol of that highest possibility of history which is called 'mankind,' and which itself points to that which transcends reality—the Kingdom of God." The highest possibility of history is mankind, a united mankind in which all men participate. It will never arrive—it "transcends reality"—yet it remains the ultimate toward which men should strive.[110]

110. *Boundary*, pp. 95–96.

CHAPTER 6

Critics and Criticism

We have come to that point in the critique where the author stands back to appraise his subject. Tillich has been criticized from many viewpoints but primarily from that of religious conservatism. This is unfortunate. The traditionalist critics, wedded as they are to supernatural belief, have generally mistaken Tillich's message for a watered-down and possibly unorthodox version of their own. That is, they have taken his overt supernaturalism seriously (if sometimes electing to call it metaphysics) and have proceeded to castigate him for straying too far from tradition and, often, for confused thinking. My own lack of belief has perhaps helped me to avoid this pitfall. At any rate, I perceive a different set of objections, the validity of which rests on the accuracy of the insights presented in the preceding chapters. In this concluding chapter I hope to distinguish between what might be called nonbeing and being in the realm of criticism—between traditionalist objections which have missed the point and legitimate criticisms which, I trust, will come to grips with the real substance of Tillich's thought.

SOME FALSE STARTS

Numerous critics have indicated, explicitly or implicitly, that they take seriously Tillich's claim to be a Christian theologian. For my part, I cannot take Tillich's claim to be a theologian the least bit seriously. Tillich's theology, as theology, is a sham from beginning to end, and nobody knew it better than Tillich. Attempts to elicit serious supernatural or metaphysical meanings from Tillich's thought will inevitably channel criticism of that thought into blind alleys. This is exactly what has happened. Criticism from within the theological fraternity has lost its way among (a) pointless attempts to discover logical fallacies in a system that does not rest on logic, (b) abortive discussions about the merits and meaning of symbolism, (c) complaints that Tillich's description of God lacks consistency, and (d) dogmatic protests over Tillich's failure to endorse the faith of our fathers.

The Question of Logic

The main thrust of J. H. Thomas, who regards himself as Tillich's "logical critic,"[1] is toward proving that Tillich's thought is overburdened with logical fallacies. So vigorously does Thomas press this point that some reviewers felt his analysis might have a terminal impact on the era of Paul Tillich. As pointed out in Chapter 2, however, Tillich does not base his thought on logic. In seeking to effect his Grand Synthesis of theology and philosophy, he has adopted the theological approach of arguing from authority (with tongue in cheek, to be sure)—whence the title, *Systematic Theology*. In his student days he had hopes of achieving a synthesis through philosophy, and for a while he thought Schelling's "Christian philosophy" might do the trick. But Tillich later espoused his mature position that an apologetic theology represents the correct approach to synthesis. This approach combines analogical correlation of theological and philosophical concepts with the apologetic method of giving alien substance to the theological concepts one is defending. The basic characteristic of the approach, as far as the logic issue goes, is that it purports to take the side of authority in the confrontation between authority and reason, theology and philosophy.

In recognizing Tillich's explicit intent to remain in accord with biblical authority, David Kelsey is closer to being right than Thomas.[2] Tillich is taking the Bible's description of Jesus as the

1. J. Heywood Thomas, *Paul Tillich: An Appraisal* (Philadelphia: Westminster, 1963), p. 186.
2. See David H. Kelsey, *The Fabric of Paul Tillich's Theology* (New Haven: Yale University Press, 1967), pp. vii, 1.

Christ and using it as an authoritative central premise ("the norm") for developing all of his conclusions. The christological norm is used to interpret a wide range of "revelatory" source material, including other material from the Bible. Everything rests on the authority of the Bible and related theological sources, as interpreted "under the norm." Authority, not reason, is king. Reason does enter through the back door, so to speak; hence philosophy is represented in the synthesis. What Tillich does is place theology and philosophy on two levels, general and particular. Authority provides the general concepts and reason directs Tillich to particular interpretations of these concepts. This two-level structure is designed to give rational content to the irrational supernaturalism of tradition: reason is, for the most part, loosely construed as anti-irrationality rather than as formal logic. The closest Tillich comes to formal logic is in denying that one individual can be 100 percent human and 100 percent supernatural at the same time and "deducing" from this paradox that God and man are the same. Beyond this there is also a lot of analogy building, but Tillich's analogies are symbolic rather than logical.

As Thomas sees it, Tillich's fundamental error of logic is to assume that because a concept exists, a genuine reality must stand behind that concept. "The fallacy that the existence of a word means the existence of a thing results in a great deal of confusion in Tillich's thought."[3] The word Thomas has in mind is "being." He thinks Tillich uses it in a metaphysical sense to denote a mysterious supernatural something or other which, as God, is the essence of reality. Tillich supposedly believes that the concept of being proves a hidden reality and, thinks Thomas, this displays Tillich's "confusion" about the concept, "the whole of reality."[4]

Some people do think this way: I once read some popular theology in which the author, a clergyman, asserted that atheists prove God exists when they use the word "God" to deny his existence. But to accuse Tillich of this sort of foolishness is grossly unfair and only reflects Thomas' own confusion. There is nothing metaphysi-

3. Thomas, *Paul Tillich*, p. 72.
4. *Ibid.*, p. 67. Compare Thomas' interpretation with Tillich's statement that "the ontological way is not a logical conclusion from the idea of the Unconditional to its existence (*Sein*), a procedure that, of course, is impossible" (*Religion*, p. 129).

cal about "being" in Tillich's thought, even though he tries (and succeeds with Thomas) to create the opposite impression within the larger audience. Depending on the context, Tillich gives being such meanings as humanity (the principal meaning), the God of theism, New Being, life, physical reality, existence, and truth. In the last sense, being includes the nonbeing (nonexistence, untruth) of God, of a life hereafter, and of any other supernatural reality; being includes the nonbeing of metaphysical being.

Issues About Symbolism

Tillich's fondness for symbolism, assisted by the many red herrings he drags through his discussions of the topic, has generated further issues having some relationship to the question of logic. These issues concern whether Tillich's symbols have or can have ultimate meaning and whether Tillich has tripped over fallacies of ambiguity.

ULTIMATE MEANINGS. Some critics have in effect construed Tillich's symbolism as an exercise in logic. In particular, the suggestion has been repeated that Tillich employs symbolic chains: a symbol is a symbol of a symbol, ad infinitum. Here the implication is that a symbol is never linked to nonsymbolic ground and that a chain of logic therefore falls apart for want of a solid premise—or perhaps a chain of meaning leads to no meaning. Any such idea reveals a serious misunderstanding of Tillichian symbolism. Tillich's symbols aren't all that complicated. There are no symbolic chains; symbols don't symbolize other symbols.[5] A symbol is simply a doctrine, concept, or term, not necessarily religious, which relates by analogy to a Tillichian concept. Thus, as we have seen, "resurrection" symbolizes man's rising from the figurative death of estrangement

5. A minor qualification is necessary. Once in a while one symbol points to a concept which in other contexts is itself a symbol for something specific, but that is as far as things go. "Destiny" (predestination) thus symbolizes the concept of God, leading to the point that God and man are identical—man in this instance is symbolized by "freedom" (free will). In this context, however, Tillich is making a statement about God, in an abstract sense of the word rather than in the symbolic sense of humanity. He is saying that God (the abstraction) is humanity, not that humanity is humanity. In the quotation which concludes Chapter 5 we saw Tillich using America to symbolize the Kingdom of God, which in turn symbolizes universal humanism. But this can hardly be called a chain, and neither does it leave us with nothing specific at the end.

from his fellow man into the New Being—new life—of union with the rest of mankind. One might question the relevance of some of Tillich's symbolic meanings to social reality, but certainly the meanings are not themselves symbols.

Closely related to the question of symbolic chains is the view that Tillich uses a type of symbolism in which one metaphor is explained by another or a series of others but never ultimately by a statement which can be taken literally. Because the reader cannot supply the literal equivalent, Tillich's thought becomes unintelligible and meaningless. In an intriguing article on "Professor Tillich's Confusions," Paul Edwards develops this point. He starts out from the premise that Tillich is a metaphysician in the sense of one who "tries to make God as unlike human beings as possible." (Edwards, who identifies himself as an unbeliever, is an exception to the general rule that supernaturalistic interpretations of Tillich come largely from supernaturalists.) A lot now hinges on what God really means, and Edwards is ready to deny that it means anything. Denying this becomes in fact a central point in the discussion, and little if any distinction is made between the particular point that being-itself is unintelligible and the general one that Tillich's symbolism is unintelligible. Edwards argues that, with Tillich, one metaphor merely leads to another. God, or being-itself, is thus explained as "the ground of everything personal." Tillich "never seems to have noticed that even in his basic statement, when elaborated in terms of 'ground' and 'structure', these words are used metaphorically and not literally." Therefore, "one metaphorical statement is replaced by another but literal significance is never achieved."[6]

If Edwards' assumption that none of Tillich's metaphors can be reduced to literal meanings were correct, his thesis that Tillich's symbolism is ultimately meaningless would also be correct. And if we acknowledge that few readers of Tillich—certainly not casual readers—have any way of knowing the esoteric meanings assigned to various symbols, particularly the meaning that being-itself is humanity, Edwards' conclusions enjoy an ample measure of validity. Yet his analysis is itself ultimately lacking. To begin with,

6. *Mind*, LXXIV, no. 294 (April 1965), 192–204.

being-itself is greatly overemphasized at the expense of other symbols whose metaphor is easier to penetrate. It is comparatively easy, for instance, to deduce that "absolutism" symbolizes God. Now "God" might itself sound like a metaphorical term. But if we have also deduced that absolutism's opposite, relativism (many), symbolizes man, Tillich's abundant hints that absolutism and relativism must be merged lead straight to the conclusion that God and man are one. Similarly, a rereading of the Chapter 4 material on the crucifixion analogy will show that Tillich is fairly explicit that the Christ symbolizes, among other things, the death of the supernatural. In other words, there are metaphorical analogies which can be exploited; the problem is to find them.

To get back to being-itself, the analogy between it and humanity —both are absolutes—is admittedly too ambiguous to lead us directly to humanity. But there is plenty of evidence scattered about in Tillich's writings (see Chapter 3) which supports the conclusion that God is man. At the same time, Tillich says in plain English that God is being-itself, which means that being-itself also symbolizes man. Once you recognize this, the formerly unintelligible symbolic statements come to life. You can then see in what sense being-itself is the ground of everything personal: humanity is the source or basis of our existence as persons. Or, in dialectical terms, humanity in its potential unity is the ground or thesis from which emerges the antithesis of every person's being estranged from humanity (unrequited love). Tillich therefore *is* intelligible (sometimes), but only when you abandon the metaphysical premise and interpret being-itself as humanity.

AMBIGUOUS TRUTH. Despite the lack of foundation for the criticisms just discussed, there is implicit in Tillich's system a potentially significant fallacy. Whether it is actually significant, however, depends on whether the implied argument, rather than serving as a ploy, is meant to be taken seriously. Tillich *seems* to argue that Christianity merits allegiance because its doctrines are valid because, as symbols, they accurately describe reality. Such an argument involves the fallacy of ambiguity. If for the sake of argument we concede that the symbolic analogies accurately describe reality, the fact remains that the symbols thereby validated and the Christian doctrines at issue are the same in name only. Anyone with an elementary understanding of logic knows that you can't prove a proposition (e.g., that Christian doctrine embodies truth) by redefining the terms. Thus, in a debate on communism, the negative cannot legitimately deny the proposition, "Resolved: that the Reds have a party line," by (a) redefining "Reds" to mean the Cincinnati Reds, (b) redefining "party line" to mean a two-party telephone hookup, and (c) proving that the baseball club has nothing but private lines. By the same token, you don't prove the truth of supernatural concepts by giving them nonsupernatural meanings.

Superficially, then, Tillich has committed a grievous error of logic. The question is: are his symbols meant to be taken seriously? In Chapter 2 it was suggested that in converting Christian doctrines to humanistic symbols Tillich is just providing cover for his subversive activities. Likewise, it was pointed out that Tillich himself has admitted that his use of symbolic analogies is more a matter of protesting than of affirming. And the point was made that a major purpose of symbolism is not to preserve old doctrines but to encipher the hidden message. This is not to deny that Tillich has a strong emotional attachment, dating back to childhood, to the Christian Church. But this attachment is not intellectual; it does not require preservation of archaic doctrines; it can be satisfied with music, liturgy, and participation in religious affairs. No doubt Tillich is happy when someone, perhaps a minister suffering the pangs of creeping agnosticism, trades superstition for symbols. Mainly, however, Tillich is interested in purging the supernatural. It really doesn't matter whether the old just dies or, alternatively, becomes a symbol. Therefore, the logical fallacy of ambiguity is unrelated to the real substance of Tillich's thought.

The Empty Picture

A different critical tack is taken by David Kelsey. He centers his analysis on Tillich's professed desire to write a theology based on the biblical *picture* of Jesus as the Christ. (Kelsey does not make Thomas' mistake of assuming that Tillich is trying to base his system on logic.) However, Kelsey immediately goes astray by crediting Tillich with accepting the supernatural origin of the biblical picture of the Christ and with taking the Bible seriously. Moreover, Kelsey does not see the picture Tillich sees, namely, the picture of a God who is man (fully God and fully man). Kelsey's errors lead to several unwarranted criticisms. His most general criticism is that a picture is a work of art which ipso facto cannot make claims and that, in any case, the picture Tillich describes has conflicting contents. The picture of the Christ, thinks Kelsey, is sometimes described as having a powerful impact on men's lives (an allusion to Tillich's "power of being") and sometimes as having structure or meaning, concepts which Kelsey doesn't clarify. Tillich's claim that the Spirit unites power and meaning is empty, because no systematic connection between them has been shown. In the same way, Tillich's description of God has two contents, power and form, which again seem mutually exclusive. The best Tillich can do with his mixed-up picture, suggests Kelsey, is to stress vaguely defined attitudes rather than positive beliefs. Therefore, instead of merely correcting the flaws of biblical literalism, Tillich manages to basically warp the New Testament.

Tillich surely does warp the New Testament, but Kelsey's judgment is otherwise faulty. First of all, a picture *can* make claims if one wants to use it for that purpose; anyone who has ever seen a political cartoon should know this. Tillich's verbal picture of Jesus, which is loosely based on the Bible's, makes the claim that God is man. As for Kelsey's charge that power conflicts with form, Kelsey offers nothing resembling an understandable explanation of what he thinks Tillich means by form, structure, and meaning. He just takes the words from Tillich and seems to imply that they either have no meaningful content or that their content depends on revelatory sense impressions. Yet how can we say that A conflicts with B if we cannot say what B is?

Let us review the meanings of power and form and see where Kelsey goes astray. Power has several related meanings in Tillich's thought. The power of being means the power to overcome nonbeing (of God, salvation, divine law, and the like), and in this sense power refers to courage or motivation. Tillich is speaking figuratively, of course, just as a clergyman speaks figuratively in saying that God is love. Power is also used by Tillich as a shorthand notation for the religious side of the trinitarian synthesis. When he asserts that the Spirit unites power and meaning, he is speaking of the religious concepts of God and revelation becoming united with philosophy's key elements, man and reason. "Meaning," along with form and structure, refers to the philosophical side of the synthesis. Reason gives meaning to the concepts promulgated by authority; reason shapes the abstract concept of God into the concrete form of man, giving it a definite structure.

What about the charge that Tillich uses the biblical picture to stress attitudes rather than beliefs? This objection also errs. On the negative side, Tillich places a great deal of stress on believing that the supernatural, especially the supernatural God, is unreal. On the positive side, Tillich stresses the need to believe that mankind is the God on which life should focus. If someone wants to call these attitudes rather than beliefs, I won't quibble, but they certainly are not the meaningless attitudes, lacking definable content, that Kelsey has in mind. Thus when Kelsey objects that "accepting the acceptance" calls for nothing but a vague attitude, he fails to recognize that the phrase is an enciphered version of Hegel's "negating the negation." Kelsey therefore misses Tillich's call to synthesis—to the belief that God is man.

Dogmatic Objections

Finally, among those who accept Tillich as a serious theologian writing seriously supernaturalistic theology, there are the critics who base their objections on divine revelation, as incorporated in the doctrine and dogma of Christian tradition. These are the religious conservatives, who take their Bible very seriously if sometimes rejecting the most primitive mythology (e.g., the devil, Adam and Eve, the virgin birth). They have God's Word as to what is real, and since Tillich doesn't believe it he is wrong.

The best representative of this school of criticism is Kenneth Hamilton. His book, *The System and the Gospel*, is devoted to proving that Tillich's system "is incompatible with the Christian gospel."[7] Hamilton is quite disturbed that Tillich has converted God from a being to a metaphysical-mystical-pantheistic entity. He is equally disturbed that Tillich has reduced Jesus to a symbol, no longer the Son of God. He thinks Tillich has too much tendency to accept modern man's view of the universe, a view about which

7. Kenneth Hamilton, *The System and the Gospel: A Critique of Paul Tillich* (New York: Macmillan, 1963), p. 227.

Hamilton is openly skeptical. To his credit, Hamilton has not been deluded into looking upon Tillich as basically orthodox, although he does accept Tillich as a supernaturalist who believes in revelation.

A more restrained member of the revelatory school is Alexander McKelway. McKelway has formulated a predominantly literal interpretation of Tillich. This interpretation assumes that Tillich's God is a being who should not be called a being because the word has anthropomorphic connotations, or something like that. (It is all right, however, to say "he" and "his" in reference to God and to speak of God's revealing "himself" to man in Jesus; this is somehow less anthropomorphic.) Reading Tillich this way, McKelway doesn't share Hamilton's view that the biblical God has been corrupted—which helps to explain McKelway's restraint. On the other hand, McKelway firmly rebukes Tillich for his lack of emphasis on Jesus. Although he can't decide whether Tillich believes Jesus was divine—at several points he says Tillich's Jesus is the Christ but later he wonders if Tillich hasn't robbed Jesus of his divinity— McKelway finds Tillich guilty of failing to affirm the incarnationist viewpoint that Jesus was God's revelation of himself to man.

Father Tavard is not unlike McKelway. He sees no cause for war in Tillich's interpretation of God; no dogmatic spears are hurled in this direction. But Tillich's Christ is another matter. "It is unbiblical. It is not in keeping with the traditional formulations of the early Councils. It is incompatible with the theology of the Fathers and that of the medieval Doctors." It can't even be reconciled with the faith of the Protestant Reformation. In a word, it is "heretical."[8]

It is pretty hard to argue with revelation: either you have it or you don't. I will simply state that criticism of the Hamilton-McKelway-Tavard variety is essentially emotional. Certainly it has no intellectual content beyond various degrees of recognition that Tillich rejects traditional belief. Instead, it depends for its validity on doctrines presumed to represent the Word of God. It also depends on the critic's intuitive confidence that his own beliefs, among the many conflicting ones "revealed" to man, are correct. No doubt many readers who share the conservative beliefs at issue,

8. George H. Tavard, *Paul Tillich and the Christian Message* (New York: Scribner's, 1962), p. 137.

particularly the belief that Jesus was divine, will accept these criticisms. To those for whom revelation is the touchstone for human thought, I can only suggest that a willingness to consider additional objections resting on philosophical grounds may lead to an even firmer conviction that Tillich is wrong.

TO WORSHIP MANKIND

Tillich's fraternal critics may have missed the mark, but Tillich remains an inviting target for criticism. To strike home, however, objections to Tillich's philosophy should treat it as just that: philosophy. The supernaturalistic premises which make theology theology aren't there, and the contemporary abundance of pseudo-theology written by men who have lost their faith in no way vitiates the criterion. Viewing Tillich's thought as philosophy, I find objectionable its wish to deify man. By way of reservation, I am well aware that much of Tillich's obvious exaggeration and his more extreme statements can be written off either as system or as mock piety. Among his levels of meaning, Tillich's deepest message is a simple No to God and Yes to man. Above this level we encounter so much foolishness that it is sometimes hard to guess how much is intended to be taken seriously. Nevertheless, one cannot excuse an unlimited amount of double talk on grounds that the philosopher really didn't mean what he said, and the fact that the ideas in question are outside the pale of supernaturalism suggests an intent to flesh out the Yes and the No with more elaborate substance. Tillich's effort to say something original leads to the assumptions that (1) most if not all persons are grasped by a single, "ultimate" concern, (2) it is a practical possibility with almost anyone for this concern to be humanity, and (3) humanity should be everyone's ultimate concern. These assumptions get Tillich into severe trouble, trouble which can be traced to his insistence on maintaining the analogical integrity of his symbolism.

The Fiction of Ultimate Concern

One of the main concepts of Tillich's philosophy is ultimate concern. Ultimate concern brings the gift of New Being, the dialectical synthesis which brings life to its unifying climax. The term is ambiguous in that it can refer to (*a*) humanity, the infinite concern to which finite concerns must be transparent if they are "true," (b) preliminary concerns transparent to humanity, that is, indirectly expressing concern for all mankind, and (c) opaque preliminary concerns, those reflecting concern for less than all mankind. At the moment we are considering the last two—finite concerns which represent an ultimate without being that ultimate. A concern for honest government illustrates true ultimacy (transparent to humanity); success and the church are false ultimacy, or demonism (transparent to self and group).

It is important to understand what Tillich means by "ultimate." There is, in his system, only one ultimate concern per person. Thus in one sense an ultimate concern is whatever is most important to an individual. But this oversimplifies. Ultimate concern is absolute concern; it is not ultimate merely in relation to lesser concerns or even to the sum total of all lesser concerns. It is a matter of infinite —unlimited—"passion." It demands "total surrender" by the person who is grasped. One's entire mental life is unified by the ultimate concern, which becomes the "integrating center" of one's existence. If a concern is ultimate, there can be absolutely no reservation about it. Speaking of science as an illustration, Tillich has indicated that the scientist's willingness to sacrifice everything, even his life, for science delineates the ultimacy of the concern.

When ultimate concern is described this way, which is exactly how Tillich describes it, one begins to wonder if Tillich has not spent too much time in the ivory tower. Most people are concerned about any number of things. Some concerns are indeed more important than others, but how many people have one single concern which is not only more important than any other but more important than all others put together? How many people have built their lives around something which will not be relinquished no matter how much else has to be sacrificed to maintain the integrating focus? It strikes me that most concerns are subject to trade-offs: concern A might be more important than anything else but would be abandoned before B, C, and D combined would be set aside.

One could argue, I suppose, that if concern A were really a matter of infinite passion, it wouldn't be sacrificed under any circumstances. This is most obvious when concern A is a person like one's wife, mother, child, or brother. Love can certainly be infinite. And it can be directed in quite a variety of directions: toward animals, humans, gods, societies, artistic creations, and so on. But therein lies the problem. If two or more quantities are infinite, how can just one of them be ultimate? Suppose a canoe upsets in the middle of a lake and a father is forced to choose between saving one or the other of his identical twin sons. He may make an arbitrary decision or grab the nearer, but does this prove that the twin who is saved was more ultimate than the other? Or suppose that a devoutly orthodox Jewish girl wishes to marry a Catholic boy who, out of love and respect for his own faith, insists that she accept Catholicism. Her devotion to both the boy and Judaism is infinite. If, in desperation, she makes an emotional choice which could have gone either way, has a meaningful ultimacy been established?

The absurdity of trying to identify a single concern which, for an average individual, is "ultimate" or "god" has been thoughtfully stated by Walter Kaufmann:

Not only frivolous people lack any ultimate concern and are in an important sense uncommitted but the same is true of millions of very serious college students who wonder what they should do with themselves after graduation. There is nothing to which they greatly desire to give themselves, nothing that matters deeply to them. They are not shallow; they are not playboys; they enjoyed many of their courses and appreciate the opportunity to discuss their problems with sympathetic professors. They do not say: nothing matters to me. What they do say is: no one or two things matter more to me than anything else.

Kaufmann proceeds, in what is some of the most trenchant criticism of Tillich I have encountered, to challenge the relevance of ultimate concern to concrete individuals. "What is my 'God'—if these theologians are right and everybody ultimately has his 'God'? I am not non-committal, not adrift, not hard put to find some project to devote myself to. I feel no inclination to pose as a cynic, saying: nothing is holy to *me*. But what, specifically, *is* holy to me?" Observing that a humane person is apt to have several deep concerns which balance one another, Kaufmann concludes that "one can safely generalize that those who, spurning more than one

concern, insist on a single commitment either abandon humanity
for fanaticism or, more often, engage in loose talk."[9]

Is Demonism Avoidable?

Tillich holds that people not only are ultimately concerned but
that salvation arrives when a person adopts a concern transparent
to humanity. Humanity is offered as a salvation open to anyone;
hence, it is appropriate to inquire whether this is actually the case.
If it develops that most persons, being merely human, cannot
muster the altruism which Tillich's New Being demands, then salvation is a practical possibility for at best a small minority.

Conceding for the sake of argument that it is correct to say that
everyone has an ultimate concern, I wonder if most of us are not
doomed to live with what Tillich calls demonic concerns. Tillich
thinks, or at least pretends to think, that infinite and unconditional
concern for all mankind can be found by anyone with the wisdom
to seek it. But can it? Aside from the fact that love and concern are
emotions not subject to conscious manipulation, how can the average human avoid having his deepest concern directed toward that
which Tillich calls demonic? I am suggesting not that people are
basically selfish—though many are—but that what matters most to
most people is loved ones, country, or both. If anything is a matter
of total surrender, the one cause which will not be abandoned, a
thing for which one would die, surely for most individuals that
concern is the family. (I am trying to be charitable: many persons,
handicapped by a perfectly natural fear of death and often without
meaningful family ties, regard nothing more highly than their own
lives.) The teacher, the social worker, the statesman, and all the
other dedicated humanitarians, not to mention the unfortunate citi-
zen of merely average interests, usually have one or more loved
ones for whom they would abandon their lifetime project or profession if it became a life and death matter. Lacking loved ones,
they would at least sacrifice their quests to defend and perhaps die
for their country.

Where does this leave Tillich? It leaves him with a salvation that
is irrelevant to all but a handful of saints and fanatics—primarily

9. Walter Kaufmann, *The Faith of a Heretic* (Garden City: Doubleday,
1961), pp. 95–97.

the latter. It leaves him with a faith which is universalistic in theory but rigidly exclusive in practice. Because concern for family, *if* the concern is *ultimate*, is one of the worst forms of demonism in Tillich's scheme of values: the group which is God is unusually small and nonuniversal. As for the nation, it is Tillich's prime example of the demonic. Therefore did God, as translated by Tillich, utter "the command to leave the gods of soil and blood, of family, tribe and nation" to Abraham.[10]

I suspect there are those who would argue that family and country are really transparent to humanity. All kinds of things can be rationalized if one really tries. But any effort to recast these "false" ultimacies as "true" renders the Tillichian struggle between humanism (all humanity is God) and demonism (part of humanity is God) meaningless. Estrangement and reunion become indistinguishable. Humanity cannot be the Unconditional and still be subject to the condition that some people are more unconditional than others. If, in the final analysis, God doesn't have to be *all* humanity, then New Being and demonism are one.

The point that any ultimate concern (but not necessarily non-ultimate ones) transparent to less than *all* humanity is demonic leads to another aspect of the problem. Even if it were granted that the average person has or can have an ultimate concern transparent to more than family or nation, the demand for universality would still bar the way to true ultimacy. Let it be clearly understood that, in line with the requirement that it be fully ultimate as well as fully concrete, humanity must be treated as a universe in the "unconditional" sense of the word. Divinity cannot be compromised; no element of humanity can be left out. Nobody. Don't assume that Tillich is a reasonable man who, in meeting specific problems, would qualify his demand for a universal God. He has made it perfectly clear that he wouldn't. He can't—not without compromising his system. For the system is based on analogy, and humanity is the analogue of both God and being. God, on the one hand, is a universal God whose omnipotence and omnipresence are not conditioned by the tiniest outpost of immunity. Being, for its part, is patterned mostly after Hegel's Absolute Spirit, which consists of

10. *Culture*, p. 35.

every last particle of reality: Spirit becomes Absolute Spirit when, in Hegel's words, it "attains the form of universality" through subject's becoming conscious that *every* object is itself, that is, that "it is *all* reality."[11] Reasonableness, then, is irrelevant to Tillich. What is relevant is that humanity must be so structured as to support two analogies, neither of which permits any diminution of the Absolute's universality.

How does universality bar the way to New Being? The answer is that hardly anyone is capable of being concerned, through a preliminary concern or otherwise, about every last member of the human race. Admittedly, some people may like to think they are. Concern for *all* humanity is superficially appealing, for it implies opposition to nationalism, prejudice, and the like. Moreover, many persons have been raised to accept, if only in the abstract, the admonitions to "love thine enemy" and "turn the other cheek." But how many really do? In real life all but the most pious take their stands this side of heaven by making exceptions in appropriate cases. To how many people does it really make sense, does it even seem human, to have a sincere concern for the happiness and welfare of each and every human being? To many of us, love for all humanity is a contradiction in terms: to wish one person well can mean wishing misfortune, suffering, or death to others. But Tillich's philosophy doesn't see things this way. Accordingly, it lays down conditions for salvation which are beyond the reach of ordinary mortals.

Man as the Answer

Even if we assume that people have ultimate concerns and that demonic ones are avoidable, Tillich's case for deifying man is thoroughly unconvincing. Tillich's position is that an individual reaches the highest attainable level of personal as well as moral maturity when he elects to make reverence for mankind the guiding principle of his life, which he then builds around some concern mirroring this principle. To this position I would object that the mature life requires no ersatz gods. I would also argue that, insofar as some individuals do have focal points in their lives (but not

11. G. W. F. Hegel, *The Phenomenology of Mind*, trans. J. B. Baillie (New York: Harper Torchbooks, 1967), pp. 795, 414 (my italics).

necessarily ultimate concerns as defined by Tillich), there are other interests and values as worthy as humanity.

Some people, it seems, cease to believe without ceasing to want to believe. Intellectually, they abandon religion; emotionally, they cry out for it. They therefore convince themselves that primitive man was in principle correct in creating gods. Where man went astray, they tacitly assume, was in turning to imaginary gods instead of some true god to be found within the scope of reality or human values. A person with this outlook, one who has rejected the substance of religion (supernaturalism) without losing the religious attitude, may turn to an ersatz faith and an ersatz god. The new god will then be defended with the same vigor and enthusiasm once extended to the defense of the old. In particular, the claim is apt to be made that the ersatz god is superior to any other and that commitment to this god is the hallmark of maturity and wisdom. Tillich in effect makes such a claim about man.

Rather than being a mark of maturity, however, the substitute faith can actually be a mark of immaturity. As Tillich explains his concept of humanism, it is in part an attempt to overcome a feeling of emptiness and insecurity which supposedly accompanies a loss of faith. I have already suggested that he exaggerates for effect when he speaks of despair as a concomitant of unbelief, yet it is clear enough that he wants to ascribe more than a modicum of therapeutic value to New Being: persons who are troubled about the meaninglessness of life find meaning and are healed emotionally. What this implies is that these people lack the maturity to accept life as it is. Deprived of God, who once made life meaningful, they find no peace of mind until a new god satisfies their inner craving for allegiance to a sacred cause. I suspect that such individuals are hard to find: the gradual realization that one's childhood beliefs are fantasy is not a traumatic experience for an emotionally stable person. Nevertheless, wherever a person is found who does lack the courage to face life without the support of a god, be it alcohol or humanity, there is an immature individual.

Most humanists, it must be conceded, are not running away from anxiety. They are not people who find it difficult to face life without a substitute religion; they are mature individuals. But does this mean that one must dedicate one's life to a cause with humanitarian overtones to become fully mature? To clarify this question, it should be understood that with Tillich we are talking about more than ethical humanism. Ethics is part of the picture, but Tillich's humanism is a matter of making humanity the indirect focus of one's life—indirect because humanity is the ultimate concern to which some preliminary concern is "transparent." Ethical behavior in human relations therefore becomes incidental to a pattern of living that centers on humanity. This means that the issue is not whose system of ethics is best but whether one man's principal interest in life belongs to a higher category of interests than the next man's. Tillich's position is that any ultimate concern not grounded in humanity is not only inferior but "demonic."

My own view is that no one category of human concerns can be termed better than all other categories. There are, to be sure, any number of concerns which I would be willing to call inferior or even unworthy, but this does not imply that every concern can be given a precise rank. Concerns are matters of taste, interest, and judgment, and what seems important to one man may seem distinctly unimportant to the next. It is one thing to believe in decent behavior toward one's fellow man; it is quite another to make a fetish of human decency or love, arguing that there can be no higher truth. Other truths are just as honorable. To give two examples, concern for the welfare of animals and ordinary scientific curiosity are, in my judgment, just as honorable as concern for human beings.

Take the case of animals. Among the many persons affiliated with the SPCA and animal rescue leagues there surely must be some whose lives reflect greater concern for the welfare of animals than for the welfare of human beings. It isn't that they are unconcerned about their fellow humans, much less that they are unethical; they just happen to be more concerned about dogs and cats. Tillich may think that these people are a shade less mature or admirable than humanitarians but, if so, he is simply prejudiced. Some of those concerned about the welfare of animals objected when, in 1967, the automobile industry used live baboons in crash tests designed to save human lives. Let us assume that the supervising engineers were more concerned about safety—hence indirectly about humanity—than anything else in the world. Personally, I have no inclination to take sides in the dispute, but Tillich definitely belongs on the side of the engineers. Is his judgment beyond debate? Other men are concerned about preserving grizzly bears and sea otters from extinction. The issue is easily confused if one imagines that these men are thinking strictly in terms of opportunities for future generations of human beings, so let us assume if necessary that admiration and empathy for lower creatures supplies the real motive. Why must such concerns rank below humanitarian ones? And why, for that matter, must they impart less inspiration or motivation?

The other example is scientific curiosity. It is easy to assume that scientists are an altruistic lot who do everything they do out of direct or indirect concern for the welfare and future development of mankind. Realistically, however, it must be recognized that scientists have numerous motives, not the least of which is earning a living. Curiosity is one of these motives. There are a few scientists who spend almost every waking hour in the laboratory and for whom their research approaches the "infinite passion" which Tillich says describes an ultimate concern. For some it is knowledge for the sake of knowledge; their curiosity is insatiable. To be sure, these men (most of them) are ethical humanists; but science for its own sake, not humanity, is their number one concern. Concerns like this are, to Tillich, "idolatrous" and "demonic." Are such epithets warranted? Are these men, by virtue of their driving curiosity, somehow less than completely honorable? Are their humanitarian colleagues at least a trifle more mature and respectable? Also, do the curious derive less "meaning" and satisfaction from life than Tillichian humanists?

System versus Reality

The main reason Tillich gets into so much difficulty with his theology of man is that he permits his system to dictate the content of his thought. Now there is nothing wrong with having a system. Almost any intellectual endeavor requires some sort of system, if only for the purpose of organizing facts and ideas. The trouble is that Tillich's system is geared to cleverness and deception rather than to the discovery of insights about reality. As cleverness, the system attempts to execute the Grand Synthesis of theology and

philosophy which holds Tillich in thrall; as deception its function is
to camouflage the hidden message and thereby protect Tillich's
standing in the Church. I have my doubts about what Tillich has
accomplished by way of uniting theology and philosophy—and
about the value of such an enterprise. The deception, it must be
conceded, has been remarkably effective. But to get to the point,
the system has been utterly unable to serve the quest for wisdom,
an end for which it was not designed. Instead of the system being
a servant of the philosopher (with respect to wisdom), the philosopher has become a slave to the system. Rather than leading the
philosopher to the truth, the system has distorted truth into
abstractions bearing scant resemblance to the reality purportedly
described.

THE ANALOGICAL GOD. The basic difficulty lies in Tillich's use of
analogy. Analogy is the keystone of the system. Tillich seeks to
establish triangular resemblances between theological concepts,
philosophical concepts, and synthetic humanistic concepts. The
theological and philosophical concepts become symbols. Their analogical relationship to each other is called correlation, and the
analogous Tillichian concept which is their synthesis pretends to
describe reality. Only it doesn't. Or, if it does, that reality is limited
to the commonplace wisdom that (a) there is a lot of strife among
men, (b) the supernatural is a creation of the human imagination,
for which reason religious solutions to human conflict can be ruled
out, and (c) human relations will improve to the extent that individuals and groups show greater consideration for each other.
Beyond this elementary understanding of the world, Tillich's
thought is replete with fancy, emptiness, and narrow-mindedness.
It is not that Tillich is naive—he undoubtedly knows better—but
that he is more concerned with the structural integrity of his system than with the validity of its conclusions. Consequently, it
becomes more important that a Tillichian idea remain true to the
theological and philosophical symbols which jointly define it than
it is that reality be accurately described.

Tillich's fanciful ideas about ultimate concern, his insistence that
man be treated as a god, his requirement that humanity be conceived universally even to the point of including its own enemies,
his unwillingness to respect other "gods" beside his own—all this

underscores the clumsiness of the system. Here Tillich is building analogies around the concepts of God and being. These are the theological and philosophical absolutes: God is the ruler of the universe and demands absolute loyalty; being is the essence of reality which renders all else superficial. As an avowed theologian, Tillich needs a God to write about; as a *systematic* theologian he intends to correlate his God with being. So, copying a string of German philosophers (Kant, Hegel, Schelling, Feuerbach, Marx, Nietzsche) who postulate the full or partial equivalence of man and God, Tillich elevates mankind to the status of a deity. In doing so he demands that all humans, bar none, be so revered. This is where he goes astray. It is one thing to exhibit respect, concern, and admiration for humanity; to embrace humanistic ethics; and to make the betterment of the human race one's own cause. It is quite another to place humanity on a pedestal as an absolute to be worshiped and beside which the deepest concerns of other men must be attacked as demonic and superficial. The pitfalls of this attitude I have tried to illustrate. Suffice it to repeat that Tillich's formal outlook betrays a severe want of catholicity.

The analogy route to God presents further hazards by passing through concreteness on the way. It was suggested that as long as love and emotion engender concern for loved ones, family, and country, "true" faith will remain beyond the grasp of most of us. Tillich might have partially avoided this difficulty by dropping his insistence that God have two sides, the ultimate and the concrete. If concreteness were abandoned as a requirement, preliminary concerns could be bypassed, and Tillich could simply demand that preservation of the human race rank highest in a scheme of values. He could then argue that, if the future of humanity were at stake, quite a few people would be willing to sacrifice themselves, their families, or their country to save it, even though their generation might otherwise be spared. Unfortunately, preliminary concerns cannot be ignored without wrecking the system. Tillich's most fundamental analogy is that between his God and the Christian God pictured in the biblical description of Jesus as the Christ. The Christ was fully God and fully man, or as Tillich prefers, both ultimate *and* concrete. Ultimacy, we have seen, describes the impersonal side of the divine and the union of all elements of divinity in one universalized divinity; it is the "fully God" aspect of the Christ. Concreteness combines manifestation in a personal life with a multiplicity of disparate "incarnations"; it is the "fully man" aspect of the Christ. Tillich insists that his God, true to the Christ picture, be a blend of ultimacy and concreteness. Humanity, the abstraction, is ultimate; the preliminary concern, "incarnated" in a concrete person, provides concreteness. Remove the preliminary concern and, as in mysticism, ultimacy swallows all concreteness. The finite side of God is lost. And so is Tillich's system.

RELATED PROBLEMS. Symbolic analogies create similar problems in other areas. Theology has traditionally been concerned about the plight of man, as precipitated by a fall from innocence into sin. Therefore, Tillich's theology must have its own Eden, fall, and sin. Here we are discussing the concepts in a socio-historical sense, not to be confused with the personal sense in which "dreaming innocence" is sometimes used to describe theistic belief. The system demands that theological concepts be correlated with philosophical ones, so innocence is linked with essence, the fall with the transition from essence to existence, and sin with existence. The analogical syntheses, which constitute Tillich's own version of reality, emerge as a mixture of sophistry and barbershop wisdom. Unable to find anything historical which would pass for innocence or essence, Tillich hypothesizes a state of latent or potential humanism among men—no prejudice, no hatred, no injustice, no war. Man theoretically could have attained universal humanism upon becoming man, but he did not. This falling short of potentiality was his fall into sin. Sin, because Tillich dislikes the word, is preferably referred to as "estrangement" or "man's existential predicament." What can be said about such philosophy? Humanistic potentiality, as the analogue of innocence-essence, might strike some as a profound and convincing description of reality, but it has no practical validity. Tillich tacitly acknowledges this when he says that his Kingdom of God can never be achieved. To repeat an earlier quotation, human improvements "do not affect the freedom to do good and evil as long as man is man."[12] As for the imperfect state of human relations, what has Tillich said that we did not already know?

12. *Boundary*, p. 77.

Theology's answer to the plight of man is salvation. As a process, this correlates with the transition from existence back to essence; as a state, for which the term New Being is preferred, it *is* essence. For Tillich, salvation is becoming a humanist. This is not humanism in a purely ethical sense, however, but in the broader sense of becoming utterly involved in a concern which, insofar as it is realized, will aid at least part of humanity. That part does not delimit one's interest in humanity but is a proxy for all humanity. Through "being grasped by" such a concern, you and I are supposed to experience all the joy, security, and satisfaction which others have attributed to religious salvation and to essence. The wondrous effects credited to New Being are a bit too lengthy to restate here. Briefly, though, New Being is to Paul Tillich as positive thinking is to Norman Vincent Peale and a decision for Christ is to Billy Graham. That marks it as a powerful antidote for trouble and anxiety. I, for one, am not at all convinced that dedication to some quest or interest is suddenly going to dissolve all worries and problems—even if the analogy says it should. For that matter, neither am I convinced that a humanistic concern must offer greater satisfaction than some other, perhaps even an ignoble one. Indeed, is it not possible that a purely selfish concern about getting to heaven can, aided by all the emotion which superstition can muster, produce greater personal contentment than a humanistic attitude? From all appearances, Tillich's desire to build an analogy between New Being and salvation has led him to make exorbitant claims which serve the analogy (and therefore the system) but which throw his conclusions seriously out of alignment with the actual human situation.

One other set of analogies should be mentioned: those that underlie Tillich's philosophy of history. Tillichian history correlates theology's story of man with the dialectical histories of Hegel and Marx. Its goal, universal humanism, is analogous to the Kingdom of God and to various philosophical utopias, most notably Hegel's Germanic monarchy and Marx's world communism. Tillich apparently feels that a theology—or perhaps it is a dialectical system which matters—would not be complete without an explanation of history, so he makes the effort. But he really doesn't believe that history has any explanation, and neither does he believe that dialectical forces are metaphysically guiding history toward its destiny. Therefore he quietly switches from an explanation of history to an abstract summary of man's ethical progress. The discussion is so ethereal that it becomes inane. Emphasis falls on the idea that a certain group bears history's meaning. The analogous groups are the Christian church, on the side of theology, and both Hegel's Germanic people and Marx's working class on the side of philosophy. Tillich calls his meaning-bearing group "Christianity," and most of his listeners immediately assume he is offering some appropriately Christian reading of history. Actually, of course, he is speaking of humanism, which bears a meaning pertaining to the deification of man. Humanism periodically attains a degree of hegemony within society: there is a theonomous period of progress toward the Kingdom of God, which period is recognizable as a Hegelian synthesis. This, according to Tillich, is what history is all about. Query: Does Tillichian history-by-analogy provide a useful, meaningful, or enlightening description of the world and society?

BEYOND THE SYSTEM

Although Tillich presents a philosophy that is grossly deficient in many areas, it would be a mistake to judge him strictly on the basis of the systematized formulations just reviewed. To reiterate, these do not represent the deepest level of his thought: the simple No to supernaturalism and Yes to mankind hold that position. Heavy emphasis on the formal propositions used to reveal (and conceal) the No and the Yes may therefore be unwarranted. Furthermore, the reception of Tillich's thought by the theological world must be considered in any assessment of it. If extreme, empty, or seemingly naive formulations have served the calculated purpose of convincing others that Tillich is a committed Christian, thereby winning for him a respectful audience, the formulations must be judged partly in terms of their efficacy in achieving this objective. Finally, there is an issue of intellectual honesty to consider. This issue relates to whether Tillich's strategy of deception exceeds the limits permitted by integrity.

Earlier we reviewed Tillich's description of how men have dug (i.e., should dig) through level after level to get at the truth. The deepest truths offered by Paul Tillich are not to be found in the deification of man, the unrealistic assumptions about the depth and character of human concerns, and the hollow formulations produced by analogy. They are to be found, rather, in the basic duo of No and Yes. Apropos the No, I have tried to stress in explaining Tillich's use of symbolism that he is far more interested in destroying supernatural beliefs than in gaining acceptance of the analogous humanistic concepts he offers as substitutes. At least some of the excesses of Tillich's symbolic statements can be excused on this account. Regarding the Yes, I have already mentioned the difficulty of deciding how much of Tillich's philosophy of ultimate concern can be taken at face value, as opposed to being treated as a complex statement of the simple Yes. It is hard to believe that the extreme shade of humanism called for by the system is not at least partly an abstraction representing a more conventional sort of humanism Tillich really has in mind. When he speaks of the "latent church" evidenced by widespread humanism among the unchurched, we certainly do not visualize people with a fanatical, single-minded outlook on life. While it is true that philosophers, not to mention theologians, have produced all kinds of foolishness which from dream-world vantage points they have managed to take seriously, I wonder if Tillich isn't sophisticated enough to know more about the nature of human concerns than his thought reveals. Maybe there is a distinction to be drawn between what he really believes and the imaginative constructs he so carelessly employs in his academic toy, the system. I am suggesting the likelihood that Tillich knows his analogical version of reality isn't true to life but is unwilling to compromise because the system would suffer. This is not to excuse Tillich's many rash statements about ultimate concern or his snubbing of nonhumanistic concerns, but it may help place certain ideas in perspective. Anyhow, regardless of what is or is not meant seriously, it must be recognized that the generalized Yes to humanity is basic and the rest is detail.

As a denial of the supernatural and simultaneous affirmation of humanity, Tillich's message is unique of presentation but not of substance. It is humanism, which in its purest form is antisupernaturalistic. Humanism is a fairly popular substitute for religion, especially among intellectuals. Personally, I see no value in establishing substitute religions, antisupernaturalistic though they may be, when one's original faith disappears. I dislike the implication that lack of *some* affiliation is undesirable, if only because of what others might think or because unalloyed atheism is too negative. The notion that ethical viewpoints must be formalized and labeled strikes me as a throwback to religion. It hints at the familiar situation of a person who has stopped believing but wants to go right on being religious. On the other hand, the humanistic ethic holding that man must decide for himself what is right and wrong on the basis of consideration for others is eminently sensible. Accordingly, I find no fault with the substance of Tillich's basic message and, indeed, strongly concur in his objections to the supernatural.

Nevertheless, were Tillich to be judged by the message alone he would rate a low score. He has said nothing original. He offers no new insights into the frailties of religion. His writing is not particularly eloquent or persuasive; it relies more on dogmatic assertion—"absurd" and "nonsense"—than on reasoned opinion. Huxley's *Religion without Revelation* and Lippmann's *A Preface to Morals* are far more adequate statements of the humanist position. Religious supernaturalism has been more effectively challenged in such works as Santayana's *Reason in Religion*, Mencken's *Treatise on the Gods*, and H. W. Smith's *Man and His Gods*. If Tillich has a claim to greatness, it does not emanate from the substance of his thought.

A Successful Masquerade

On the positive side, Tillich deserves substantial credit for successfully executing a bold masquerade designed to undermine Christian theology, education, and belief from within the Church. Tillich's theology is not genuine, but it has been accepted as bona fide by most of his readers and critics. Pretending to believe in an indescribable god, one that struck some interpreters as very much like God, Tillich produced volumes of mystical-sounding prose expounding about being-itself and "his" relation to man's existential predicament, that predicament being estrangement from being-itself. Analogical and dialectical formulations, not often recognized as such, were discussed in profound tones and presented as "onto-logical" truths. Theologians read Tillich, scratched their heads and praised his profundity even while chiding him for errors, and ele-vated him to the top of their profession. One only needs to browse through the growing body of literature on Tillich to appreciate how thoroughly the theological profession has been hoodwinked.

There have always been, it is true, a certain number of atheists among ministers and theologians—men who have lost their faith without losing the desire to retain their status. It is easy enough to get away with theological dissimulation if one professes to believe in God while holding the private reservation that God is truth or love or concrete reality or some such abstraction. What makes Tillich's case impressive is that he made his theology sufficiently convincing to win for him the number-one rank in Protestant the-ology while at the same time making his atheistic views clear enough to be recognized by careful readers.

As not merely a recognized theologian but American Protestant-ism's leading spokesman, Tillich was in a position to wield consid-erable influence. And wield it he did: the proliferation of paperback editions of Tillich's books, the posthumously published lectures, and the continuing flow of commentary attests to his wide reader-ship. Granted, relatively few of his readers understood much of what they read. However, one needn't be able to follow Tillich's systematic formulations to perceive his incessant attacks on Chris-tian tradition. Although even the No, or most of it, presumably escaped many readers, it seems likely that others found confirma-tion for incipient doubt. Tillich's skepticism proved, it must have seemed, that one need not believe all those suspicious tales of the supernatural to be a Christian. It would be temerarious to venture a firm opinion on whether Tillich really influenced a substantial number of persons, but I suspect that the No reached quite a few, including some studying for the ministry. (The seminary, with its introduction to religious history and biblical problems, is a time of awakening for some; and for youngsters conditioned to religious authority, an authoritative statement of liberal opinion is likely to exert occasional influence.) Certainly it is true that Tillich, assisted by Bonhoeffer and Bultmann, managed to convert to atheism a bishop of the Church of England: John Robinson's *Honest to God* bears Tillich's stamp on page after page. Moreover, Tillich's relatively open assault on theistic conceptions of God—most of his critics caught on—undoubtedly helped nourish the God is Dead theology.

The Question of Honesty

The fact of Tillich's successful fifth column activities and related deception raises an issue of integrity. Has Tillich been dishonest with his listeners and perhaps even with himself? If so, how does this affect his stature?

ENDS AND MEANS. At the outset, let it be understood that Tillich has not lied to anybody. In claiming to believe in God, pretending to be a Christian (and a Lutheran at that), and calling himself a theologian, he has misled most people, and not by accident; but he has two defenses. First, he has warned that his propositions are symbolic, not to be taken literally, and that his God is not a being; he has even provided sufficient clues for his symbolic meanings to be discovered. Second, he has given words like God, Christianity, and theology secret interpretations which, in his eyes at least, suffice to make his statements technically truthful—however deceptive they may be. Tillich, in other words, merely equivocates.

Equivocation, of course, is well short of complete honesty. Do we therefore censure Tillich for being deceitful? I suspect that many religious conservatives will, while some moderates and liberals who may employ similar tactics themselves might hesitate to do so. For my part, I am not ready to say that deceit per se is wrong: the end can justify the means. Who is to condemn the store manager who, asked at gunpoint to open a safe, pretends to be a clerk who doesn't know the combination? What about the FBI agent who infiltrates the Ku Klux Klan, playing the role of a bigot? Similarly—this question is addressed to clergymen—if you don't believe in the resurrection but give an Easter sermon the ambiguities of which lead part of the congregation to assume you believe the myth, does the end (what is it?) justify the means? The point is that if a person has, or thinks he has, a legitimate objective whose benefits outweigh any harm associated with means, it is not dishonorable to use means which would ordinarily reflect badly on their user. Hence if Tillich thinks that the conquest of religious superstition and religious bigotry justifies deception, there is nothing intrinsically wrong with his acting accordingly.

I do not imply that Tillich's precise mission is worthwhile. As long as his motives are impersonal, that is for him to decide. For the record, my own minority opinion is that the cause is worthy but the scheme of limited value. To judge by some of the encomiums awarded Tillich, his seeming pieties may have fortified more than a few believers even while the rest were being seduced.[13] In any case, I prefer an individual who stands up for what he believes, lending whatever dignity he can muster to the side he thinks is right. Still, if Tillich thinks he can help his cause best by deception, he is entitled to differ.

EMOTION AND ART. The foregoing comments assume that Tillich's motives are impersonal. If they are not, the balance between ends and means is altered. And, in fact, the evidence indicates that Tillich's motives are really a mixture of the impersonal and the personal. There is without doubt a sincere concern, quite impersonal, about the way religion continues to jeopardize human progress and human relations. But, to reiterate, Tillich is also motivated by an emotional attachment to Christianity and by an artistic desire to effect the Grand Synthesis of theology and philosophy. These last two ends bear closer review.

Religion, we have seen, was a vital part of Tillich's early life. The son of a minister, he came from a deeply religious family and grew up in a small, conservative town. His training was in theology. Although skepticism took root before he completed his education, religious momentum carried him first into the ministry and then into wartime service as a chaplain. By this time he was gripped by an indelible love for the religious and the sacramental, a love which he himself has eloquently described. Religious edifices, music, sermons, and Christian holidays were a way of life which,

13. Sidney Hook, in his essay on "The Atheism of Paul Tillich," voices this opinion: "But I am not really persuaded that Tillich's ambiguities can get the idol-worshipers [Tillich's terminology] out of the temples; there is some evidence that his ideas provide the rationalizations for those to remain who would otherwise have left." *Religious Experience and Truth: A Symposium*, ed. S. Hook (New York: New York University Press, 1961), p. 63.

he has confessed, played a crucial role in his decision to remain a theologian. Under comparable circumstances, other ex-believers have sacrificed conviction to emotion by remaining active Christians and even ministers. These people have lacked the courage of their convictions. Personal integrity has yielded to feelings and to esthetic and social—perhaps even economic—considerations. Tillich is hardly a stereotype but, given his acknowledged emotional commitment to the church, it is difficult to assume that his theological activity is purely a matter of humanistic strategy.

With the Grand Synthesis, Tillich's deception again steers a personal course. Tillich is captivated by the idea of effecting a union of theology and philosophy, an idea which seems to have been popular during his student days. He wants to correlate a wide range of analogous theological and philosophical concepts. The goal is a humanistic synthesis which will stand as a philosophical theology. This is an innocuous project and essentially reflects the artist's impulse to be creative. Creativity in this instance requires theological credentials, however. Tillich gets them by claiming to be a Christian. The cause is not ignoble, but is exercising the imagination an end sufficiently impersonal and otherwise worthy to justify the means of deception?

I do not pretend to know the relative importance of the several motives that underlie the deceit in Tillich's thought. It is doubtful that he knew either. Human beings have a way of rationalizing selfish motives by, among other means, ignoring them in favor of any worthy objectives. Perhaps Tillich convinced himself that emotion and art were strictly incidental to his fight against supernatural belief. If so, he deceived not only his larger audience but himself. Personal considerations may have been primary or secondary, but they were present. This being the case, one could easily entertain reservations concerning Tillich's intellectual integrity.

SUMMING UP

Although not exactly intended as such, the "systematic theology" of Paul Tillich is in many respects a broad satire on Christian theology. In what amounts to a devastating assault on those who allegorize or otherwise find imaginative God-spoken meanings in a Bible they can no longer take at face value, Tillich in effect pretends the scriptures were written by ancient humanists. With audacity which should bring envy to any self-respecting neo-orthodox interpreter, and without cracking a smile, he utilizes the Bible and tradition to concoct a "theology" that mocks theology, albeit covertly. The basic features of traditional belief are reconstituted as humanistic, which is to say antitheological, images and described in solemn tones as religious truths. God is duly praised as the ground of our being and our ultimate concern, appellations which some conservative critics have found both meaningful and appropriate. Admixed with this theological hokum is a generous amount of ontological claptrap which, given anything approaching a literal understanding, is so nonsensical as to belie the straight-faced air of profundity that gilds the presentation.

The theological world—Catholic side as well as Protestant—has taken it all very seriously. Men have listened attentively and accepted Tillich as a dedicated Christian striving to elucidate a higher reality. This reality has struck many observers as metaphysical, but to others it is nothing higher than the spiritlike deity of the liberals and moderates, for whom God has junked his anthropomorphic frame while hanging onto his anthropopathic psyche. The theologians, notwithstanding their frequent disagreement with Tillich on crucial issues, have repeatedly bowed to his wisdom and insight. Some commentators have even ventured the suggestion that Tillich is Christianity's chief hope for a reconciliation of Protestantism and Catholicism.[14]

What is especially remarkable about Tillich's enterprise is that he remained widely accepted despite the abundant evidence of his atheism. (During the last decade or so atheistic theology has become fairly commonplace, but this was not the situation when Tillich was breaking ground.) Enough observers commented on his substantive atheism to alert Christianity to what was going on. Moreover, Tillich himself provided sufficient information about his

14. See Walter M. Horton, "Tillich's Role in Contemporary Theology," *The Theology of Paul Tillich*, ed. Charles W. Kegley and Robert W. Bretall (New York: Macmillan, 1952), pp. 41–44. A less sanguine yet still highly complimentary opinion about Tillich's ecumenical qualities appears in Carl J. Armbruster, *The Vision of Paul Tillich* (New York: Sheed and Ward, 1967), pp. 307–8.

God's character to point his colleagues in the right direction. In particular, his emphasis on apologetics and his identification of secular humanism as the target of his apologetic message, when taken in conjunction with his definition of apologetics as finding a common criterion and his use of the Logos as an example, should have alerted many. If identifying God with the Logos gave ancient Christianity a common criterion vis-à-vis the pagans, what must God be identified with to give modern Christianity and humanism a common criterion? Also, suspicion should have been raised by Tillich's insistence that the Chalcedonian formula is correct in holding that the Christ was fully God and fully man and that concepts treating the Christ as merely a half-god are wrong. Why should Tillich, who doesn't even believe in the divinity of Jesus (a fact recognized by many), attach any importance to a particular version of an ancient superstition? Why, unless his system depends on an imaginative solution to the arithmetic paradox?

Perhaps the explanation for Tillich's success lies in the strong proclivity of the theological mind to adhere to supernaturalistic modes of thought. Perhaps it was the unwillingness of Protestant Christianity to accept the possibility that its leading American spokesman was an impostor. Whatever it was, the fact is that Tillich did convince most of the world that what he called being-itself was in one way or another supernatural. The practical significance of this accomplishment is highly conjectural. If nothing else, it certainly gave Tillich a wide audience. This enabled him to reach people who would never have listened to an avowed skeptic. How did his listeners receive him? Confusion was probably the leading response. However, as said before, it seems likely that a fair number of individuals were led to more enlightened world views and that at least a few were helped to the realization that the supernatural exists only in man's imagination.

Less a cause for renown but deserving acknowledgment is Tillich's heartfelt concern—his personal ultimate concern—for emancipating those he could reach from bondage to religious supernaturalism. Tillich offered a theology (as it was assumed to be) designed to lead each person to whatever level of religious sophistication that person was prepared to accept; and if Tillich's motives reflected a certain ambivalence toward religion, his desire to mitigate the corrosive effects of religious prejudice and superstition was nonetheless genuine.

Beyond subversion and good intentions, there may be some who will wish to credit Tillich with an artistic masterpiece of significant proportions—an ingenious synthesis of theological and philosophical concepts. Any plaudits from this sector will have to come from others, though, since interdisciplinary synthesis is an art form I have not learned to appreciate. Besides, most of Tillich's correlations were invented by Hegel, who patterned much of his own system after Christianity.

Little of a favorable nature can be said about the content of the Tillichian system. Antisupernaturalism and humanism, the two main ingredients in Tillich's cleverly garnished theological stew, provide a potentially nourishing base, even though the neoreligious flavor of humanism is mildly offensive. Unfortunately, so much analogy has been added to the mix that the final product is thoroughly distasteful. Tillich would have each of us adopt a single-minded attitude in life, that attitude centering on a particular concern. The concern, which can be anything so long as it is "transparent to" humanity, should be deified; all other concerns must, if they interfere, be sacrificed to the one which is God. Even one's family must be subordinated since, where two or more concerns conflict, the lesser must give in to that which has been designated as the bearer of ultimacy. Thus, if a family crisis arises in the life of a bacteriologist whose ultimate concern is finding a cure for tetanus, and if resolution of the crisis would jeopardize the medical endeavor, family welfare must be sacrificed. Tillich would also challenge the propriety of our choosing guiding concerns which derive their ultimacy from something other than humanity. There is something demonic about trying to save the sea otter, assuming that its benefactor just happens to admire these lovable creatures and is not at all worried about keeping them around for others to enjoy. Also flirting with demonism is the astronomer whose only motive for searching the heavens is an overpowering curiosity about the universe.

My point is that whenever we move beyond the basic propositions—the Yes and the No—to matters of detail everything becomes so exaggerated and preposterous, so out of touch with what is real or tenable, that it can only be characterized as naive—if not, in its own peculiar way, bigoted. Let me emphasize that there is no intent to accuse *Tillich* of naiveté or bigotry. Rather, I am saying that he has been so carried away with analogy that *his philosophy* becomes an accidental form of fanaticism which Tillich would never endorse if it were stated in simple, direct language. While reluctant to play the role of mindreader, I find it very hard to believe that Tillich would agree that our friend who wants to preserve sea otters for strictly personal reasons, not out of concern for future generations, is practicing demonism. Nor do I believe that Tillich would deprecate science for its own sake. (My hunch is that, if pressed and forced back at every attempt to equivocate, Tillich would try to rationalize the concern-for-animals case: he might argue that, if a project is beneficial to humanity, it is transparent to humanity regardless of its architect's motives. This would mean, of course, that any concern entailing incidental benefits to humanity was thereby transparent—even if the underlying motives were utterly selfish ones like wealth, prestige, or self-advancement; humanism and demonism would no longer clash. Regarding scientific curiosity, perhaps Tillich or a disciple of his would again rationalize by holding science to be transparent to humanity—which begs the question of whether scientific quests always help and never ultimately threaten mankind.)

The concession that Tillich might not accept the baldly stated implications of his philosophy does not, however, belie the fact that the implications are there. They not only are there but represent the real meat (beyond the bare-bones Yes and No) of the system. The unreasonable character of the finer points of the system poses a dilemma: either we reduce Tillich's thought to such basic simplicity that his ideas become trite, almost pedestrian, or we accept the fact that the details of the system give it an aura of foolishness and extremism. Because of this dilemma, any accolades bestowed on Tillich will have to rest not on what he said but on what he did.

His immediate accomplishment was to delude almost everyone, followers and critics alike, into accepting him as some type of supernaturalist. Considering his top-ranking position in American theology, this deception is remarkable—but not itself a mark of greatness. Greatness demands a more practical accomplishment, which in this instance would have to be success in leading people away from religion and toward humanism. Was Tillich successful? Objective conclusions are exceedingly difficult to draw. We cannot doubt that he had many readers and listeners, yet there is simply not much evidence one way or the other as to how they reacted. Conceivably, the future will present later analysts with something more concrete, maybe a new movement of Christian humanism bearing Tillich's name. (I don't expect such a movement to materialize.) But at the moment there is no persuasive reason to suppose that Tillich had an effect commensurate with his popularity or that most of those he addressed responded with anything but befuddlement. I must therefore reaffirm the opinion that his impact, though generally favorable and significant, was limited and occasionally negative. Tillich's chief claim to fame will be that he fooled a lot of people.

Index

277

Doubt, 23–30, 45–46, 53, 215–17, 248, 268. *See also* Atheism; Death of God; Meaning of life

Dreaming innocence, 28, 61, 77, 95, 205, 207, 210, 215, 263. *See also* Eden; Ideal, the; Innocence; Potentiality

Dualism, 138, 139, 141, 142, 223

Dynamics, 82, 108, 126, 133–34, 189

Ecstasy, 5, 121, 183, 203

Eden, 30, 75, 228, 237; correlated, 2, 56, 84, 87, 136. *See also* Dreaming innocence; Innocence; Potentiality

Edwards, Paul, 246–47

Elements, dialectical ("ontological"): in Hegel, 75, 76, 221–22; in Tillich, 82, 118, 119, 121, 125, 129, 130, 132–35, 214, 221–22, 235. *See also* Dialectics; Particularity; Universality

Emotionalism, 127

Enlightenment, the, 172, 224, 229

Eschatology, 85, 87, 154, 161, 162, 163. *See also* Doomsday; Heaven; Hell; Kingdom of God; Last judgment; Messiah; Zoroasterism

Essence: in dialectics (*see* Dialectics, essence and existence, and separation and return); metaphysical (*see* Being, philosophical; Ontology; Pantheism; Spirit, Hegel's; Ultimate reality); potential (*see* Dreaming innocence; Eden; Fall, the; Ideal, the; Innocence; Potentiality); realized (*see* Actual, the; Kingdom of God; New Being; Salvation; Self-realization; Self-transcendence)

Estrangement (existence), 21–22, 56, 57, 90–98, 100, 101, 132, 241, 247; and the Christ, 84, 170, 179, 185–86, 191; as dialectical, 67–76, 78, 79, 80, 81, 95, 97, 98, 132, 185–86, 191, 192, 207, 208, 211, 219, 221, 228, 230, 237, 238; G. Hammond's interpretation, 11, 207–8; Hegelian, 22, 71, 74–76, 94–101 *passim*, 109, 131, 132, 133, 222, 237, 238; as the human predicament, 90, 91, 177, 184, 268; Marxian, 69, 74, 94, 109, 237, 238; overcome, 2, 170, 174, 196, 218, 245; as sin, 23, 56, 62, 84, 86, 152–

53, 175, 189, 205, 206, 238, 263; in Tillich's ontology, 121, 133, 134, 135, 136, 137, 190; transcended, 108, 109. *See also* Actual, the; Despair; Dialectics, essence and existence; Fall, the; Finitude; Nonbeing; Plight of man; Separation and return

Eternal Life, 58, 232. *See also* Immortality

Ethics: of Jesus, 147, 153–63, 179–80, 184–85; of Tillich, 269–71; in ultimate concern, 259, 262, 264, 267

Existence, "characteristics" of, 130, 135–36

Existence, of God: the God above God, 96–98; metaphysical gods, 41–47, 130, 244*n*; the traditional God (*see also* Atheism; Death of God), 18–19, 20, 37–41, 51, 96–97, 100, 111, 180–82, 216–17, 218, 219–20

Existence, as a philosophical concept. *See* Actual, the; Dialectics, essence and existence; Estrangement; Fall, the; Finitude; Nonbeing; Plight of man

Existentialism, 8, 13, 16, 77, 92, 116

Faith: demonic, 149, 150; Tillichian, 55, 58, 112, 115, 176, 193, 195; traditional, 33, 36

Fall, the: in Hegel's thought, 68, 205; in theology, 23, 30, 31, 56, 205, 228, 263; in Tillich's thought, 23, 56, 57, 80, 84, 85, 95, 136, 205, 263. *See also* Eden; Estrangement; Innocence; Potentiality; Separation and return; Sin

Father: in Jesus' teachings, 155, 158, 161; in the Trinity, 22, 37, 202, 203, 205, 239

Ferré, Nels F. S., 34

Feuerbach, Ludwig, 68–69, 101, 188, 262

Finitude: examples of, 35, 42–43, 109, 150, 151, 153, 162, 167, 253; in Hegel's thought, 68, 134, 222; in Tillich's ontology, 82, 125–29, 135–36, 138. *See also* Particularity

First cause, 46

Forgiveness, 37, 154–55, 174

Form, 82, 127, 133–34, 189

Formalism, 127

Incarnation: belief in, attributed to Tillich, 5, 8, 50, 165; as a dialectical thesis, 21, 178, 180, 190, 239, 240; in history, 228, 229; and humanity, 127, 128, 167, 232; and New Being, 175, 193; rejected by Tillich, 36, 164, 251; in theology, 114, 116, 124, 125, 144, 145, 166, 200, 203, 222; and ultimate concern, 21, 116, 117, 127, 128, 166, 236, 263. *See also* "Jesus as the Christ"

Individualization, 133–34, 139, 213–15, 218, 220–22. *See also* Particularity; Self

Infinity, 2, 42–43, 93, 95, 125, 135, 138; in Hegel's thought, 68, 71, 205, 222; and humanity, 82, 132, 167, 252; as unlimited concern or love, 39, 109, 135, 136, 253. *See also* Transcendence; Ultimacy; Unconditionality; Universality

Innocence, 23, 92, 205, 237, 238, 263. *See also* Dreaming innocence; Eden; Potentiality

Islam, 105, 115

Jesus, 15, 32, 46, 52, 66–67, 105–6; belief in divinity of, 5, 6, 28, 34–36, 50, 51, 113, 164, 187, 251, 273; the historical, 26, 48–49, 147, 153–63, 178, 179, 185, 193, 224. *See also* Christ, the; "Jesus as the Christ"

"Jesus as the Christ," 89, 218, 248; as final revelation, 125, 127; in history, 228, 232; and the Holy Spirit, 198, 199; misinterpreted, 50; as mythological, 34, 117, 164, 168; as the norm, 113–14, 116–17, 138, 151, 163–68, 236, 244, 262; as a symbol, 21, 168–73, 177–87, 190, 198. *See also* Christ, the; Christology; Jesus; New Being; Norm, the

Jews, 51, 52, 152, 158, 159, 223–24. *See also* Judaism

John, gospel of, 78, 123, 178, 182

Judaism, 106, 223. *See also* Jews

Justification by faith, 36

Kairos, 22, 228–30

Kant, Immanuel, 66–67, 68, 101, 188, 262

Kaufmann, Walter, 18, 19, 62n, 76n, 254–55

Kegley, Charles W., 1

Kelsey, David, 14–15, 199, 243, 248–50

Kierkegaard, Sören, 8

Kingdom of God, 83, 84, 187, 227, 228, 241, 245; in Christian history, 52, 223–24, 228; in dialectical histories, 72, 87, 238; and Jesus, 154–61 *passim*; in Tillichian history, 22, 58, 79, 98, 223–26, 230, 232, 265. *See also* Theonomy

Last judgment, 156, 175

Latent church, 104, 231, 266

Law, divine. *See* Divine law; Great Commandment; Ten Commandments

Law, Jewish religious, 52, 159

Law of love, 56, 60, 96, 112, 145, 146, 166, 175, 187, 203, 219, 234

Levels of meaning, 19–20, 49–51, 60, 187, 252, 266, 273. *See also* Ambiguity

Liberalism, 30, 31, 36, 51, 140, 147, 148, 161, 272; and Tillich, 25, 149, 187

Life: God as, 11, 207–8; philosophy of, 212–22; divine (*see* Divine life; Separation and return)

Lippmann, Walter, 267

Literalism, 39–40, 50, 58–63 *passim*, 89, 207, 249, 251, 269, 272. *See also* Symbolism

Logic, 89, 243–45, 247–48

Logos, 117, 118, 119, 120, 121–24, 144–46, 149, 176, 187; in apologetic theology (as God), 106, 123, 129, 188–89, 273; as the Christ (Son), 8, 36, 123, 165, 166, 175, 178, 202, 204; as reason, 118, 119, 122, 123, 173, 203, 210, 234

Lord's prayer, 154–55

Love, 5, 80, 111–13, 145, 146, 171, 203, 218, 236, 255. *See also* Law of love

Luke, gospel of, 159, 163

Luther, Martin, 200

MacIntyre, Alasdair, 18, 19

McKelway, Alexander, 5–6, 16, 37, 41, 138, 183, 251

McTaggart, J. M. E., 10

sophical anthropology, 14–15; Tillich's, 22, 80–81, 87, 129–37, 138, 189, 220–22, 234–36; Tillich's misinterpreted, 4, 9, 10, 13, 47. *See also* Being, philosophical; Metaphysics; Pantheism
Osiris, 35
Overman (*übermensch*), 102–3, 111

Panentheism, 3, 4, 9, 16, 38, 138
Pantheism: attributed to Tillich, 3, 4, 10–16 *passim*, 38, 51, 167, 250; defined, 4, 43–44; in Hegel's thought, 68, 102; imitated by Tillich, 131; and polytheism, 139; rejected by Tillich, 7, 9, 42–44, 45, 47, 108, 109. *See also* Being, philosophical; Metaphysics; Naturalism; Ontology; Ultimate reality
Parable: and Jesus, 48, 155–56; and Tillich, 77, 87–88, 208, 209, 233, 239
Paradox, 37, 111, 144, 204, 244, 273
Participation: metaphysical, 7, 15, 44, 167; Tillichian, 133–34, 213–15, 218, 220–22. *See also* Mysticism, as a symbol; Universality
Particularity: in Hegel's thought, 20–21, 74–77, 120, 221; in Tillich's thought, 22, 81, 118, 119, 121, 130, 188. *See also* Concreteness; Elements, dialectical; Finitude; Individualization; Self
Passover, 159
Paul, Saint, 51–52, 105–6, 187, 225
Peale, Norman Vincent, 264
Personal God. *See* Being, God as a; Existence, of God; Theism, God of
Peter, Simon, 157, 181, 184
Philosophy: Christian, 88, 89, 243; correlated with theology, 54, 82–90, 233–34; German, 66–77, 100–3, 110–11; of nature, 101–2 (*see also* Naturalism). *See also* Correlation, method of; Grand Synthesis
Plato, 10, 66, 77, 208
Plight of man, 23, 37, 90, 94. *See also* Despair; Estrangement
Polarities, 9, 77, 128–29, 132–35, 213–15. *See also* Coincidence of opposites; One and many, problem of the; Principle of identity

Polytheism, 138–43 *passim*, 152, 201, 211, 235
Pope, the, 32, 73*n*
Potentiality (potential essence): in Hegel's thought, 76, 81, 82, 97, 120, 238; and innocence, 56, 57, 84, 205, 238, 263; in Tillich's thought, 22, 79, 80, 84, 95, 118–19, 125, 129, 132–37 *passim*, 170, 189, 191, 207, 221, 237, 238, 247, 263. *See also* Dreaming innocence; Eden; Fall, the; Ideal, the; Innocence
Power of being, 1, 6, 9, 61–62, 114, 176, 202, 207, 219–20, 225, 249
Predestination, 48, 134, 163, 226, 245
Preliminary concerns: described, 21, 86, 116–17, 153, 167, 175, 236, 262; and ontology, 81, 119, 120, 122, 128, 137; as opaque (idolatrous), 121, 150, 168, 171; as transparent, 21, 116, 117, 126, 127, 128, 168, 172, 225, 253, 256, 257, 259, 274, 275
Principle of identity, 133, 143, 144, 145, 214, 236. *See also* Coincidence of opposites; One and many, problem of the; Polarities; Synthesis
Proletariat, 73, 79, 95, 109, 231, 238
Prophets, 148
Protestantism: acceptance of Tillich, 1, 8, 54, 268, 272, 273; discussed, 28, 29, 32, 105, 204, 210–11; redefined, 85, 218; violated, 251
Protestant message, 28, 29, 30
Protestant principle, 28, 29*n*
Providence, divine, 36–37, 176, 181

Realized essence. *See* Self-realization
Reason, 113, 117–29, 190, 203, 244, 250; as an antithesis, 21, 197, 198, 212, 233–34, 239; conflicts in, 81, 124–29, 190; as a correlate, 84, 85, 89, 122, 124, 196, 233–34; objective, 81, 119–21, 122, 125, 190, 203, 235; ontological, 81, 117–19, 125, 190, 235; subjective, 81, 119–21, 122, 125, 143, 190, 202, 212, 235; technical, 117, 118, 211. *See also* Logic; Logos, as reason
Reconciliation. *See* Reunion, frag-

mentary; Self-realization; Separation and return
Reformation, the, 229, 251
Reincarnation, 193, 194
Relativism, 57, 81, 126–27, 145, 247
Religion, 176, 213–15, 232, 258, 267, 270, 275; non-Christian, 194, 223–24; typology of, 138–44, 190, 201, 211, 230, 235
Resurrection: of the dead, 34, 52, 154, 175, 223; of Jesus, 30, 31, 35, 183, 230, 269; as a symbol, 21, 62, 85, 174, 178, 182–83, 190, 196, 239–40, 245
Reunion, fragmentary, 11, 56, 90, 91, 96, 97, 109, 170, 190–91, 192, 207, 226, 227–28. See also Dialectics, union and separation; Self-realization; Separation and return
Revelation, 6, 7, 14, 16, 250, 251; and correlation, 82, 84, 85, 89, 122, 124, 196, 233–34; as a thesis, 21, 212, 239; final, 125, 126, 127, 182; in Tillich's ontology, 81, 119, 121–29, 190, 235; as a value judgment, 2, 24, 44, 78, 173, 195, 197, 198. See also Divine law; Word of God
Robinson, Bishop John A. T., 18, 111, 269
Roman Catholic Church. See Catholicism
Rowe, William L., 12, 44, 96
Ruah, 194
Russell, Bertrand, 1

Salvation, 2, 6, 23, 30, 51, 209; correlated with return, 84, 87, 92, 174, 196, 205, 238; and dialectics, 75, 78, 80, 92, 95, 136, 237; and New Being, 173–74, 186, 255, 264; promised by Jesus, 154, 156, 157, 159, 160; supernatural type rejected, 29n, 34, 62, 181, 215, 217. See also Immortality; Kingdom of God
Santayana, George, 1, 267
Saoshyant, 223
Sartre, Jean-Paul, 8
Savior-gods, 35
Scharlemann, Robert, 15–16
Schelling, F. W. J. von, 26, 88, 89, 101–2, 188, 214, 243, 262
Schleiermacher, F. E. D., 105

Schonfield, Hugh, 48
Schweitzer, Albert, 48, 162–63
Second coming, 31, 175, 224, 228
Self, 16, 93, 130–33, 136, 190, 221, 231; in Hegel's thought, 81, 94, 95, 120, 130–31, 153; in Marx's thought, 73, 94. See also Elements, dialectical; Finitude; Individualization; Particularity; Spirit, Hegel's
Self-affirmation. See Self-realization
Self-alienation. See Estrangement
Self-consciousness. See Self-realization
Self-realization, 11, 14, 39, 75, 101, 176, 208, 238, 264; in German philosophy, 67, 68, 71, 72, 73, 82, 97, 101, 102, 109, 131, 205, 206, 224, 231; as personal salvation, 182–83, 186–87, 191, 213, 217, 218; in Tillich's ontology, 22, 79, 82, 90, 97, 130, 132, 134, 136, 201, 207. See also Self-transcendence
Self-transcendence, 38–39, 102, 107–10, 132, 134, 136, 171, 238. See also Self-realization
Separation. See Dialectics, union and separation; Divine life; Estrangement; Sin; Separation and return
Separation and return: as based on Christian themes, 22, 75, 78, 87, 170, 178, 183, 185, 201–2, 205, 233; Hegel's version, 72, 75, 79, 95, 131, 236–37; Marx's version, 74, 79, 236–37; Tillich's version, 78, 79, 80, 95, 132, 170, 178, 184, 198, 200, 201, 204, 207, 208, 237, 238, 239. See also Dialectics, union and separation; Divine life; Reunion, fragmentary
Sermon on the Mount, 159
Signs, 55
Sin, 37, 55, 58, 174, 175, 186; as estrangement, 21, 23, 62, 84, 86, 92, 93, 94, 136, 152–53, 189, 205, 206, 238; Tillich's, as analogous to classical, 23, 56, 75, 87, 228, 237, 263. See also Estrangement
Skepticism (Greek), 222
Slavery, 72, 74, 185, 237
Smith, Homer W., 267
Socialism, 13, 171
Son, the, 37, 123, 164, 180, 199, 228; as analogue of dialectical "life," 78, 87, 178; as symbol for

separation, 22, 201, 202, 203, 205, 239
Son of man. *See* Messiah
Soper, David, 5
Soul, 33, 78, 193, 194, 224
Space, 136–37; gods of, 151–52
Spinoza, Baruch, 13, 43, 44
Spirit, divine. *See* Divine Spirit
Spirit, Hegel's, 68, 70–73, 74–77, 101, 120, 206, 222, 224, 231, 236, 237, 238; as analogue of depth of reason, 81, 118, 119; compared to Tillich's God, 20, 79, 81, 130–31, 134, 188, 256; as estranged, 22, 75, 90*n*, 94, 95, 97, 98*n*
Spiritual presence. *See* Divine Spirit
Stoicism, 222
Subject: in Hegel's thought, 68, 75–76, 119–20, 121, 206, 257; in Tillich's thought, 9, 80, 81, 82, 130. *See also* Reason, subjective; Self
Substance: as a "category," 136–37; metaphysical, 43, 44
Suffering servant (of Isaiah), 157
Superstition, 4, 31, 33, 35, 121, 204, 216, 248, 270, 273, 274
Symbolic statements, 58
Symbolism, 2, 16, 44, 50, 55–66, 82, 93, 94, 161, 163, 189, 204, 207, 208, 245–48, 252, 263, 266, 269; in "Christ," 26, 43, 89, 147, 148, 165, 167, 169, 177–87, 190, 191, 228, 232, 240, 250; and correlation, 84, 85, 86, 261; in "God," 14, 39, 41–42, 47, 84, 115; in "Holy Spirit," 193, 195, 196, 198; in miscellaneous religious symbols, 21, 34, 35–36, 87–88, 168, 170, 173–77, 199, 200, 205, 210, 214, 230; in nonreligious symbols, 57, 77, 90, 92, 103, 111, 124, 125, 128–29, 172; parables as, 48, 209, 233. *See also* Literalism
Synthesis: and correlation, 84–90, 94, 107; dialectical (in general), 22, 29, 66–82 *passim*, 95, 97, 140, 142, 146, 183, 192, 206–12 *passim*, 217, 226, 228; divine Spirit as (dialectical), 22, 84, 196–98, 203, 204; New Being as (dialectical), 29, 169–70, 177–78, 182, 183, 186, 190, 191, 192; as Tillich's basic method, 86–90, 103–5, 107, 188, 189, 232–40; in Tillich's (dialectical) ontology, 119, 125, 129–38 *passim*, 190. *See also* Coincidence

of opposites; Dialectics; Grand Synthesis; Negation of the negation; Principle of identity; Theonomy
System, Tillich's, 10, 55, 82, 94, 145, 243, 252, 256, 260–66 *passim*, 268, 274. *See also* Correlation, method of; Dialectics; Grand Synthesis; Symbolism
Systematic Theology, 7, 42, 50, 52, 54, 56, 61, 87, 88, 104, 108, 113, 128, 129, 150, 182, 188, 191, 192, 193, 202, 204, 243, 271–72

Tavard, George, 6–7, 28*n*-29*n*, 183, 251
Temple, 159, 181
Temptation, 162, 184
Ten Commandments, 32, 158
Theism, 9, 17, 38, 40, 107, 213–15, 218, 221, 234–35; attributed to Tillich, 3, 5–8; God of, 3–4, 15, 16, 17, 20, 30, 34, 40, 45, 46, 52, 96, 97, 99, 111, 180, 181, 206, 214, 220; as a symbol, 78, 170, 178, 204, 205, 209, 239. *See also* Being, God as a; Death of God; Existence, of God
Theologians, 13, 52, 117, 148, 187. *See also* Tillich, Paul, as a theologian
Theology, 4, 52, 55, 90, 93, 105, 149, 163, 164–67, 173–74, 175, 212, 271, 272; correlated with philosophy, 54, 82–90, 233–34; philosophical, 88–90, 187, 271. *See also* Apologetic method; Correlation, method of; Theologians
Theonomy, 22, 80, 126, 210, 229, 237, 265. *See also* Kingdom of God
Thesis, dialectical. *See* Dialectics; Elements, dialectical; Heteronomy; Incarnation, as a dialectical thesis; New Being, as dialectical; Potentiality; Revelation, as a thesis; Theism, as a symbol
Thomas, George F., 9, 16, 138
Thomas, J. Heywood, 9–10, 37–38, 89, 164, 199, 243–45, 248
Tillich, Paul: biographical data, 24–28, 53–54, 270–71; ethics of, 269–71; as a theologian, 8, 14, 54, 60, 87, 242, 252, 262, 267–69, 272, 273, 275, 276
Time, 136–37

DATE DUE
